HIKING TRAILS
of
NOVA SCOTIA

MICHAEL HAYNES

HOSTELLING INTERNATIONAL – NOVA SCOTIA

GOOSE LANE EDITIONS

Published by Goose Lane Editions and Hostelling International – Nova Scotia with the assistance of the Nova Scotia Trails Federation and the Nova Scotia Sport and Recreation Commission, 1995.

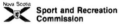

Nova Scotia
Sport and Recreation Commission

Cover photograph by Scott Cunningham of Coastal Adventures, 1994. Reproduced with permission of the artist.
Back cover photograph taken at Victoria Park, Truro, by John Haynes.
Book design and maps by Brenda Berry.
Edited by Charles Stuart and Laurel Boone.
Printed and bound in Canada by Gagné Printing.

10   9   8   7   6   5   4   3   2

Canadian Cataloguing in Publication Data
    Haynes, Michael, 1955 -
    Hiking trails of Nova Scotia

Co-published by: Hostelling International – Nova Scotia.
Includes bibliographical references and index.
ISBN 0-86492-165-9

1. Trails — Nova Scotia — Guidebooks.
2. Hiking — Nova Scotia — Guidebooks.
3. Nova Scotia — Guidebooks.   I. Hostelling International – Nova Scotia.   II. Title.

GV199.44.C22N64 1995   796.5'1'09716   C95-950170-3

Goose Lane Editions
469 King Street
Fredericton, New Brunswick
Canada E3B 1E5

HIKING TRAILS OF NOVA SCOTIA

ACKNOWLEDGEMENTS

So many people deserve thanks that I can be certain of only one thing: I will fail to mention some of them. This project benefited from the skills and talents of each, and if I missed you, please accept my sincerest apologies.

Those who hiked with me: Lindsey Arnold, Claudette Hammock, Matthew Haynes, Peter Haynes, Alan Logan, Ian Purdy, Catherine Chandler-Smith, Stuart Smith.

Those who helped me find information: Clifford Boudreau, James Bridgeland, Iris Byrnes, Ken Cavanaugh, John Cotton, Charles Dill, Heather Drope, Trevor Franker, Kevin Gay, Charles Harrison, John Haynes, Peter Hope, Susan Hruszowy, Lyman Jones, Alan Jean-Joyce, Lilli Ju, Brian Kinsman, John Leduc, Heather MacDougall, Roland MacKenzie, Colin MacKinnon, Marlene Melanson, Alex Middleton, Mike Nicholson, Margaret Reed, Debbie Ryan, Bill Schwartz, Ted Scrutton, Robert Semple, Stan Slack, Diane Smeltzer, Debbie Smith, Eric Smith, Norma Symonds, Elaine Wallace, Ike Whitehead, Alex Wilson, Tom Wilson, Bob Young.

My employers deserve special thanks: The Duke of Edinburgh's Award, the Nova Scotia Trails Federation, the Nova Scotia Underwater Council, and the Orienteering Association of Nova Scotia all tolerated, and even encouraged, my efforts to work full time and undertake this book simultaneously.

One person deserves particular mention. Without the urging of Dr. Don Arnold, I never would have had the confidence to start this project. I owe him a tremendous debt.

Michael Haynes

CONTENTS

Preface   9

Introduction   13

Trails at a Glance   23

COBEQUIDS – NORTH SHORE   **27**
Region Map   29

SOUTH SHORE – ANNAPOLIS VALLEY   **75**
Region Map   77

CENTRAL – EASTERN SHORE   **125**
Region Map   127

CAPE BRETON ISLAND   **175**
Region Map   177

CAPE BRETON HIGHLANDS NATIONAL PARK   **223**
Region Map   225

KEJIMKUJIK NATIONAL PARK   **269**
Region Map   271

Afterword   317

Useful Addresses   319

Selected Bibliography   321

Index   323

Fresh bear tracks, Hillards Lakes. MICHAEL HAYNES

PREFACE

The Canadian Hostelling Association – Nova Scotia, now Hostelling International – Nova Scotia (HI – Nova Scotia) is proud to present the new edition of Hiking Trails of Nova Scotia (HTNS). HTNS has been the foremost guide to hiking in the province for over 30 years. This, the 7th edition, represents a significant change for the book and illustrates the depth of focus and commitment in the hostelling movement as we near the next millennium. We hope the reader finds this book carefully researched, clearly presented, and, most importantly, a practical and useful guide to some of Nova Scotia's most beautiful trails. Nova Scotia is blessed with a rugged beauty second to none in the world and an attempt to fully capture this in HTNS would require multiple volumes — far too heavy to carry on your travels! Through a careful screening process we have put together a collection of trails we hope you will find enjoyable, challenging, and professionally presented in a pocket-sized version for use on the trails.

HI – Nova Scotia has its roots in the out of doors. The first hostels were located in private homes or were temporary structures providing basic accommodation for young people hiking or biking across the province. Over the years, with the advent of international tourism and changing trends in recreation, the demand for larger and better-equipped hostels continues to grow. One of the most significant changes for hostelling, and indeed for all outdoor recreation, is the realization that recreation is not just for the 18-25 age group. Hostelling and its related recreational pursuits in Nova Scotia are now the domain of seniors, families, organized youth groups and foreign travellers. To meet the demands of these active and varied groups, HI – Nova Scotia has had to upgrade facilities in urban settings while maintaining the charm of the country hostels. This unique blend of hostels could not be possible without the dedication of our Associate Hostel Operators, who provide hostels in beautiful locations like Sandy Bottom Lake, St. Peter's, Twin Rock Valley, Darling Lake, LaHave, and Barrington.

One of the most significant developments in the facilities has been the purchase of a new hostel in Halifax. With moderate enhancements, the Halifax Hostel will be a first-class facility all Nova Scotians can be proud of. The Wentworth Hostel has been a long-time favourite, particularly with the readers of this book. With access to 70+ km of trail, the hostel is a frequent host to hikers and skiers alike; however, at 130+ years of age, the hostel is well past its prime, and so we are planning stages for replacing the building in 1998-99. This will be our first purpose-built hostel, and it will be an exciting development in the provision of recreational opportunities in the province. Through a joint effort with our counterparts in New Brunswick, we operate a recreation-based hostel in Fundy National Park, and, in addition to the skiing opportunities at Wentworth, members also have access to an HI – Nova Scotia-owned ski hostel at Val d'Irene, Quebec.

Hostels evolved in Nova Scotia out of a need by recreational enthusiasts like the readers of this book. Through publication of this book, the building or licensing of hostels, and the development of organized outdoor activities, it is our goal to encourage all Nova

Scotians to take advantage of our province's unparalleled beauty. We welcome your comments and suggestions on our efforts. If you would like more information about HI – Nova Scotia hostels, organized activities, membership or volunteer information, please contact us at Hostelling International – Nova Scotia, PO Box 3010 South, Halifax NS B3J 3G6, or call (902)425-5450, ext. 324.

We hope we are able to improve your enjoyment of Nova Scotia through this book, and we look forward to seeing you on the trails and in the hostels. On all your adventures we wish you "Happy Trails."

Alan D. MacLennan, President
Hostelling International – Nova Scotia

Beach below look-off, Cape Mabou. MICHAEL HAYNES

INTRODUCTION

Nova Scotia is blessed with abundant woodlands, rugged ocean coastlines, and scenic natural vistas. More than 85% of the land area of the province is covered in forest, ranging from the stunted, ice-blasted balsam firs in the Cape Breton Highlands to the magnificent 300-year-old hemlocks in the southern interior. The ocean, never more than 60 kilometres away, enfolds the province in more than 6000 kilometres of harbours, beaches, and hidden bays. Views from the towering cliff-tops facing the Minas Channel or the endless restless swell of the Atlantic Ocean seen from Martinique Beach can capture the heart of even the most jaded traveller.

Hiking Trails of Nova Scotia will introduce both the novice and the experienced walker to some of the thousands of kilometres of paths, trails, and old roads that crisscross Nova Scotia. Most are in parks owned and maintained by government; these tend to be the highest quality trails available, well marked and maintained, with abundant supporting textual material obtainable. However, quite a few of the most interesting areas of the province contain no large preserved areas. With the exception of Prince Edward Island, no province in Canada has a smaller proportion of its land area in public ownership — only 23%. Most of that is in Cape Breton Island and the unpopulated interior mainland. So a fair number of the hiking opportunities presented in this book will be completely wild: abandoned rail-lines, coastal walks following game trails, and former coach tracks. And unlike the park trails, few of these possess signage or services of any kind.

This is a thrilling time for hikers in Nova Scotia. More trails of all types — snowmobile, cross-country ski, mountain bike, hiking, and multi-use — are under construction in almost every corner of the province than have ever been built before. And for the first time, instead of being restricted to provincially or federally owned lands, as most of the existing public trails are, these new pathways are being developed everywhere, including on the properties of supportive woodlot owners and farmers. Each year, the opening of more routes increases the exciting recreational possibilities in an already rich and varied panorama of natural delights. As well, the proposed Trans-Canada Trail is certain to make an impact on trail development in every corner of the country in years to come.

I hope that the trails you find in this book fulfil all your expectations of a good hike and leave you with many fond and lasting memories.

How to Use This Book

Hiking Trails of Nova Scotia is not a comprehensive guide to all the trails in this province. There are thousands of pathways, abandoned roads, animal trails, and parks found in every county, with new trails being developed each year, and no one has a complete inventory. I learned of places to hike from old books and brochures, through word of mouth, and by accident. Some of the most popular pathways in the province, such as the famous Cape Split, Cape St. Marys, and the Boisdale Hills Firetower, lie on private property, and I could not always obtain the landowner's permission.

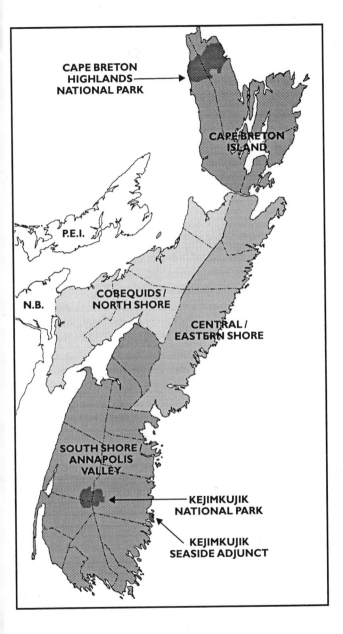

CAPE BRETON
HIGHLANDS
NATIONAL PARK

CAPE BRETON
ISLAND

P.E.I.

N.B.

COBEQUIDS /
NORTH SHORE

CENTRAL /
EASTERN SHORE

SOUTH SHORE /
ANNAPOLIS
VALLEY

KEJIMKUJIK
NATIONAL PARK

KEJIMKUJIK
SEASIDE ADJUNCT

Instead, I have selected an assortment of hiking possibilities somewhat arbitrarily. (If your favourite has been overlooked, let me know.) Dividing the province into six geographic regions, I chose ten hikes within each, varying between short and long, easy and difficult, coastal and inland. Every region begins with a brief introduction including a map indicating the starting points of the trails. Each trail constitutes a separate entry, incorporating a reproduction of the most recent topographical map of the area scaled to fit the book's pages.

A capsule description begins each trail outline:

Length: given in kilometres and miles, rounded to nearest the .5 km.

Time: based on an "average" walker's rate. Do not assume that this reflects the precise amount of time that you will require to complete any particular hike. Everybody hikes at a different pace, which will vary according to weather conditions, the length of the trail, and the individual's fitness level.

Type of trail: indicating the footing that will be encountered.

Rating: a designation from 1 to 5, with 1 suitable for all fitness and experience levels and 5 recommended for experienced and very fit hikers only. These ratings represent nothing other than my own opinion, and I have attempted to base them on an "average" individual's fitness (enlisting friends and relatives as guinea pigs; forgive me all!). If you are a novice, choose level 1 and 2 hikes initially, and work your way up as you gain experience. Starting at level 4 or 5 will only ensure that your hiking career includes punishment from the beginning.

Uses: including cross-country skiing, horseback riding, snowmobiling, and riding ATVs.

Facilities: telling if services such as washrooms or water will be found on the hike.

Gov't topo map: the national topographic map of the terrain covered by the trail.

Each trail outline is divided into the following sections:

Access Information: how to get to the starting point.

Introduction: background about the trail, including historical, natural, or geographical information, as well as my personal observations or recommendations.

Trail Description: a walk-through of the hike, relating what I found when I last travelled the route. In every case I describe junctions and landmarks from the perspective of someone following the trail in the direction I have indicated. If travelling in the opposite direction, remember to reverse my bearings.

Cautionary Notes: information on hunting season, wood ticks, cliffs, high winds, raging seas, or anything I believe you should take extra precautions about. In some cases I highlight environmental concerns, such as piping plover nest sites. Please take these warnings seriously.

Future Plans: what, if anything, is intended in the way of changes to the trail or park in the next few years.

Further Information: many trails, particularly those in parks, have a separate brochure available. If so, I will mention it here. A list of addresses for all agencies mentioned is included in the back of the book.

Where I have no information for Cautionary Notes, Future Plans, and Further Information, these sections will not appear in the trail outline.

A chart of all trails on pages 23-25 shows their lengths and degrees of difficulty at a glance.

About Equipment

Particularly for city dwellers, the forest is a place we do not often visit. We know there are things we should never leave the house without when we go downtown, such as money, ID, and keys, and we automatically pick them up on our way out the door. Similarly, there are a few items that, if we get in the habit of always carrying with us when we enter the forest, should help ensure that every hiking experience is a safe and enjoyable one.

Few people know that they are required by law to carry matches, a knife, and a compass when they travel in the woods in Nova Scotia. The law also requires that hikers know how to use the compass correctly, something surprising few people can actually do (most recreation departments offer courses in map and compass reading). Proper footwear is essential, and care should be taken in selecting what you will wear when hiking. There are other items that are equally indispensable and that you should always include, even in the summer.

Map: I always obtain a map of the area. For some places, particularly provincial or federal parks, a special map of the area exists. Otherwise, I purchase the government topo map. With a map, I get a sense of the terrain that I will be hiking through. Is it swampy? Are there cliffs? Are houses nearby? If I get lost, what direction do I follow to find help? Looking at the map, I know what special equipment may be required and gain an understanding of any special safety considerations.

Water: Perhaps nothing is more important than water. You can live for two weeks without food, but you may die in as few as three days without water. Finding water in Nova Scotia is not usually a problem, but being certain you can safely drink it is. I always carry one litre per person on a hike of up to 10 km, more if the distance is greater, if the day is particularly hot or humid, or if I am taking children with me. Dehydration occurs rapidly while hiking, and the accompanying headaches or dizziness diminishes any pleasure from the hike. Drink small sips of water often, and do not wait until you are thirsty to do so.

Food: Though food is not really necessary on a day hike, I always carry something to snack on while I walk. Apples, trail mix, bagels—anything rich in protein, vitamins, or carbohydrates is good.

Whistle: If you get lost and want to attract attention, a whistle will be heard far better than your voice, and it is less likely to wear out from continuous use. (If you do not believe that, take one outside the house and give a couple of blasts. See how much attention you attract.)

First Aid Kit: When you are out in the woods, even minor injuries may become major disabilities. A small first aid kit with bandages, gauze, tape, moleskin, etc., permits you to deal with blisters and bruises and other common problems.

Garbage Bag: Sadly, this is one of the most used items that you will carry into the woods. First, you should always put all your own trash into the bag and carry it out with you: food wrappers and even apple cores should go into the bag. In addition, particularly if you are hiking on a well-used trail, you will always find litter left behind by others. I always put as much as I can into my garbage bag. If you don't do this, it probably will not get done.

Warm Sweater and/or Rain Jacket: Nova Scotia weather is highly changeable, and forecasts are not always accurate. Rain and wind often combine for uncomfortable and possibly life-threatening conditions. No matter how good the weather seems to be, I always have some heavier clothing with me. Some days, especially in the fall, this might be a wool sweater, while on other trips it may be a rain jacket.

Backpack: You need something to carry all this, and I recommend that you invest in a good quality day-pack. Mine is 1000 dernier nylon (Cordura), and it wears extremely well. It has adjustable shoulder straps, a waist strap, a large inner pouch and two roomy outer pockets. I use it almost every day, both in the city and in the woods, and it carries everything I need. The essential items fit easily inside a good pack, and it will sit comfortably on your back. After one or two trips, it becomes just another part of walking. In fact, I find it difficult to hike without my pack.

Optional (but Recommended) Equipment: Sunscreen, hat, bug repellent, camera, binoculars, field guides, toilet paper, writing paper and pen.

Really Optional Equipment: Extra socks, tarp, rope, eating utensils, flashlight, towel, bathing suit, small stove, fuel, toiletries (toothbrush, paste, soap), sleeping bag.

About Hazards

There are few dangerous plants and animals in the Nova Scotia woods. All four species of snake, for example, are harmless. But there are a few things to remember before you enter the woods.

Ticks: Introduced to Nova Scotia in the early 1900s, the American dog tick is found in the South Shore–Annapolis Valley and Kejimkujik National Park regions, and it is active from as early as April to as late as July. The Nova Scotia population has never produced a confirmed case of Lyme disease.

Bears: Black bears live in Nova Scotia, although they are rarely sighted. Parks Canada has an excellent brochure that I recommend obtaining.

Poison Ivy: Rare in this province, it will be encountered in Kejimkujik National Park and in a few other places. Intense itching is caused by an oil produced by the plant.

Moose: Bulls weigh up to 550 kg (1200 lbs) and can be unpredictable, especially during the fall rutting season. These animals are not just big deer. Treat moose with as much respect and fear as you would a bear.

Hunting Season: Hunting is permitted in many of the areas covered in this book. Usually starting in early October, hunting seasons vary from year to year and according to different types of game. Contact the Department of Natural Resources for detailed information before going into the woods in the fall. No hunting is allowed on Sunday, but always wear some bright orange garment for safety.

Weather: Changeable and unpredictable, Nova Scotia weather must be taken into account. High winds along the coast are common, and the windchill factor can become significant. (For example, as you start hiking inland, the temperature is +16°C [61°F]; when you reach the coast, winds gust to 60 kph [38 mph]; the windchill equivalent becomes +6°C [43°F].) When windchill combines with water chill from ocean spray, fog, or rain, hypothermia becomes possible. It's always a good idea to bring sweaters and rain gear.

TRAILS AT A GLANCE

Trail Name	Difficulty Level 1	2	3	4	5	km (mi)
COBEQUIDS — NORTH SHORE						
Amherst Point Migratory Bird Sanctuary	X					4.0 (2.5)
Beaver Mountain Provincial Park		X				5.0 (3.0)
Cutie's Hollow			X			5.0 (3.0)
Five Islands Provincial Park			X			11.0 (7.0)
Gully Lake					X	26.0 (16.25)
Munroes Island Provincial Park		X				10.0 (6.25)
Refugee Cove					X	18.0 (11.25)
Wallace Bay National Wildlife Area	X					4.0 (2.5)
Wards Falls		X				7.0 (4.5)
Wentworth Hostel Look-off		X				3.5 (2.25)
SOUTH SHORE — ANNAPOLIS VALLEY						
Blomidon Provincial Park			X			13.0 (8.0)
Chebogue Meadows Interpretive Trail		X				5.5 (3.5)
Delaps Cove		X				9.5 (6.0)
Graves Island Provincial Park	X					3.0 (2.0)
Liverpool Rail Trail				X		25.0 (15.5)
Mushpauk Lake		X				10.0 (6.25)

Trail Name	Difficulty Level 1	2	3	4	5	km (mi)
Port L'Hebert Pocket Wilderness	X					3.0 (2.0)
Sable River Rail Trail					X	52.0 (32.5)
Uniacke Estate			X			12.0 (7.5)
Upper Clements Provincial Wildlife Park		X				8.0 (5.0)
CENTRAL — EASTERN SHORE						
Abrahams Lake	X					6.5 (4.0)
Duncans Cove			X			8.0 (5.0)
McNabs Island	X					7.0 (4.5)
Middle Musquodoboit	X					3.5 (2.25)
Musquodoboit Harbour Rail Trail					X	25.0 (15.5)
Old St. Margarets Bay Coach Road					X	40.0 (25.0)
Pennant Point		X				13.0 (8.25)
Queensport Road				X		18.0 (11.25)
Salmon River				X		12.0 (7.5)
Taylor Head Provincial Park			X			18.0 (11.25)
CAPE BRETON ISLAND						
Cape Breton				X		15.0 (9.5)
Cape Smokey Provincial Park			X			11.0 (7.0)
Gull Cove		X				12.0 (7.5)
Highland Hill	X					7.5 (4.75)
Mabou Highlands					X	14.0 (8.75)
Meat Cove				X		16.0 (10.0)
North River Provincial Park				X		18.0 (11.25)
Pringle Mountain			X			12.0 (7.5)
Usige Ban Falls	X					7.0 (4.5)

Trail Name	Difficulty Level 1	2	3	4	5	km (mi)
Whycocomagh Provincial Park		X				2.5 (1.5)
CAPE BRETON HIGHLANDS NATIONAL PARK						
Aspy			X			9.5 (6.0)
Clyburn Valley		X				9.0 (5.5)
Coastal			X			11.0 (7.0)
Corney Brook		X				8.0 (5.0)
Fishing Cove				X		16.0 (10.0)
Franey Mountain			X			6.5 (4.0)
Glasgow Lakes		X				8.0 (5.0)
Middle Head	X					4.0 (2.5)
Skyline		X				7.0 (4.5)
Trous de Saumon			X			13.0 (8.0)
KEJIMKUJIK NATIONAL PARK						
Channel Lake					X	26.0 (16.0)
Fire Tower			X			12.5 (7.5)
Gold Mines	X					3.0 (2.0)
Hemlocks and Hardwoods		X				6.0 (4.0)
Liberty Lake: Big Dam – Campsite #43				X		18.0 (11.25)
Liberty Lake: Campsite #43 – Campsite #37					X	23.0 (14.5)
Liberty Lake: Campsite #37 – Mersey River				X		18.5 (11.5)
Luxton Lake			X			14.0 (8.75)
Peter Point	X					3.0 (2.0)
Seaside Adjunct		X				12.0 (7.5)

Cutie's Hollow. MICHAEL HAYNES

COBEQUIDS – NORTH SHORE

This region connects Nova Scotia to the rest of Canada and comprises Antigonish, Colchester, Cumberland, and Pictou counties. Running through the entire length is the Cobequid-Chignecto fault line, and the Cobequid Hills, once perhaps as high as the Alps, still provide elevation and variety enough to offer challenging hikes. Along the Northumberland Strait the drowned coastline, lower elevations, and softer soils offer a distinctly different but no less enjoyable experience.

Although the stated combined total distance of hikes in these four counties is the lowest of any region in the province, adding the 60 km (37.5 mi) of paths near the Wentworth Hostel boosts it to the highest. Locations such as Wards Falls and Refugee Cove are exceptional, and the Amherst and Wallace Bay bird sanctuaries offer fun strolls with almost guaranteed wildlife viewing. Munroes Island is always a wonderful experience. The interconnected network at Five Islands enables walkers to select distances suitable for any fitness level, as do the stacked loops of Beaver Mountain. Thanks to the work of the Colchester YMCA, the Crown land at Gully Lake is accessible to the novice and experienced hiker alike. Cutie's Hollow may be difficult to find and rough to reach even when you know where you are going, but I can guarantee that you will be pleased once you are there.

Because I have a certain weakness for hilly terrain and waterfalls, the Cobequid Hills have long been a favourite haunt. Hikes like Economy Falls transform me into a playful adolescent, and the abandoned roads of Cumberland and Colchester counties offer limitless possibilities for exploring. Abandoned railways from Springhill to Parrsboro, Oxford Junction to Pictou, and Ferrona Junction to Guysborough could be superior linear trails if they were acquired by the province and developed by community groups. The proposed route of the Trans-Canada Trail, entering the province at Amherst and heading to Cape Breton, suggests that this region has exciting outdoor recreation potential.

Remember that hunting is permitted in the areas crossed by the Cutie's Hollow, Gully Lake, Refugee Cove, Wallace Bay National Wildlife Area, and Wards Falls trails. Usually starting in early October, hunting seasons vary from year to year and according to types of game. Contact the Department of Natural Resources for specific information before going into the woods. Wear orange for safety even on Sundays, when hunting is illegal.

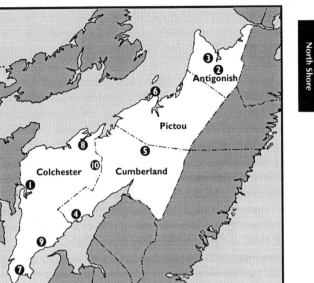

COBEQUIDS / NORTH SHORE

1.	Amherst Point Migratory Bird Sanctuary	*30*
2.	Beaver Mountain Provincial Park	*34*
3.	Cutie's Hollow	*38*
4.	Five Islands Provincial Park	*42*
5.	Gully Lake	*48*
6.	Munroes Island Provincial Park	*52*
7.	Refugee Cove	*56*
8.	Wallace Bay National Wildlife Area	*60*
9.	Wards Falls	*66*
10.	Wentworth Hostel Look-off	*70*

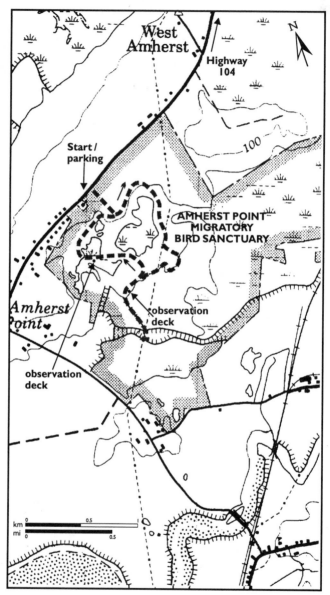

Amherst Point Migratory Bird Sanctuary

Amherst Point Migratory Bird Sanctuary

Length: 4 km
  (2.5 mi) return
Time: 1-2 hrs
Type: walking paths
Rating: 1

Uses: hiking, cross-country skiing
Facilities: none
Gov't Topo Map: Amherst 21 H/16

Access: From Highway 104, take Exit 3 and drive southwest on an unnumbered road away from Amherst toward Nappan. Three kilometres (2 mi) past the Wandlyn Inn, a blue Canadian Wildlife Service sign on the left signals the entrance to the sanctuary's parking lot.

Introduction: Although relatively small, Amherst Point has much to offer. Designated a Migratory Bird Sanctuary in 1947 at the request of neighbouring landowners, it assumed its present size of 433 ha (1070 a) in 1980. A surprising variety of habitats lie within the sanctuary, but 66% of its area is either open water, marsh and bogs, or controlled water-level impoundments—an environment ideal for waterfowl.

The enclosed wetlands, specifically the impoundments created by the dykes and sluices built by Ducks Unlimited in the 1970s, are among the best breeding grounds in Nova Scotia. More than 200 bird species have been observed at Amherst Point, which is a regular nesting site for regionally rare varieties such as gadwall, redhead, ruddy duck, Virginia rail, common gallinule, and black tern.

Gypsum deposits underlie the entire area, and from 1935 to 1942 a commercial mine operated near the sanctuary. Conical depressions called sinkholes pepper the site and create an unusual and rugged topography in places.

Trail Description: Follow the road linking the parking lot to the highway. A metal gate prevents vehicles from continuing, and the wide track leads 200 m/yd to a three-way junction at the top of a hill overlooking Laytons Lake. An interpretive panel here displays a map showing the trail network. I recommend taking the left route, which follows the ridge line along abandoned upland fields northeast for 400 m/yd.

No sign marks the right turn downhill, and a distinct path continues straight, but at the first junction descend toward the woods and Laytons Lake. A beautiful spruce canopy provides shade as the trail follows the water's edge; a solitary rough-hewn bench looks out on a tiny cove. Following a ravine inland over a tiny bridge, the trail winds through woods, giving occasional views of Quarter Moon Lake on the left. Rejoining Laytons Lake, the path follows the bank fairly closely until it connects to an abandoned rail line.

Turn left and follow this track to the power line. Continuing straight leads 300 m/yd to the dyke separating impoundments 2a and 2b. But on your right, 25 m/yd before the power line, a path re-enters the forest and wanders 400 m/yd through lovely woods to another junction and one of the few directional signs in the sanctuary. Turn left here and walk 200 m/yd to a new observation deck tucked in the trees. Continue a further 50 m/yd and find where the dykes connect to the land. From here many kilometres of additional walking is possible, although the dykes are not part of the formal trail network.

Retrace your steps to the signpost and proceed left on the path separating forest and field. At the next junction turn left again, and almost immediately you encounter a small bridge spanning a brook. Laytons Lake is once again on your right. Just beyond the bridge is an X-junction; right leads up the hill 500 m/yd to the start, left goes into the field back towards the dykes. Continue straight instead, and 300 m/yd later find another observation deck overlooking The Cove on your left. Another bridge separates two ponds, and on the other side you re-enter the trees, a gorgeous stand of eastern hemlock, and come to a trail junction and your second directional sign, guiding you right.

This is the only difficult walking of the hike. A handrail assists the climb up between steep-sided sinkholes. Note the sudden and dramatic change in the land. The trail traces the narrow crest of the ridges separating several depressions until it reaches a small clearing called The Glen, where five interpretive panels describe the sanctuary's features. Completing the loop, only 200 m/yd farther along the path, is the initial junction on the top of the hill. Turn left again, after maybe one more look around, to return to the parking lot.

Cautionary Notes: Hunting is not permitted within the Amherst Point Migratory Bird Sanctuary. Even so, be cautious in the fall and wear orange vests or hats.

Although ATV and snowmobile use are prohibited, both occur, especially underneath the power lines, along the sanctuary's access road, and along the dykes.

Remember that this is a sanctuary, and that at times throughout the year you will come upon nests. Please resist the temptation to touch the eggs or interfere in any way. Do not take dogs into this area; they will certainly disturb nests.

Future Plans: The Amherst Hiking Club is attempting to build a trail across the Tantramar Marshes connecting the Amherst Point Sanctuary with the Sackville, New Brunswick, Waterfowl Park.

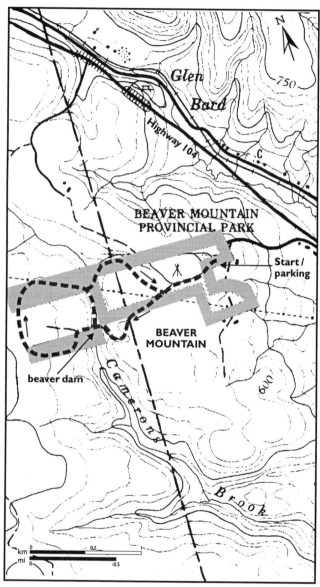

Beaver Mountain Provincial Park

Further Information: The Canadian Wildlife Service (CWS) has a 1981 brochure with more historical and natural information and a checklist of birds. To obtain a copy, write: CWS, PO Box 1590, Sackville NB E0A 3C0.

Beaver Mountain Provincial Park

Length: 5 km
(3 mi) return
Time: 2 hrs
Type: pavement,
dirt road, walking paths
Rating: 2

Uses: hiking, cross-country skiing
Facilities: outhouses, tables, campsites, fireplaces
Gov't Topo Map:
Merigomish 11 E/9

Access: From Antigonish, take Highway 104 11.5 km. (7 mi) west toward New Glasgow. At Exit 30 head south (left) and take first right road (sign in place). Follow for 5 km (3 mi); park at the end of the pavement.

Introduction: Nestled in the Antigonish Highlands, Beaver Mountain offers great summer camping and outstanding winter recreation. Within its 133 ha (329 a) are 47 campsites, which are available from May to September. When snow is on the ground, the trail system is always well used, and nearby Keppoch Mountain permits skiers to enjoy a downhill experience on the same day.

From the park entrance, the spectacular view of the St. George's Bay lowlands, stretching east toward Antigonish, is reason enough to attract visitors. Beaver Mountain is also a marvellous site to take a family for a picnic. The trail is a stacked loop system, and either a 3 km (2 mi) or a 5 km. (3 mi) option is available. The extensive hardwood and softwood stands, the abandoned fields, and the beaver colony offer a variety of habitats and wildlife to see.

Trail Description: Start your walk at the park entrance and administrative centre. From here follow the paved road straight. In the fall and winter you should soon sight ski trail signs, and on occasional trees also notice red rectangular trail markers. Continue until reaching campsite #41. A dirt track heads left for 50 m/yd to a well-signed junction where skiers, and hikers, too, unless they feel ornery, are directed left again. Passing underneath a powerline and across its cleared right-of-way, the trail enters an area of densely packed white spruce perhaps 30 years old.

As the trail descends, the road continues right while trail users are directed left, briefly outside the park boundary. For hikers this is relatively easy walking on a wide and often grassy track. Signs warning of hills ahead become more common now, and markers are frequent. Reaching Camerons Brook, the trail makes a sudden sharp right turn and crosses over an interesting bridge next to two beaver dams. These animals are primarily nocturnal, and sightings are best made at either dawn or dusk; they are very rarely seen in winter.

From here, those who wish a shorter walk should turn right and follow a path paralleling the creek until they reach the next junction. Another right turn, and they are heading back to the start of their 3 km (2 mi) constitutional. Those who wish to walk the full distance should turn left at the bridge instead and start the hike's first uphill push.

Once you start climbing, the woods become exclusively hardwood, mostly maple and beech, with trees tall enough to provide shade. Although the trail is much narrower here, it remains distinct. Several deep gulleys are well bridged and small bogs are skirted, ensuring dry footing. The route hugs the outer limit of the parkland, and the protected nature of your surroundings may become evident as the trail makes its first 90° turn. The land on the left, just outside the park, has been clear-cut, and for most of the next 2 km (1.25 mi) this tract is a constant, thought-provoking companion.

The second sharp right turn occurs as the trail approaches the power line right-of-way, and you are now on your way back. The hardwoods here are gorgeous, with visibility in all directions for several hundred metres. With the turn, the trail begins to descend again towards Camerons Brook, and the next kilometre is mostly downhill. Former logging roads are common, but the frequent trail markers should prevent confusion. Just before reaching the creek the grade gets very steep, and skiers should be warned that they must turn sharply at the bottom with no warning.

This junction is the connector with the short loop. Turning right will return you to the beaver dams; turning left will lead you back to the start. Immediately you emerge from the woods, leaving the maples behind, and cross under the power line for the last time. Crossing the creek, you climb into a stand of white spruce that has reclaimed former cleared fields. Continuing uphill, you remain enfolded by softwoods as the trail passes behind many of the campsites (on your left), and even though both they and the power line are very close, the density of the stand provides a sense of seclusion.

You abruptly find yourself back at the junction on the dirt track where the signs first directed traffic left. From here, turn left and retrace your initial route back to the park entrance.

Further Information: The Department of Natural Resources has a free brochure available on the cross-country ski trails.

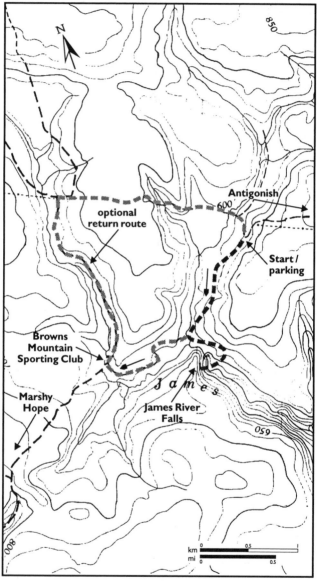

Cutie's Hollow

Cutie's Hollow

Length: 5 km
(3 mi) return
Time: 2 hrs
Type: former road,
walking paths
Rating: 3

Uses: hiking, mountain
biking, cross-country
skiing
Facilities: water
Gov't Topo Map:
Merigomish 11 E/9

Access: The roads into this site are tough and confusing. From Antigonish, drive on Highway 245 to the turnoff to Browns Mountain and Pleasant Valley. At the second intersection, follow the right branch; the road becomes increasingly rough during its climb to the top of Browns Mountain. Continue for about 10 km (6.25 mi) past the transmitter towers until the road makes a sharp left turn and descends to Cutie's Hollow. Look on your right for a spring; on your left on a tree is a small hand-painted sign that says "Cutie's Hollow." Park anywhere along the roadside.

Introduction: This is a gem I discovered in the summer of 1994 following a conversation with the Recreation Director of Annapolis Royal, who had gone to university in Antigonish. Consulting a topo map, I saw a notation of a waterfall on the James River and decided to investigate. I could not believe what I found. The tiny, slow-moving brook turns into a 15-20 m/yd (50-65 ft) waterfall spilling dramatically into a rocky bowl surrounded by cliffs on all four sides; the only safe access is along the stream bed.

Once settled and farmed, the hills are now almost completely deserted, and I felt more isolated here than I did anywhere else in the province. (Maybe it was the pack of coyotes that chased their prey past my tent on Browns Mountain.) Expect to work to see this waterfall, even before you get out of your car. I have given this hike a moderate degree of difficulty, but the drive in rates a 4.

Trail Description: Across the road from the trailhead is a water tap that regulates the flow of a spring. Get a drink before you start. The spring is clean, and nothing tastes better than fresh, cold spring water. The path starts along an old road running parallel to the James River. Shown on the provincial map of 1924, the road has long been abandoned. The trees are quite old in some spots, although the abundance of young hardwoods suggests recent logging. Initially, the path can be extremely muddy. Apparently, the ground water does not confine itself to the spring. Also, mountain bike use appears to be very heavy, churning the wet spots into gooey morasses; ATV tracks can be seen as well. Large deadfalls have been skirted rather than cleared, creating a winding path.

After 1 km (.5 mi), the old road veers right to approach the river. Instead, follow a flagged trail left up a hill. Perhaps 300 m/yd later, another junction appears, and you should continue to keep left under the pine canopy. The trail begins to curve left, climbing as it does, and returns to mixed forest. Once again it widens, looking like another old road. At 2 km (1.25 mi), you will hear the falls to your right, and a side-trail leads off towards the river. This descends very, very steeply down the hillside into a hidden canyon. There are no guardrails, the earth is loose underfoot, and the grade is nearly vertical. Patience on the main trail is worthwhile, because it continues another 200 m/yd and gently descends to river level at the end of the ridge. Flagging tape marks the approach route to the water, then the path works back upstream to the falls.

Be prepared for a surprise. If you saw the languid river, especially in summer, you might expect a simple cascade over the exposed rocks of a modest drop. Instead, you discover a grand bowl carved at least 20 m/yd deep into the landscape, with sheer rock faces rising on all sides. The harder volcanic basalts, revealed by the eroding river, have had their covering of softer sandstones and siltstones stripped away, leaving behind this remarkable formation. Beneath the cataract is a clear circular pond begging for someone to swim in it (which, I am told, is a favourite pastime). Remember that the bottom is all rock. Water marks reveal that levels vary greatly in this hollow; expect limited access during spring runoff and after heavy rainfalls. However, in summer there are many smooth rocks on which to sit and rest and enjoy the sound of the falls. When you are ready to leave, the way in is also the way out.

The more adventurous may consider a different return path. About 400 m/yd from the falls, a prominent ATV trail crosses the James River and heads toward Marshy Hope. After less than 1.5 km (1 mi), the trail emerges from the low wet ground at the buildings of the Browns Mountain Sporting Club. Turn right, and follow the road as it meanders beside a creek, then parallels power lines about 5 km (3 mi) back to Cutie's Hollow. Be cautious among all the side routes; attempt this alternative route only with a good map and compass.

Cautionary Notes: The roads to this hike are rugged and potentially damaging to a family car. Four-wheel drives and trucks are recommended. Also, I found the road network confusing, especially because of new logging roads. Before you turn off the pavement, make sure you have a good map and a full tank of gas.

The terrain around the waterfall is steep cliffs, and the path has been created by use, not thoughtful planning. Be *extremely* careful descending into the river canyon; the risk of a fall is great, and you are far from

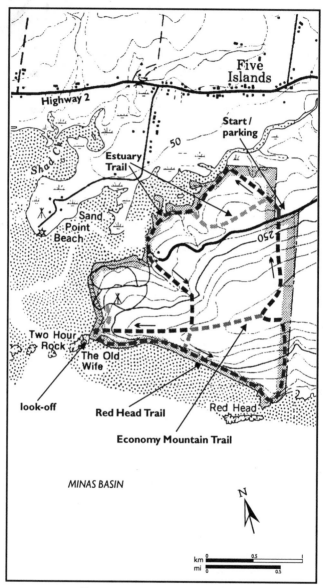

Five Islands Provincial Park

assistance. Do not attempt to scale the cliffs aroun waterfall, and do not do this walk alone.

Hunting is permitted on these lands.

Five Islands Provincial Park

Length: 11 km
(7 mi) return
Time: 4 hrs
Type: walking paths,
fields, roads
Rating: 3

Uses: hiking, cross-country
skiing
Facilities: outhouses, water,
campsites, firewood,
showers, tables, benches,
playground
Gov't Topo Map: Parrsboro
21 H/8

Access: From Truro, drive west along Highway 104 to its junction with Highway 2 at Glenholme. Turn onto Highway 2 and continue past Lower Economy. Road signs advise of the park entrance on your left. Total distance from Truro: 57 km (35.5 mi). From Parrsboro, drive east along Highway 2 through the village of Five Islands. Road signs for the park entrance are on your right. Total distance from Parrsboro: 32 km (20 mi).

Introduction: The five islands at the foot of Economy Mountain, for which the park is named, are prominent in Native legend. Beaver, that energetic but destructive force, ravaged the medicine garden of Glooscap, the powerful Mi'kmaq God-Chief. Infuriated, Glooscap chased after Beaver, hurling five huge rocks at him. The stones all missed and landed in the Bay of Fundy, where they became the islands we see today.

A different version of the islands' formation suggests they are part of the mostly eroded volcanic basalt cap protecting the underlying stone of the red cliffs. Geologists have found minerals such as chabazite, stilbite, calcite, and agate on them. Rockhounding is a popular attraction all along this coast, where the rapidly changing shoreline reveals new finds every year. In Parrsboro, a geological museum offers guided tours. Visitors require permits to collect rocks, minerals, and fossils in provincial parks.

The park includes a 90-site campground within its 452 ha (1117 a) boundaries. Clam digging is popular activity on the 1.6-km (1-mi) mud flats revealed twice daily at low tide, but remember the speed with which the tide changes and do not venture too far from the high water mark.

Trail Description: From the park entrance sign on Highway 2, drive 1.5 km (1 mi) down the paved access road to the first gate and parking lot on the right. When the campground is open, between May and October, so is this gate, and the administrative centre is a further 1.5 km (1 mi) beyond. However, for hiking purposes, I recommend that you begin here. The Estuary Trail enters the woods on the west side of the parking lot, where a large sign and many red rectangular trail markers fastened to trees mark your route. The path is distinct and wide although punctuated with numerous roots. Several pleasant bridges bordered by white spruce are found immediately at the start, as the trail begins to curve north and head downhill toward the East River.

The first junction is with the returning Estuary Trail, but stay right and continue downhill. The path widens as you walk underneath softwoods surrounded by a carpet of sphagnum moss. At East River, the trees change to mixed hardwoods and the footing becomes wetter. For the next kilometre you parallel the river, and several look-offs allow you to view the extensive salt marshes.

Red Head, Five Islands. MICHAEL HAYNES

After 500 m/yd the trail turns inland to another junction. Continuing straight uphill returns you to the first intersection and your start, so bear right and go down the steep hill, around the sharp turn, and over the bridge, through an area cut by several deep, narrow gorges. A further 500 m/yd and you emerge onto grassy fields near the administration centre, where you will find washrooms.

The trail enters the woods again below the administration centre at the back of a small grassy field opposite campsites #88 and #89. Look carefully for the tree-obscured ingress. Crossing a power line cut, the path heads uphill along a marvellous ridge 10 m/yd above a brook in a steep gorge. After nearly a kilometre uphill, an open clear-cut planted with pine appears on your left and continues until you reach the four-way junction.

Turn right, walking for 300 m/yd to emerge into the camping area through campsite #75. Continue left along the gravel road until it starts to curve right, then cut left for 25 m/yd to rendezvous with the Red Head Trail. Turn right and follow the path until the junction with the look-off side trail. Follow it for 300 m/yd to its end, where you arrive at the most spectacular sight in the park, the Old Wife, a highly sheared, jointed ridge of basalt knifing skyward out of the ocean. Directly beyond is Moose Island and the remainder of the Five Island chain.

Leaving this side trail, you turn right and follow the Red Head Trail , which is well signed. For the first kilometre, a steel-link fence on your right parallels the 90 m/yd cliffs. Your path is level and wide, easy walking, with the campground on your left. Reaching a junction after 1.5 km (1 mi), continue straight ahead and gently downhill for another kilometre. Watch for look-offs, some thoughtfully equipped with benches. The remainder of your hike will be more challenging as you approach the deeply eroded slopes around Red Head. The path narrows and descends steeply as it nears this point, and a side trail takes you onto the promontory. The view of the sandstone cliffs over which you walked is magnificent.

After Red Head, the route follows the ridge line, with occasional detours into deep gorges and stops for impressive views, for less than a kilometre before it turns inland for the final climb to the top of Economy Mountain. You face a very steep ascent through mostly dead forest. The bench you find part way up may be a welcome relief. Your final junction is with the Economy Mountain Trail. You may wish to use the bench here, because there is still some climbing to be done. The adjacent sign displays a map, and you can see that you turn right to get back to the parking lot. At first you continue to ascend, but mercifully the trail soon begins to slope downward. Less than 1 km (.5 mi) of continuous steep downhill remains, and you emerge at the gate opposite where you entered the Estuary Trail, completing the grand loop.

Cautionary Notes: Much of the Red Head Trail follows steep, actively eroding cliff edge. When I was last there, in 1993, at least one of the safety barriers was moveable.

During low tide, large areas of sand are exposed, including a connection to Moose Island. Do not walk there. Tides rise up to one metre in 20 minutes, stranding the unwary, and the tidal currents are irresistible. Access is only by boat, which can be chartered locally.

Further Information: The Department of Natural Resources has a free brochure with trail map and outline of services.

Gully Lake

Length: 26 km (16.25 mi) return
Time: 8-10 hrs
Type: former roads
Rating: 5

Uses: hiking, mountain biking, cross-country skiing, horseback riding, snowmobiling, ATV
Facilities: none
Gov't Topo Map: Truro 11 E/06, Tatamagouche 11E/11

Access: From Truro, travel 15 km (9.5 mi) on Highway 104 toward New Glasgow through Kemptown. Turn north onto the Mount Thom Road. After 2 km (1.25 mi) turn left on the Proudfoot Road and drive 1.5 km (1 mi) to its end. Park here; the trail continues in the same direction as the road. (Ongoing construction on Highway 104 may affect these directions.)

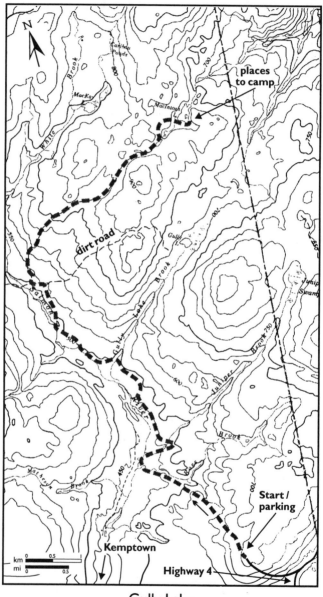

Gully Lake

Introduction: Gully Lake is located in a large parcel of Crown land midway between Truro and New Glasgow in the Cobequid Mountains. This parcel contains three lakes, four brooks, and the source of the Salmon River. Innumerable old logging tracks interlace through the area, and many of these are still well travelled and easy to find. Any combination of short, medium, long, or overnight opportunities can be created if you know the network.

I have combined a number of trails to construct a 26 km (16.25 mi) route that can be a challenging day-hike for the serious outdoorsman, or a pleasant two-day trip with an overnight camp on a lake for the more leisurely. Attempting the full distance in one day earns you the 5 rating. Extending the walk overnight reduces it to a family-oriented 3.

Trail Description: Continue on foot along the dry, hard-surfaced former road past the blueberry fields. Two can walk side by side quite comfortably here, as they can for most of the hike. Within 500 m/yd the trail crosses an old field, a remnant of an earlier homestead, and then it continues through mixed stands of young but pleasant hardwoods and softwoods for the next kilometre. Your next landmark is an old farm field beginning to return to forest. Crossing the field, your trail continues north and downhill through woods — mostly conifers — for the next 1.5 km (1 mi) almost to the Salmon River. Ross Brook parallels the path for much of this distance and in some places may seem to join it for a while. Approaching Salmon River, the trail finally crosses the brook and another well-travelled track joins on your right. If you continue straight, you encounter the Salmon River within 100 m/yd. Follow this new trail now, turning east and beginning to climb alongside a small stream on your left, called Juniper Brook. Another trail junction, this one on your left in another abandoned field, appears in less than a kilometre. Turn left, and cross the field heading north once more. If you miss the turn, your trail is quickly going to become narrow and indistinct, warning you to backtrack.

For the next 6.5 km (4 mi), the trail will follow the Salmon River on its east bank. Evidence of ATV usage will be frequent, and ATV enthusiasts maintain several railway tie bridges over rivulets. Alternating mixed tree and pure hardwood stands highlight glimpses of the river until you begin to move inland and uphill a bit. Just before the bridge over Gully Lake Brook, you will encounter another abandoned farm field. Over the bridge, the trail briefly turns left before curving around to the north again, and about 1.5 km (1 mi) beyond the brook, you will sight a significant open bog on your left. Between late July and early September the tall purple flower of the Joe Pye weed should catch your eye. During the next kilometre, the trail turns away from the Salmon River and climbs slightly. The old road gets rocky but is quite dry and still easy walking. You suddenly emerge from the trees to find yourself on the wide, gravelled Gully Lake Road. You have walked about 8 km (5 mi) so far, and the best is yet to come.

Turn left down the hill and follow the road toward ·Salmon River. This stretch is very exposed, but you only have to go about 250 metres before you can shelter under the trees again. A gravel pit on the north side of the road marks your re-entry point, and the former road on the far side is easy to find. This segment is a beautiful stroll up a gentle slope through open mixed hardwoods, suitable for almost anyone. After about 2.5 km (1.5 mi), the trail from the MacIntosh Lake Road joins on your right, coming down the hill. Continue following the slope as the trail gradually descends toward MacIntosh Lake. A beaver pond on your right 1.5 km (1 mi) later forces the road to swing wide around a small hill. White spruce starts to dominate, and as you approach the lake you will notice remnants of old fields and stone walls on your left. The lake is a popular destination and a lovely site for either a picnic or a campout, with abundant nearby grassy fields and foliage. This is your half-way point, 13 km (8 mi). Retrace your steps to reclaim your car on the Proudfoot Road.

Cautionary Notes: This is an entirely unsupervised area. There are no signs and no services, and the trails are not maintained. Before entering the woods make certain that you inform someone where you will be and when you are expected back.

Hunting is permitted in this area.

Further Information: The YMCA of Colchester produced an excellent free Observation and Trail Guide to the entire Gully Lake area of Colchester and Pictou counties through a Youth Environmental Education Program in 1993.

Munroes Island Provincial Park

Length: 10 km
(6.25 mi) return
Time: 3 hrs
Type: sand beaches,
rocky shoreline
Rating: 2

Uses: hiking
Facilities: outhouses,
washrooms, tables, water,
firewood, garbage cans,
supervised beach
Gov't Topo Map: New
Glasgow 11 E/10

Access: From the Trans-Canada Highway, Highway 104, turn at Exit 22 onto Highway 106. Continue through the Pictou rotary toward the Caribou Ferry. Af-

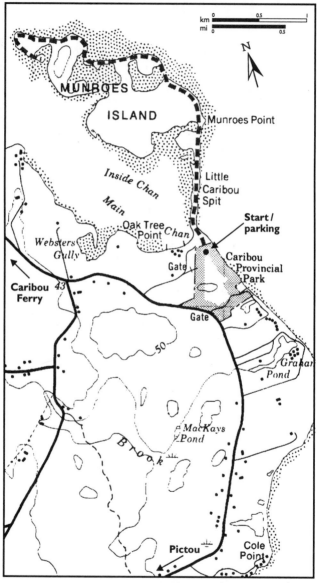

Munroes Island

ter 7 km (4.5 mi), take the last exit before the Prince Edward Island Ferry east (right) toward Caribou Islands Provincial Park. Go 3 km (2 mi) down an unnumbered road; the park entrance is on your left. Drive into the park and leave your car at the beach parking lot.

Introduction: The Northumberland Strait coastline is among the most sought-after land in Nova Scotia. Ideal as summer cottage country, the gentle sandstone, siltstone, and shale of this district sharply contrast with the rugged granites of the Atlantic coastal region. The shallow channel separating the mainland from Prince Edward Island offers the warmest salt water north of the Carolinas, and its long sandy beaches ensure easy access to it. This is one of only three true lowland areas in the province, with the topography ranging from flat to undulating. It is also a submerged coastline, the land link with Prince Edward Island having been severed by the rising ocean between 5000 and 7000 years ago. Pictou Island is a remnant of a ridge that ran through the centre of what is now the Northumberland Strait.

Most of the coastline is privately owned, and only a few small parks lie between the New Brunswick border and New Glasgow. Munroes Island represents one of the few natural settings remaining along this beautiful coast. In 1992, the Nature Conservancy of Canada donated Munroes Island to the Province of Nova Scotia, capping a three-year project initiated by a local resident to acquire the 112 ha (280 a). Local companies such as Michelin Tires (Canada) Ltd., Scott Maritimes Ltd., and the Sobey Foundation supported the project, and other major contributors include the Themedel Foundation and the Seagull Foundation.

This is a wonderful stroll for a lazy Sunday morning or afternoon. The flat, wide beaches encourage dawdling, and I find it hard to resist the urge to build a sand castle.

Bird life is abundant, and the island is home to bald eagles. Except for its length and its occasional rocky sections, this is a walk for everybody. Of course, those not interested in hiking may always remain in Caribou Islands Provincial Park. Its supervised beach is on the sandspit connecting Munroes Island with the mainland, and its picnic area is on the high ground just behind.

Trail Description: This trail requires little elaboration. In essence, you just follow the shoreline. However, a few observations might be useful to first-timers. From the parking lot, a wooden stairway leads to the beach. Pictou Island and Prince Edward Island should be visible to the north and Merigomish to the south. In the summer, lifeguards supervise a clearly marked and popular section of this beach, and you might feel a little overdressed in your hiking gear on a hot July day. Continue walking up the beach beyond the supervised area. Munroes Island, or Little Caribou as it was once called, is no longer separate from the mainland. As recently as the early 1980s, a narrow channel of water cut it off from Widow's Point, where the park is located.

For more than a kilometre you walk over a beautiful open sandspit populated only by low grasses. Stay on the park (right) side of the beach. Rounding the point at the far end of the beach, footing becomes a little rockier, especially in areas exposed at low tide. An impounded salt marsh is located on your left, home to ducks and sandpipers. Continuing along, you'll see whimbrels, yellowlegs, spotted sandpipers, and other shore birds combing the exposed shore for dinner. Just beyond the marshy area you may spot terns and gulls sitting on the rocks offshore; if you don't see them, you will certainly hear them. Another pond appears on your left, and at high tide you might get your feet wet crossing its channel to the ocean. At low tide, however, this is only a shallow indentation through the sand. The next point beyond the pond contains the roughest walking. Practically no sand fringe exists, and the shore is a small embankment between forest edge and water level. I was scolded by a pair of offended kingfishers when I last walked there.

The ferries connecting Wood Islands, Prince Edward Island, and Caribou ply the channel between Caribou Island and Munroes Island and pass very close. Another sandy beach fills the next cove. Similar to the sandspit connecting the island to the mainland, this beach is only a thin ribbon connecting the more stable tree-covered areas. Walk to the grass fringe on top, and you will look into another lagoon. I have sighted as many as 10 herons here. The final kilometre rounds a wooded point with a stony beach. Walking is never difficult, but spray-covered rocks can be slippery. You finish on a grass-covered point that curves around to provide impressive views of Caribou Island, Caribou Harbour, and the ferry terminal. Although the wide beach continues beyond this point and appears to offer an easy return, the inland side of the island is a much tougher hike, with marshy banks instead of the sand and stone of the strait shore; you're certain to get your feet muddy. I recommend that you sit on the sandy beach beneath the automated light, enjoy a lunch or snack, and return along your original route.

Cautionary Notes: Many bird species, including great blue heron, nest on Munroes Island. When disturbed, herons abandon their nests and eggs, and one person walking underneath their nesting tree is sometimes sufficient to frighten them away permanently. To minimize disruption, restrict your hiking to the forest edge.

Future Plans: The Department of Natural Resources hopes to turn Munroes Island into a natural environment park.

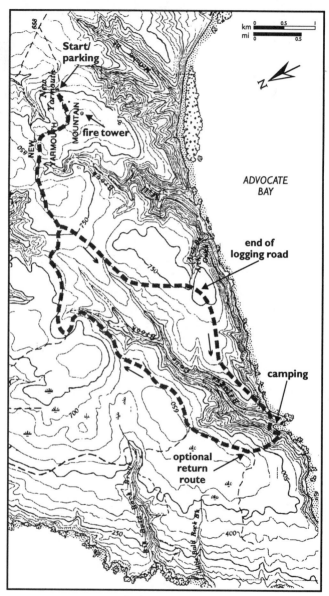

Refugee Cove

Refugee Cove

Length: 18 km
(11.25 mi) return
Time: 6-8 hrs
Type: former road,
gravel road, footpath,
woods
Rating: 5

Uses: hiking
Facilities: none
Gov't Topo Map: Cape
Chignecto 21 H/7

Access: From Parrsboro, drive 46 km (29 mi) along Highway 209 to Advocate Harbour. On the far side of town, turn left off Highway 209 toward West Advocate. Drive 1.2 km (.75 mi) on a paved road to the Chignecto Variety Store (on your right). Turn right onto an unmarked dirt road and follow it for 4.5 km (2.75 mi). Take the left fork (you can see the fire tower in the distance), and follow it for 1.5 km (1 mi). Park your car next to the abandoned hunting camps just before the fire tower. The trail runs along the northern boundary of the field.

Introduction: In 1755, when war with France for control of North America was looming, English colonial authorities decided to expel the large Acadian population living in recently captured mainland Nova Scotia. Thousands were driven from their homes, loaded onto ships, and dispersed throughout British North America. Escapees from seizures around Grand Pré and Minas Basin gathered in this tiny, inaccessible cove before moving on, and their hiding place has been known as Refugee Cove ever since.

Between 1840 and 1890, Advocate Harbour was a booming shipbuilding community, and its brigs, barques, and schooners travelled round the world. The lumber to build these vessels and the cargo to fill their holds came from the hills of Cape Chignecto, and every cove held a lumber camp.

The dirt road to New Yarmouth can be used only between May and November. For the rest of the year snow and mud make it inaccessible to regular vehicles.

Trail Description: The first 1.5 km (1 mi) of the walk follows the almost-overgrown logging road running northwest from New Yarmouth. Many less distinct tracks separate from it, but you should have no difficulty staying on the correct path. This older road intersects a Scott Paper Class 1 logging road, wide and gravelled, and you bear left. Within 500 m/yd the ground falls away on your right and you have a magnificent view of Chignecto Bay and the New Brunswick coastline.

Your route now heads into the valley created by Refugee Cove Brook. Several prominent roads separate from this main track in the next kilometre, and you must pay careful attention to landscape features to stay on the correct path. As you approach the brook, expect to see a low completely clear-cut ridge on your right. Former editions of *Hiking Trails of Nova Scotia* recommended following the creek down to the cove. Those wishing an exceptionally challenging experience may still do so. Those not so ambitious should follow the road that first parallels the valley, then slowly climbs to the hills on its left. It ends in an area of clear-cut high above Advocate Bay, but a distinct trail can be found, with some searching, at the western edge of this tract.

For the next 2 km (1.25 mi), your route follows the top of the ridge through an area of beautiful hardwoods. The ocean is on your left, and Refugee Cove Brook is on your right. The trail descends gradually to within 500 m/yd of Refugee Cove. From here, however, it falls sharply more than 150 m (500 ft) to sea level. Footing becomes very difficult, and this entire section is extremely steep. You arrive in alder thickets choking the stream bed, but you quickly emerge onto the grassy clearing. Note the old brick oven on the east side. There are numerous campsites beside the creek; remember to stay above the tide line. From the mouth of the cove, Advocate Harbour and Cape d'Or seem within hailing distance to your left, while across Minas Channel the shore of Kings County is quite prominent. To the right, 9 km (5.5 mi) away, the rugged hills of Isle Haute rise vertically out of the water.

Most hikers will return along the same route when they decide to leave. Those wishing a challenge may instead exit via the narrow gully near the mouth of the cove. Following a small stream-bed, this gorge steeply climbs to the hills above. Keep right, and when the land begins to level and the gully disappears, follow a compass heading of due north. After 300 m/yd of heavy bushwhacking, you will come upon an old logging road. Turn right.

This road has grown in quite well and provides a lovely, shaded walk for the next 4 km (2.5 mi). Although many faint trails exit in various directions, the only distinct junction occurs after 1 km (.5 mi). Keep right. This old road traces the opposite slope of the Refugee Cove Brook valley, and it continues until it intersects with another Class 1 logging road near the head of the brook. Once again turn right and follow this wide, open track until it rejoins the incoming road 2 km (1.25 mi) later. Turn left, and retrace your route to New Yarmouth, 3 km (2 mi) away.

Cautionary notes: Although it appears to be an easy walk to Refugee Cove along the coastline at low tide, never attempt it. Extremely high tides, averaging 8 m (26 ft), wash far up the sheer unbroken cliffs, and it is possible to become stranded or even washed away.

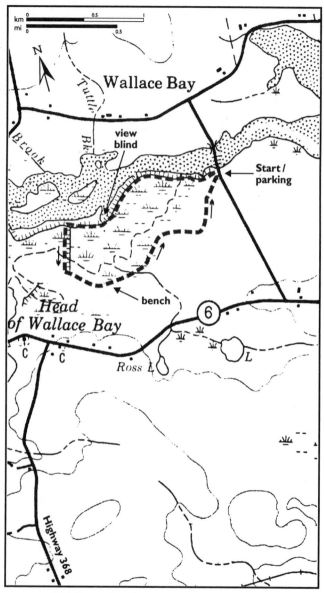

Wallace Bay National Wildlife Area

This is one of the most rugged trails outlined in this book. Make certain you let people know where you are hiking and when to expect you back. Map and compass are essential on this hike.

Hunting is permitted in this area.

Future Plans: Development of the proposed 4252-ha (10,500-a) Cape Chignecto Provincial Park awaits final approval and funding before work begins. The extensive plans include campgrounds around New Yarmouth, day-use facilities around both West Advocate and Spicers Cove, and a coastal wilderness trail from West Advocate around Cape Chignecto to Spicers Cove. At more than 20 km (12.5 mi) one way, it will be the longest hiking trail in a provincial park in Nova Scotia.

Wallace Bay National Wildlife Area

Length: 4 km
(2.5 mi) return
Time: 1-2 hrs
Type: walking paths
Rating: 1

Uses: hiking
Facilities: none
Gov't Topo Map: Pugwash
11 E/13

Access: From Pugwash, drive 8 km (5 mi) toward Tatamagouche along Highway 6. Less than 1 km (.5mi) past the Highway 368 turnoff, turn left on an unnumbered road to Wallace Bay. There is a parking lot on your left 1 km (.5 mi) down this road, just before the bridge over the Wallace River. From Wentworth, travel north first on Highway 307, then on Highway 368 until it ends at Highway 6. Turn right, toward Tatamagouche; the road to Wallace Bay is 1 km (.5mi) on your left. There are no road signs for the trail except beside the parking lot.

Introduction: In 1973, Ducks Unlimited undertook the construction of 3.8 km (2.5 mi) of dikes and five water control structures (sluices) to establish 144 ha (356 a) of impounded wetlands. In 1980, Wallace Bay was declared a National Wildlife Area and is maintained under the Canadian Wildlife Act.

Situated at the upper limit of Wallace Harbour on the Northumberland Strait, the area has long been an important migration and breeding habitat for waterfowl. The habitat management initiated by Ducks Unlimited and the protection afforded by the National Wildlife Area have contributed to significant increases in both the numbers of waterfowl hatched here and the varieties of species inhabiting the area. Other marsh birds, birds nesting in the surrounding uplands, and even bald eagles have moved into the protected territory, which includes more than the original wetlands. These wetlands make up more than 75% of the National Wildlife Area's 585 ha (1445 a); 17% of the area is forest, and the remainder is abandoned farmland.

If you like birds, this is a good place to find them. But it's not just a great birding site; it's also a pleasant little hike for the entire family. The trail is easy walking with practically no elevation change, particularly on the dike, and the distance is within most people's comfort level.

Trail Description: This is a loop trail, and either direction will return you to the parking lot, but I recommend starting your stroll on the river side. Not only is the viewing better, but the walking is easier, too. Your first 2 km (1.25 mi) is along the completely flat, unobstructed, hard-earth surface of the dike. Twenty-year-old white birches predominate, creating a fairly low but relatively thick screen of leaves for most of this section of the hike. On your left are freshwater wetlands, the protected area created by the dyke; on your right are tidal channels and salt marsh.

Birding opportunities are everywhere, so I hope you remembered to bring your binoculars. Almost as soon as you enter the trail you will notice an elevated nesting box to your left. Originally intended for wood ducks, these boxes have proven equally beneficial to the hooded merganser population. In addition to the ducks in the water on both sides of you, warblers and vireos make their homes in the trees, and several species of sparrow and the raucous red-winged blackbird populate the grasses and rushes. Half-way along the dike you will find an observation shelter with a sturdy bench, built by the CWS and the Wallace Area Development Association. From here you can observe both fresh and salt wetlands, although viewing is best on the river side. Across the river the land is cleared and is open for a considerable distance. Various hawk species patrol there regularly.

Several hundred metres past the observation stand the dike forks. Continuing directly ahead you will quickly notice that there is no longer a clearly defined path, and if you ignore this clue you will eventually come to a dead end. Instead turn left and head toward the forest. You still have water on both sides, but the vegetation is sparser and you have a wider view. Watch around this area in particular for beaver and muskrat. In late spring and summer, especially toward dusk, you will be serenaded by a froggy chorus. At the end of the dike the trail enters a hardwood stand. From this point on, brightly painted blue jay figures affixed to trees will mark your path. A unique feature on this trail, these homemade markers are abundant and conspicuous. As the foliage changes, so do the birds, with warblers, thrushes, and woodpeckers much in evidence.

Turning back toward the parking lot, the trail leads you through overgrown fields, an alder swamp (wet despite bridges), and finally into dense softwoods. Boreal and black-capped chickadees, nuthatches, and kinglets flit among the spruce. The wetlands are now out of sight on your left, but they're not far away, as the occasional loud quacking will remind you. After nearly 2 km (1.25 mi) among the widely differing groves, the trail returns to the parking lot.

Cautionary Notes: This is a wildlife preserve, set aside to provide safe conditions for waterfowl breeding. In the spring you may encounter nests anywhere, including the middle of the trail. Do everything in your power not to disturb them. Do not take dogs or other animals on this hike; they are far too disruptive to the birds and mammals inhabiting this area.

Fishing, hunting, and trapping are permitted inside this National Wildlife Area.

Future Plans: A short loop into a scenic hardwood stand is under construction.

Further Information: The CWS has historical and natural history information for this area, and a brochure is in preparation.

Wards Falls

Length: 7 km
(4.5 mi) return
Time: 3 hrs
Type: walking paths
Rating: 2

Uses: hiking
Facilities: outhouses, benches, garbage cans, picnic tables
Gov't Topo Map: Parrsboro 21 H/8

Access: From Parrsboro, drive west along Highway 209 for 8 km (5 mi) to the community of Wharton. A green and yellow sign on your right directs you onto the dirt access road. (If you pass the sign for the community of Diligent River, you have missed the turnoff by 100 m/yd.) From the pavement, the access road leads directly to the trailhead, less than a kilometre away.

Introduction: This property, a holding of more than 2000 ha (5000 a), belongs to C. Ernest Harrison & Sons Ltd. of Parrsboro, a lumber and building supply company. In memory of its founder, C. Ernest Harrison, the company has agreed to take the land around the trail out of production and maintain the trail. In 1993, Harrison's replaced all the old bridges, outhouses, and signs. All the company's lands are open for recreational use, and snowmobile clubs have many kilometres of groomed track in other locations.

Where the North Branch Diligent River cuts through the Cobequid Mountains, the resistant older rocks have eroded, carving a narrow (4 m/yd wide) gorge nearly 40 m/yd long and 20 m/yd deep — Wards Falls. In summer only a trickle of water falls innocently from the opening, and it is possible to walk inside the gorge without getting wet. During the spring, however, the narrow aperture is sometimes insufficient to accommodate the

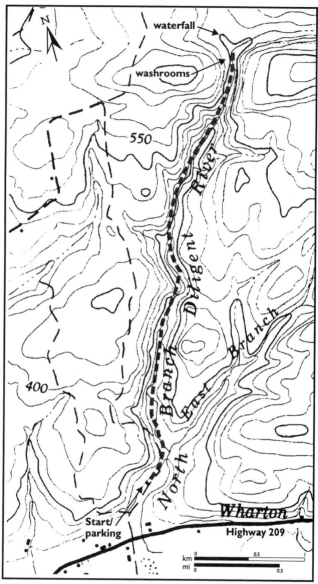

waterfall

washrooms

550

Diligent River

Branch

East Branch

400

North Branch

Start/
parking

Wharton

Highway 209

km
mi

0   0.5   1

0   0.5

Wards Falls

water passing through, with spectacular results. There are few similar sites in Nova Scotia.

Trail Description: A sign in the parking lot stands at the entrance to the walk next to a covered garbage can. At first an old road, the trail heads up the valley with the North Branch Diligent River, more of a meandering brook, on its right. Rather quickly the trail turns right off the old road and crosses the brook. There are some signs, but in the summer these might be difficult to notice. Once over the bridge, the route crosses an abandoned field planted with white pine. Soon the trail moves under the high spruce canopy that shades the remainder of the walk. As if unable to make up its mind, the path crosses back and forth over the brook too many times to count, fortunately on well-constructed bridges. The farther up the increasingly steep-sided valley you go, the older and larger the trees become. On quiet days, when a light mist rises from the brook, the scene of moss-covered rocks and old trees looks almost enchanted.

In case you start wondering where you are, mounted on one of the bridges is a large sign saying "Halfway." Also along the route are several benches and seats carved from tree stumps. If you walk quietly you may sight a blue heron fishing. These large birds, commonly seen in the tidal flats, nest in the tops of trees and work almost any body of water. Other frequent avian sightings should include chickadees, Canada jays, nuthatches, and thrushes. Pay close attention in the spring when the warblers are back. Novice birders will be amazed at the colour variations.

Two large outhouses on your left warn you that you have almost reached the end of the walk. Built the same time as the bridges, these privies are almost sturdy enough to use as emergency shelters! The trail now

Falls and ladder, Wards Falls. MICHAEL HAYNES

climbs relatively steeply for a short distance, the sound
of the falls grows louder, and a picnic table on your left
overlooks the entrance to the gorge. You are facing a
massive exposed rock wall rising directly across your
path: the Cobequid-Chedabucto fault. For most hikers,
this is where the walk ends. The more adventurous may
wish to climb the ladder from the bottom of the falls to
the entrance of the canyon, where they will be re-
warded with a fascinating view of the cave-like ravine.

From there, ropes secured by pitons permit the agile
and confident to scramble into the gap, where they may
walk a few metres further until blocked by deeper basins.
These pools, though cold, may invite some impromptu
skinny-dipping. (Not that I would ever try this, of course.)
Whatever your choice, when you are ready, retrace the
same path to return to your car, 3.5 km (2.25 mi) away.

Cautionary Notes: The entrance to the gorge is difficult
to reach and requires some dexterity on the ladder and
ropes. Rocks are often slippery from spray. After a rain-
storm, or during the spring runoff, do not enter the
restricted area of the gorge. Although some paths appear to lead beyond the falls, these are not part of the
formal trail system and are not maintained.

Hunting is permitted in this area.

Further Information: The local tourist association has
received funding to produce a brochure about the trail.
Visit the tourist bureau in Parrsboro to see if it is available yet.

Wentworth Hostel Look-off

Length: 3.5 km
(2.25 mi) return
Time: 2 hrs
Type: walking paths
Rating: 2

Uses: hiking, mountain
biking, cross-country
skiing
Facilities: none
Gov't Topo Map: Oxford
11 E/12

Access: From Truro, drive 48 km (30 mi) toward Amherst on Highway 104. Turn left (west) on Valley Road
1.5 km (1 mi) past the downhill ski area; watch for the

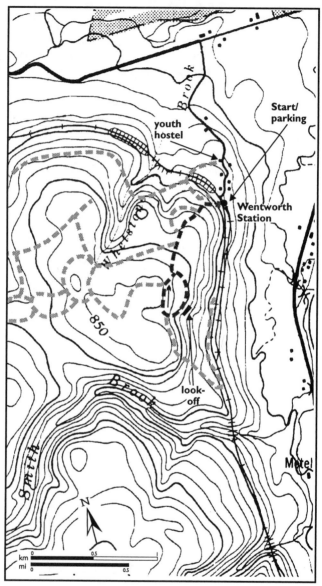

Wentworth Hostel Look-off

sign for the youth hostel. Turn left onto a dirt road 1.5 km (1 mi) later, and continue until the road ends at railway track, approximately 1 km (.5 mi) further.

Introduction: As you drive the dirt road up to the hostel, try to imagine it as it was in the early 1900s. A major stop for the Intercolonial Railway beginning in 1876, Wentworth Station boasted three hotels, two grocery stores, a carriage factory, a tailor shop, a shoemaker, a livery stable, a freight shed, a station, a rail siding, and a post office. It was the shipping and distribution centre for a large part of the Northumberland Shore, including Wallace and Tatamagouche. Today, few residences and no businesses remain.

Since acquiring the "Uncle Josh" Livingston property in 1962, Hostelling International has extensively renovated the buildings, which may now lodge 40 people. The hostel is open throughout the year. Wentworth Valley is one of the largest skiing centres on mainland Nova Scotia. In addition to the downhill slope on the opposite side of the valley, the land behind the hostel contains more than 70 km (44 mi) of cross-country trails, all of which may be hiked as well. I have highlighted only a short walk to the most striking location; days of roaming are possible in this area.

Trail Description: It is possible to start at the hostel, but better parking is available at the end of the road, the site of the former train station. From here, cross the busy train tracks quickly. The trail entrance, which is becoming overgrown, is on the hillside near old apple trees; it's less than 20 m/yd from a power pole at the end of the road opposite. Watch for flagging tape on trees. Once you have found the path, it is very easy to follow.

The first trail junction comes complete with a sign that points left and reads "Look-off," making your decision easy. The next junction, very shortly afterward, is not signed, but turn left anyway. (Actually, both paths lead to the same spot later.) You are faced immediately with a fairly steep uphill; until you reach the look-off, most of the hike will be ascending. This area is mostly young white spruce, reclaiming an old clearing.

The trail levels off briefly, and another junction points you left again. The trail you just climbed is called "Fall Line"; remember this for the return trip. Crossing a little stream, you climb again for 50 m/yd to another junction. Once again bear left, trusting the signs. Note the "No Snowmobiling" marker. Continuing uphill a few hundred metres leads to another junction, but this time the look-off trail is not the furthest left trail. The sign instead directs you to the middle of three possibilities. The "SM" on the accompanying sign stands for "Ski Marathon." The forests up here are generally hardwood. Yellow birch and sugar maples predominate, and there is very little undergrowth. When the trail almost levels and the hill slopes on your right, you arrive at the final turn toward the look-off, where a sign tells you that it is 1.4 km (1 mi) back to the hostel. Less than 300 m/yd remain, now level and gently downhill; the path is narrower here. A small boggy area on your right supports tall spruce and, judging from the tracks in the snow, a fair number of deer.

Suddenly you arrive at the bare outcropping of granite that is the look-off, which is easily visible from the Trans-Canada Highway below. From here you obtain a spectacular southward panorama of the Wentworth Valley, as well as a good view of the ski trails on the opposite slope. To return to your car, continue along the path beyond the look-off. The trail describes a short loop around a small knoll and boggy area to rejoin the main network. From now on, just remember to turn right at all junctions. However, signs are located at every intersection, and there should be no confusion. If in doubt head downhill, except at the first decision point. Do not follow "Hyslop's Hangup"; the name should be warning enough. Reaching the initial junction near the tracks, turn left instead of right, then cross the railway at the bottom of a grassy field. This trail will lead you directly to the Wentworth Hostel. From there, walk up the dirt road to the parking area.

Cautionary Notes: The look-off is a bare piece of rock with no guardrails, very slippery when wet or icy. If you take the wrong turn and become lost among the many paths, a compass bearing of 90° (east) leads to either the railroad or Highway 104.

The railway here is extremely dangerous. It is heavily used, continuously, with trains moving at high speeds. Because of the topography, there is little warning of their approach. *Do not loiter on the tracks*. Move across immediately.

Future Plans: New trails are being added every year; check with the hostel for updates. A new map of the area beyond the railway tracks is being issued in 1995.

Further Information: Extremely detailed topographical maps of the land behind the Wentworth Hostel and of the ski hill on the other side of Highway 104 are available from the Orienteering Association of Nova Scotia for $5. All trails are shown.

Delaps Trail. MICHAEL HAYNES

SOUTH SHORE – ANNAPOLIS VALLEY

Lunenburg town and the Bluenose are, for many, quintessential Nova Scotia. For others, rows of apple trees near Wolfville, their pink blossoms defiantly announcing the arrival of spring, best evoke the character of the province. Both of these areas are found in the southern portion of the province, the most geographically diverse of the regions in Hiking Trails of Nova Scotia. The rugged shoreline from Aspotogan to Yarmouth is similar to the exposed granite headlands of the Eastern Shore. The Annapolis Valley, a region of sandstone and siltstone soils protected between the basalt ridges of North and South mountains, is the most agriculturally fertile area of Nova Scotia. The Atlantic interior, rugged, boggy, and barren, stands distinct from them both.

The South Shore–Annapolis Valley region also includes some of the most thickly inhabited areas of the province, and a number of popular trails, such as Cape Split and Cape St. Mary, and the New Germany–Middleton rail trail are located on private property. I could not include these in Hiking Trails of Nova Scotia because I could not obtain permission from the landowners. Changes to property laws, such as the provincial government's proposed Occupier's Liability Act, may alter this situation in a few years, but until then to use these trails is to trespass.

Novices, young people, and those with restricted mobility will enjoy Port L'Hebert and Graves Island, short walks in beautiful settings. The slightly longer Delaps Cove, Mushpauk Lake, and Upper Clements trails demand more effort to complete. Chebogue Meadows offers a shorter but tougher hike; its excellent interpretive panels make it a "must." The Liverpool Rail Trail was the first section of abandoned railway in Nova Scotia developed for recreational usage, and its proximity to Summerville Beach and the Sable River Trail gives it a valuable position. Experienced outdoors people might want to combine the hikes, making a round trip of almost 90 km (55 mi). Blomidon Provincial Park has been recognized as a wonderful spot for generations, and you can expect to share the trail. The newly constructed Uniacke Estate trails are exciting, and if the ones opened in 1995 prove popular others might be extended into remote parts of the property or connected with community hiking paths. I hope the Uniacke Estate trails are only the first of many new trails in this beautiful area of the province.

Hunting is permitted in the lands crossed by the Delaps Cove and Mushpauk Lake trails and the Liverpool and Sable River rail trails. The season usually begins in early October, but it will vary from year to year and according to the kind of game to be hunted. Contact the Department of Natural Resources for detailed information before going into the woods. There is no hunting on Sunday, but be sure to wear hunter orange vests and hats for safety every day nevertheless.

In 1994, a tract of land surrounding the Sable River Rail Trail was designated among 31 candidate protected areas by the Department of Natural Resources. Over the next several years, the DNR hopes to work with other interested groups to develop a management policy to decide on suitable economic, recreation and conservation uses for each tract. Free copies of the proposed system plan for parks and protected areas can be obtained from the Department of Natural Resources.

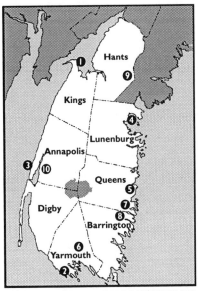

SOUTH SHORE / ANNAPOLIS VALLEY

1. Blomidon Provincial Park · 78
2. Chebogue Meadows Interpretive Trail · 84
3. Delaps Cove · 88
4. Graves Island Provincial Park · 92
5. Liverpool Rail Trail · 96
6. Mushpauk Lake · 100
7. Port L'Hebert Pocket Wilderness · 106
8. Sable River Rail Trail · 110
9. Uniacke Estate · 114
10. Upper Clements Provincial Wildlife Park · 120

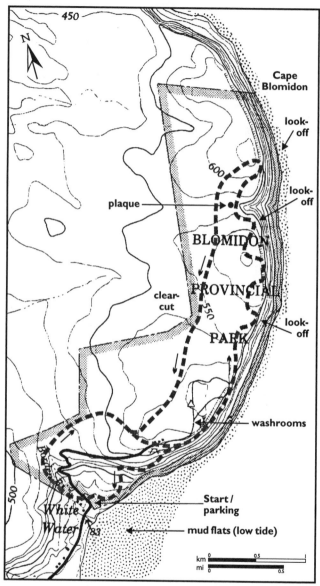

Blomidon Provincial Park

Blomidon Provincial Park

Length: 13 km
(8 mi) return
Time: 5 hrs
Type: walking paths,
fields
Rating: 3

Uses: hiking
Facilities: outhouses, water,
picnic tables, camping,
firewood, garbage cans,
showers, playground
Gov't Topo Map: Parrsboro
21 H/8

South Shore

Access: From Highway 101, take Exit 11 north to the junction with Highway 1 and Highway 358. Follow Highway 358 to Canning, and from there take the Pereau Road until you run out of pavement. The total distance from Highway 101 is 25 km (15.5 mi). You can park in the lot at the bottom of the hill or continue on the road up the hill to a lot at the top, which reduces both the hiking distance and the degree of difficulty.

Introduction: Blomidon Provincial Park occupies the top of a spectacular 183-m (600-ft) cliff overlooking Minas Basin, which dominates the entire skyline. The brick red of the sandstone hillside is mirrored in the broad mud flats exposed by the retreat of the highest tides in the world, some 12 m/yd. The spectacular views of Minas Basin and the Parrsboro shores are breathtaking, one of the principal attractions for visitors.

The 759 ha (1875 a) park includes 72 campsites and picnic areas both at the top and at the bottom of the hill. Blomidon Provincial Park was established in 1965 after much consideration as a national park.

Trail Description: From the lower parking lot, follow the road up the hill. Signs on your left clearly indicate the entrance to the Borden Brook Trail, rectangular red metal flashes denoting the path. (Seen from the other direction, the flashes are yellow.) At a junction just inside the woods, walking straight ahead takes you to a series of small waterfalls, while turning left sends you up the steep hillside along a narrow path, your toughest climb of the trek. You quickly end up on the top of the ridge on an old road. Turn right and follow the road across the bridge over Borden Brook. On the other side, you go into the woods again to your left. The alders here are great in the spring and summer for birding. Look for redstarts and northern parula warblers. Moving on, you once again join an old road for a few paces. Be cautious at the next junction. Your trail, marked by red-tipped posts, goes right. Continuing straight will send you on the road to Scots Bay, many difficult kilometres distant.

The trail soon reaches a large field originally cleared by the New England settlers who farmed this land in the 1770s. Instead of staying on the path, cross right over the field until you find either the administration building or the upper picnic area. You will see them when you reach the top of the hill in the middle of the field. Rejoin the trail near the camping area, where cliff access is restricted by a long fence. Follow along, with the ocean clearly on your right. You are now on the Joudrey Trail. Skirting through a forest of maple, birch, and beech, the trail rounds a small pond and arrives at the first look-off. The cliffs of Five Islands Provincial Park across Minas Basin are prominent. The trail continues along a well-worn route through open woods near the cliff edge. On a clear day, you can almost spot Truro in the distance. This is the portion of the hike that most people remember because of the spectacular views.

The next look-off looks towards Parrsboro and along Cape Blomidon's cliffs, following which the trail descends into a ravine to a bridge at Indian Springs Brook, where a plaque commemorating a land donation by

Low tide, Blomidon Park. MICHAEL HAYNES

South Shore

Mr. Joudrey will be found. The Look-off Trail continues through mature spruce stands to a final cliff-side panorama, two viewing areas facing northeast and southeast.

The return trip follows the Woodland Trail. Just outside the western boundary of the park the trail passes a clear-cut area. With the trees removed you can see Cape Split, Cape Chignecto, Isle Haute, and New Brunswick on a clear day. Partridge sightings are common along this section. After about 3 km (2 mi), the path begins to widen and is gravel covered. You are nearing the campground, which is off to your left, and its small interpretive trail. Continue straight, crossing the road to the group campsite, until you reach a large field. Turn left and cross the field to reach the picnic area and regain the trail at its far south end. You are on your way downhill now, and little more than 1 km (.5 mi) of walking remains.

Yellow flashes signal your route, and the trail is short and steep, with stairs providing assistance over rough sections. Near the bottom the path becomes a broad grassy field, but beware of the electrified fence on your right, especially if you have children with you. If you are lucky, the tide will be out, and you will be presented with a view of almost 500 m/yd of mud flats extending from high sandstone cliffs. Continue along the edge of the field until you spot the staircase leading you back to the lower parking lot and your car.

Cautionary Notes: The trail is very steep at both the beginning and at the end. Furthermore, much of the hike takes you near a very high, very steep, and actively eroding cliff. Exercise extreme caution near look-offs, and never venture beyond fences or other barriers.

The reddish flowers of the purple trillium cover the forest floor in the spring. Although it seems to be every-where, the purple trillium is a rare plant and the flowers should not be picked. If you do pick some, you'll be sorry. Purple trillium depend on carrion beetles for pollenation and give off a truly disgusting perfume.

Further Information: A brochure about Blomidon Park can be obtained by contacting the Department of Natural Resources.

The local tourism association prints a brochure about hiking in Glooscap country. It can be picked up at local tourist bureaus.

Chebogue Meadows Interpretive Trail

Length: 5.5 km
  (3.5 mi) return
Time: 2 hrs
Type: walking paths, boardwalks
Rating: 2

Uses: hiking
Facilities: benches
Gov't Topo Map: Yarmouth 20 O/16

South Shore

Access: From Yarmouth, drive 6 km (3.75 mi) along Highway 340 toward Corberrie. A sign advises that you are 800 m/yd from the park, but at the parking lot the sign is set in from the road and is easy to miss. Look on your right, just where the overhead power lines cross the highway.

Introduction: Most hiking trails on provincial lands are associated with picnic or camping parks, and the majority of these are simple improved paths that lead you to a particular destination, usually scenic, and back to your car. Chebogue Meadows is quite different, with only the hiking trail and the interpretive panels.

Interpretive panels have been erected at different locations in the park to point out various habitats. They describe the characteristics of each habitat type and explain its value to different species of wildlife. In addition, a side trail has been added past Station #11 at the Chebogue River. Approximately one kilometre return, this trail leads you to an elevated observation platform overlooking a watercourse managed by Ducks Unlimited.

Worthwhile just for the walk and the scenery, this trail is an interesting and informative outdoor educational opportunity. It provides valuable insights into both the natural and the managed forests of Nova Sco-

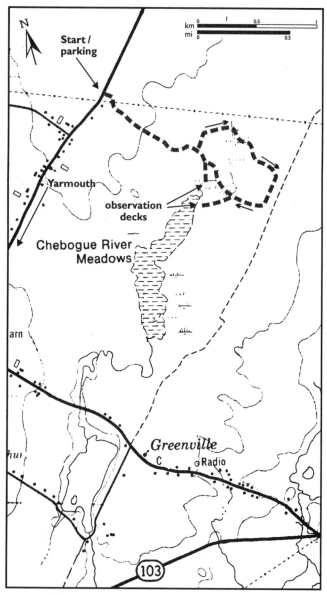

N

Start /
parking

km
mi

Yarmouth

observation
decks

Chebogue River
Meadows

arn

Greenville
C   Radio

hu

103

Chebogue Meadows Interpretive Trail

tia for people like myself, who want to know more about the woods in which we are hiking.

Trail Description: The path starts in the clearing under the power lines. About 25 m/yd in, you will find a large map showing the route and the location of the interpretive stations. This map did not include the new interpretive stations or the side-trail when I was there in August 1994. Do not be too nervous if you hear rifle fire even when it is not hunting season. The rifle range of the Southwestern Nova Scotia Muzzle Loading Association is less than 2 km (1.25 mi) away and always seems to be busy.

You move into the forest only a short distance before you encounter the new stations. Alternate #1A: Mercantable Thinning, and Alternate #1B: Remnant Removal, Clear-Cut, may be found in the first few hundred metres. The first section of the trail is in very good condition, gravelled, wide, and with long boardwalks over wet areas. It is also well signed, with rectangular red metal markers affixed to the trees. (Yellow rectangles mark the return trip.) But before the first kilometre ends, the trail becomes much worse, with numerous small rocks and jutting roots making it just difficult enough to earn a rating of 2. Although bothersome, the rocks are interesting. Note the occasional large chunks of white quartz among all the granites.

When you reach the trail fork, the sign directs you left, and just beyond it you find interpretive stations #1 and #2, and a bench if you need to sit. There appear to be several side-trails around here as well, but they are not part of the itinerary. A short distance through the softwoods, stations #3 and #4 are situated in the few hundred metres before the bridge over the Chebogue River. Crossing over the stream on a long boardwalk, you see the large, open sedge meadows on your right. Station #6, your next panel, warns about everybody's favourite problem, the dog tick. Read this one carefully, especially if you are hiking before July 1!

The trail returns to the woods, and station #7, Softwood Forest, is just inside the forest edge. Station #8, Maple Swamp, is a particularly lush-looking area and provides your best chance to see deer if you are visiting in the summer. Uphill on drier ground are stations #9 and #10, although the trees at #10 look a bit older than the 15 years suggested in the panel. Station #10A (a new one), Habitat: Clearing, Title: Diversity, is on the highest ground just before the trail makes a 90° turn to the right. A fence on your left should keep you from accidently following a former logging road. Alternate #11A, Habitat: Shelterwood, Title: Vertical Diversity, on your left just after the turn, appears to replace station #11.

Coming down the hill toward the river, you will see two signs on your left, "Look-off" and "No Exit." These mark the new side trail, a perfect diversion. About 450 m/yd over a small ridge, you find a newly constructed observation deck overlooking open wetlands. A great blue heron, marsh hawk, and several species of duck were all in sight when I arrived.

Returning to the main loop and continuing over the Chebogue River, you will be slightly surprised to find station #5 now positioned in the middle of the bridge. It is completely appropriate there, but unexpected between stations #11 and #12. Station #12, located on another viewing platform situated beside the marsh, is within sight of #5, and from #12 you can also see the new look-off. A few hundred metres beyond the viewing platform, the trail re-enters the woods and completes the loop. Your final kilometre of walking is over the same route you followed in.

Cautionary Notes: This could almost be rated a level 1 hike, but several very rocky spots along the trail might cause problems for some people.

A sign at the start of the trail warns users to wear hunter orange from September 15 to February 15. As you will see from the condition of some signs, this is good advice.

Note that this is tick country from April to July.

Delaps Cove

Length: 9.5 km
  (6 mi) return
Time: 3 hrs
Type: dirt road,
  walking paths
Rating: 2

Uses: hiking, mountain
  biking, cross-country skiing
Facilities: outhouses,
  picnic tables, benches
Gov't Topo Map: Digby
  21 A/12, Granville Ferry
  21 A/13

Access: From Annapolis Royal, drive on Highway 1 across the causeway to Granville Ferry. There turn onto Parkers Cove Road heading toward the Bay of Fundy. Turn left at the intersection at the shoreline toward Delaps Cove, and continue until the pavement ends. Total distance: 22 km (13.75 mi) from Annapolis Royal. A road sign directs you left on a steep dirt road for 2 km (1.25 mi); it ends in the parking lot.

Introduction: After the American Revolution, large numbers of the colonists who remained loyal to the British Crown were forced to leave the new republic. Almost 19,000 settled in Nova Scotia, overwhelming the 20,000 people already living here. Nearly 3500 settled

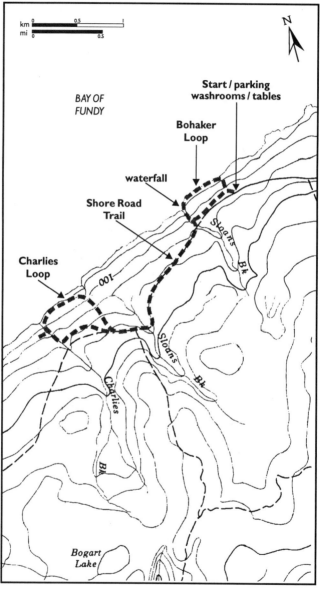

km 0   0.5   1
mi 0   0.5

N

BAY OF
FUNDY

Start / parking
washrooms / tables

**Bohaker
Loop**

waterfall

**Shore Road
Trail**

**Charlies
Loop**

100

Sloans Bk

Sloans Bk

Charlies

Bk

*Bogart
Lake*

Delaps Cove

in Annapolis County, among these nearly 500 Black Loyalists. Some of them were slaves accompanying their exiled masters, but most had been freed. As elsewhere in Nova Scotia, the best lands in the fertile areas went to influential whites and military Loyalists. Blacks, when their claims were eventually processed, were usually given smaller lots in less desirable locations.

Delaps Cove was just such a place, situated on the other side of North Mountain from the county seat at Annapolis Royal, exposed to the harsher weather of the Bay of Fundy, and located on infertile basalt rock. The 1871 census listed 70 inhabitants, with all the families but one being Black. Some managed to become fairly prosperous; James Francis owned 125 acres of land, 12 sheep, 2 oxen, a house, a barn, and a boat. The majority were not so fortunate. Just one house remains occupied today, and only the stone walls, apple trees, and foundations remind us of this former community.

The Municipality of Annapolis County opened this trail in 1985. Utilizing the right-of-way of the former road, two distinct loop systems were connected for a 9.5 km (6 mi) total hike. There is much to see on this walk: the remains of the former settlement, a waterfall, a small vein of agate, and, of course, the Bay of Fundy itself.

Trail Description: A large interpretive display at the trailhead contains a map of the path network and informational brochures. Use the outhouses at the parking lot; they are the only ones available. At the start of the 2.2 km (1.5 mi) Bohaker Loop, just past this big panel, you will find a guest book waiting for your signature. Turning right, the path quickly takes you downhill to the ocean and an interpretive sign describing tides. Following the coastline, the trail overlooks the exposed basalt ridges running from the forest edge into the water. In some places huge rectangular boulders stand separate, eroded by the constant tidal action. After 400 m/yd you reach Bohaker Brook, where a small cliff-lined cove has been etched into the basalt; the waves have jammed the cove with driftwood. At the back of the hollow is 13-m/yd Bohaker Falls. The trail heads inland now, although a side path crosses the brook, ends in a look-off at the top of the waterfall, and provides one of the nicest views of the hike.

Leaving the coast, you move inland through lovely spruce and balsam fir stands paralleling the brook. Well-constructed bridges lead you to the other side. At a junction turn left to return to the parking lot, crossing an impressive old stone wall en route, or head right towards the Shore Road and the Charlies Loop. The right-hand path connects to the Shore Road in 300 m/yd, climbing a little as it passes through mixed hardwoods of white ash and maple. This connecting segment between the two loops — the Shore Road Trail — is what remains of the former highway that used to run the length of North Mountain. There is little shade along this 2.7 km (1.75 mi) stretch, and you should wear a hat and carry lots of water on hot, sunny summer days. But because the trail is not ditched, expect it to be wet during the spring and fall. There are no landmarks through here either, except the descent to the crossing of Sloans Brook at about 2 km (1.25 mi).

Only one small sign marks the entrance to the 1.9-km (1.25-mi) Charlies Loop; do pay attention. Goldenthread, a popular folk remedy for mouth pain, grows abundantly among long beech fern, bracken fern, and bunchberries. Several side trails take you to the water's edge. The first of these comes out next to a small vein of agate, the second is bordered by bayberry scrub, and the last spur features an observation deck overlooking Charlies Cove and the coastline towards Digby Gut. On a clear day you should sight the Digby–Saint John Ferry.

Delaps Cove. MICHAEL HAYNES

South Shore

Following the brook inland, you come to the foundation of the Pomp household (see the interpretive panel), and just beyond that to a second, smaller house site.

Anyone wanting a rest or a few moments of contemplation should take the side trail across Charlies Brook. Only 100 m/yd long, it descends into the steep, narrow ravine to a bench beside and above cascading waters and enfolded by mature softwoods—a perfect place for a sandwich or even a nap. From here, you return to the parking lot via the Shore Road, about 3 km (2 mi) back along the route you walked in.

Cautionary Notes: The connecting trail between the Charlies 4 and Bohaker loops is sometimes used by ATVs. Please listen for them and be prepared to move out of the way.

Expect to encounter wood ticks from April to July.

Hunters use this area between late September and early February.

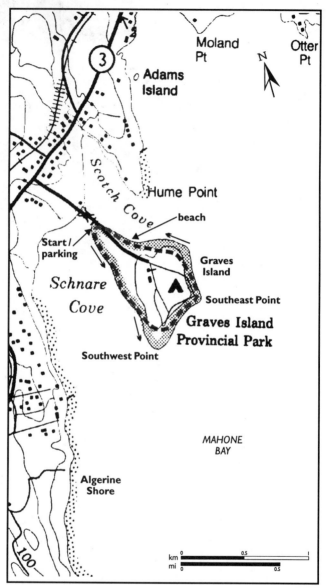

Graves Island Provincial Park

Future Plans: A local ATV group plans to cl[...]
Shore Road all the way to the community of [...]
Beach. Over the next few years they should be c[...]
directional signs.

Further Information: The Municipality of Annapolis
County offers a variety of pamphlets and guides for the
Delaps Cove Trail.

Graves Island Provincial Park

Length: 3 km
  (2 mi) return
Time: 1-2 hrs
Type: walking paths
Rating: 1

Uses: hiking
Facilities: outhouses,
  campsites, picnic tables,
  playground, beach,
  water, fireplaces, garbage
  cans, benches
Gov't Topo Map: Chester
  21 A/9

Access: From Halifax, drive south on Highway 103 to
Exit 7. Continue south on Highway 3 for 5 km (3 mi).
The park entrance is on your left and is well-signed.
Drive on the paved road across the causeway, and
either park your car upon reaching the island or continue to the parking lot by the administrative office. In
winter the gate is closed at the causeway.

Introduction: Graves Island is one of the shortest hikes
in this book, a pleasant little scenic stroll suitable for all
fitness levels. Graves Island Provincial Park includes the
entire 50-ha (123-a) island. Its 64 campsites boast the
highest occupancy rate of any provincial campground
in Nova Scotia. In addition, it enjoys a small sand beach

that is well used in the summer, a wonderful picnic ground, a boat launch, a large modern playground, and a fantastic location on the popular South Shore only 70 km (44 mi) from the Halifax-Dartmouth metropolitan area.

The island is actually a drumlin, as are most of the other nearby islands. Deposited by glaciers, drumlins are small oval hills of sandy loam that overlie the dominant granite rock of the district. The drumlins scattered over the landscape in Lunenburg County give the area around Chester its rolling topography, and their better drained, more fertile soils explain why you will find cleared fields and old farmhouses covering most of them. Graves Island itself was once farmland.

This is an ideal excursion for the entire family. The distance is short, the trails are wide and well-maintained, and there is practically no elevation change. The trails are not wheelchair accessible, however. The beach and playground offer alternatives to hiking, and this is a popular campsite. As a beginning hike for young children, this has much to recommend it. And considering the beauty of its surroundings, adults should find it pleasant if not challenging.

Trail Description: You may start your walk anywhere. The path network uses the spoke system, a circular trail linked to the centre via numerous short connecting paths. This enables walkers to complete as much or as little as they chose, terminating their hike when they reach any of the connector paths. In summer, I recommend starting at the picnic grounds near the entrance and beginning on the south side of the island. This enables you to finish at the beach on the north side, a good choice on a hot July day. If you stay on the perimeter trail, you never have to climb the small hill in the centre of the island, making the stroll even easier.

Otherwise, park at the administrative centre, where water is available, and follow the path immediately behind it to descend to the coast. Once there, turn left.

Nova Scotia's South Shore has been a vacation destination for generations, and looking around Mahone Bay you will understand why. From the south side of Graves Island you will see numerous cottages, some quite large, on the coastline opposite. As you round the outer point, the many small islands dotting Mahone Bay will come into view, along with the host of sailboats always active in these waters. Several benches at look-offs permit a relaxing examination of these busy sailors. You might even be able to sight Tancook Island in the distance, or the daily ferry that connects it with Chester and costs only $2 for a round trip.

The north side of Graves Island faces the Aspotogan Peninsula, on which are the villages of Blandford, where a whaling station used to operate, and Deep Cove, a favourite hiding place of the rum-runners. If you leave the trail and walk down to the ocean, you will discover that the shallow water running over the cobble beach is actually quite warm. But if you stay under the canopy of the softwood forest, you can amble alongside the remains of stone fences erected by the original settlers of Graves Island, farmers for whom the comparatively rich soil of the drumlin was a boon. Expect black-capped chickadees and golden crowned kinglets to keep you company in the woods. Some of these may be tame enough by the end of the summer to take seed from your outstretched hand. Make sure you have a treat for them.

Completing the circle, you reach a sandy beach next to the causeway. Maybe you have not worked up too much of a sweat, but a swim in the warm salt waters of Mahone Bay will still be refreshing. Otherwise return to your car and have a picnic before you start for home.

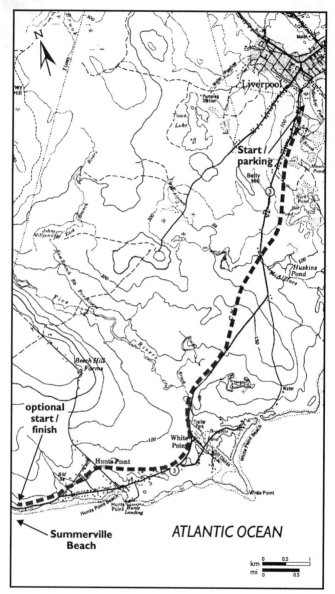

Liverpool Rail Trail

Further Information: Camping rates at provincial parks vary. Firewood is extra, and age and extended stay discounts exist. For a complete rate schedule, contact the Parks and Recreation Division of the Department of Natural Resources.

Liverpool Rail Trail

Length: 25 km
(15.5 mi) return
Time: 7-8 hrs
Type: abandoned
railway bed
Rating: 4

Uses: hiking, mountain biking, cross-country skiing, horseback riding
Facilities: outhouse, picnic tables
Gov't Topo Map: Liverpool 21A/2, Port Mouton 20P/15

Access: Leave downtown Liverpool on Highway 3 toward Yarmouth. Still inside the town limits is the Queens County municipal office building. West Street is just before it, on your left. Turn there and drive for about 100 m/yd; you will find parking on your right and the start of the trail. The path can also be entered at several other places along the route, although there are no other specific parking areas.

Introduction: The CNR abandoned its railway line on the South Shore in 1984, removing the tracks the following year. Even before that day a citizens' group in Liverpool began working to develop a section as a recreational trail. They required years of negotiation and labour to achieve their goal, but in 1990, with the assistance of the Liverpool-Queens Development Commission, the Department of Natural Resources, the Municipality of Queens, the Town of Liverpool, and many dedicated volunteers, the first declared "Rails-to-Trails" route in Nova Scotia was opened.

Like most rail trails, the Liverpool line is broad and level, with very gentle grades. The original gravel bed, composed of large coarse stones that were difficult to walk on and impossible to bicycle through, was removed and replaced by much finer material. The result is footing that is a pleasure to traverse. The trail is somewhat long for families, particularly if they make the trip both ways, but it is a wonderful alternative to walking or biking on the highway, especially because it can be entered at so many spots. Connecting the town of Liverpool with the immensely popular Summerville Beach, and from there with the Sable River Rail Trail, this path permits a number of recreational options.

Trail Description: The hike begins at a small nature park behind the Queens County municipal offices. Climb a low hill from the parking lot to the rail trail, then walk left along its gravel surface until the path crosses Bog Road. Here an information panel provides a map and description of the trail. Note that all non-motorized uses are permitted. In order to prevent vehicular access, large boulders have been placed in the middle of the trail at all road intersections.

Continuing past the sign, the trail starts arrow-straight and quite level. You notice numerous footpaths joining from both sides, and even unofficial entrances for vehicles, such as one on the right from Highway 3 by the Shell station just 200 m/yd along. Even the most cursory glance at the trail shows deep ATV tracks in the gravel almost from the start. Also in the first kilometre are several excavated areas on both sides, and a junk yard, but once you're past this area the view improves considerably, and young hardwoods are beginning to grow thickly alongside the cleared area.

The first intersection, an optional entrance or exit, is 3 km (2 mi) from the start at McAlpines Brook, where the trail crosses Highway 3. From now on, the road will be on your left. A custom-built superstructure has been added to the railway bridge at McAlpines Brook; planks cover the gaps between the ties to enable bicycles to cross, and guardrails have been affixed on both sides for added safety. Beyond the brook more spruce and pine appear by the trail edge. Watch the ground for coyote scat; it was plentiful when I was last there. For perhaps a kilometre the trail moves away from the road, and this is the most remote section of the walk, but soon you begin to notice houses on your left, and then the trail returns to parallel the road no more than 15 m/yd away.

South Shore

Another custom-built bridge crosses Five Rivers, 7 km (4.5 mi) from Liverpool, and by White Point, 500 m/yd later, the trail becomes almost a sidewalk for the highway. At one point a driveway even crosses the path. Beyond here the trail moves inland again through an area of abandoned fields and thick alder growth. About halfway to Hunts Point, just past a derelict house, is a spot where spring runoff has nearly washed out the track. The ground throughout this section is soft whenever the weather is wet. Reaching Hunts Point, 10 km (6.25 mi) from Liverpool, you cross three roads separated by a few hundred metres. Blocking every intersection are the ubiquitous rocks. Expect to meet local residents jogging or walking their dogs through here, especially in the summer when this popular vacation area gets quite busy.

The trail ends abruptly on Highway 3 at Summerville opposite house #7201, only 1.5 km (1 mi) from the entrance to Summerville Beach Provincial Park. There is no parking space at this end of the trail, although there is another interpretive panel similar to the one on Bog Road. Unless you have someone to drive you back, turn around and retrace your route to the start.

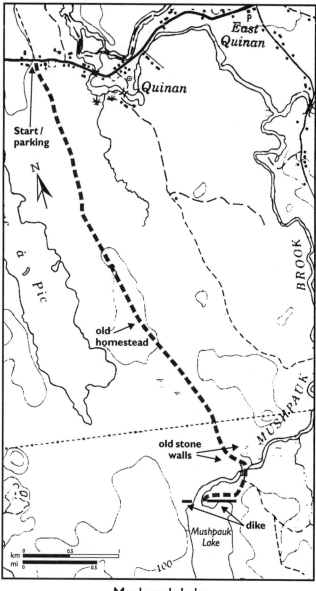

Start /
parking

N

old
homestead

old stone
walls

dike

Mushpauk
Lake

km 0   0.5   1
mi 0   0.5

Mushpauk Lake

Cautionary Notes: Although No Hunting signs are found at trail entrances, most of the land bordering the trail is privately owned and will be used by hunters. Wear orange safety clothing every day during fall months, even though hunting is prohibited on Sundays.

Expect to encounter wood ticks from April to July.

There are no warning signs on Highway 3 at either McAlpines Brook or the entrance/exit at Summerville. Be careful of traffic, especially at McAlpines, where the speed limit is 90 kph (55 mph) and the road is curving. Be cautious at all intersections.

Future Plans: The existing trail is intended to be only the first phase of an ambitious plan to extend a maintained trail far down the South Shore.

Further Information: The local committee has produced a trail brochure which can be obtained at the Liverpool tourist bureau.

Mushpauk Lake

Length: 10 km
   (6.25 mi) return
Time: 2-3 hrs
Type: former road,
   walking paths
Rating: 2

Uses: hiking, mountain
   biking, cross-country
   skiing, horseback riding,
   ATV, snowmobiling
Facilities: none
Gov't Topo Map: Tusket
   20 P/13

Access: From Yarmouth, drive on Highway 103 to Exit 33. Turn left on Highway 308 toward Springhaven and Quinan. One kilometre (.5 mi) past the Quinan Road sign, 200 m/yd past the Springhaven Canoe Outfitters sign, turn right off the road into the parking lot immediately before St. Agnes Catholic Church (no name posted). The community hall (no name posted) is behind the church. The trail entrance is unmarked but distinct in the right (west) corner of the lot. Total distance from Yarmouth: 25 km (15.5 mi).

Introduction: This trail follows the remains of an old coach road that ran inland from Pubnico when the area was settled by United Empire Loyalists after the American War of Independence. After the farms were abandoned, the road fell into disrepair. Stone walls and old foundations can often be seen alongside the path, and on the banks of Mushpauk Lake you will find the vestiges of an impressive stone and earth dike.

This is not the most scenic walk, but it does grow on you. History buffs like myself will be excited by the ruins and delighted by the beautiful stretch under a spruce canopy bordered by stone walls on both sides, and the dike is simply astonishing. But everyone may not be equally enthused over a pile of rocks. Perhaps you might prefer to search for the lost loot from a postal coach robbed on this road in the mid-1800s. The thieves went to their graves with the secret, but the money is said to be buried nearby. Whatever your pleasure, Mushpauk Lake makes a very nice place to have a picnic, and the walk there is very easy.

Trail Description: This trail proceeds straight to Mushpauk Lake, with no significant turns along the entire route. Although there are several intersections with ATV trails, continue straight ahead and you will be fine. This road has been abandoned for many years, so the canopy overhead is quite thick. Though the forest is predominantly hardwood, wet areas seem to harbour spruce instead. Notice a parallel road, not marked on your topo map, close on the right. This new gravel track leads to cottages on nearby Lac à Pic and shadows the trail for more than 3 km (2 mi). In wet weather, large pools form in the old road, and wading or detours will be required.

At the top of the first noticeable rise, you come across an abandoned farm on your right. The old apple trees provide the first clue of its existence; turn off the trail and wander into the field. You will find the remains of the stone fences surrounding the homestead and the house foundation, which in the summer is covered in ferns. Remember: the trail is a public right-of-way, but the land around you is private property.

Continue along the path. At the top of the next hill you will find another stone fence, and the trail becomes more open and easy to visualize as a cart track. As you come down off the higher ground, a large cleared area opens on your right, and you can see electrical power lines in the distance cutting across your route. The clearing seems part clear-cut, part open bog, and it covers a substantial tract. The trail skirts it, turning into the trees briefly before emerging into the cleared area beneath the two power lines.

On the other side of the power lines, the alders close in, almost enveloping the path, and an old house on your left no longer has any yard. But after less than 500 m/yd, the brush gives way to a stand of mature spruce, and prominent stone fences border both sides of the path. This is the most attractive portion of the hike: the stones are covered in moss, the path is wide and covered in spruce needles, and a high canopy provides shade. A large grassy field appears on your left, and you arrive at Mushpauk Creek. When I was there two youngsters were dangling a small net from the old bridge. They were fishing for "kaicks" (pronounced "kayaks," the local term for baby gaspereau) to use as bait. Although rickety, the bridge has been repaired to permit ATV use.

On the other side of the bridge, the trail gets somewhat confusing. Many paths fan out in all directions in a field. Keep right, even though other tracks appear more distinct. Some underbrush obscures the trail entrance at the forest edge, but it soon clears. The trail continues straight a short distance, then turns right, seemingly to avoid a ridge. This is the dike, and Mushpauk Lake is on the other side. Continue a further 300 m/yd; here the trail ends at the mouth of Mushpauk Creek, where you'll see the remains of the level-control mechanisms. This is a nice place to have a snack, although I personally favour the bridge. The lake is also safe for swimming, though unsupervised. Return along the same route to finish your hike.

Cautionary Notes: There are no signs and no services, and the trail is not maintained. Before entering the woods, inform someone where you will be and when you expect to be back. Carry a compass and map. Many small trails connect with Mushpauk Lake. Be prepared to bail out if you become uncertain of your route. Expect wood ticks from April to July in these woods.

Hunting is permitted in this area.

Further Information: The Yarmouth Tourist Bureau issues a brochure listing hiking trails in the area. Some of these are unsigned, like the Muspauk Lake Trail; more importantly, the Cape St. Marys Trail is not only unsigned, it is on private property.

Port L'Hebert Pocket Wilderness

Length: 3 km
(2 mi) return
Time: 1 hr
Type: walking paths,
boardwalks
Rating: 1

Uses: hiking
Facilities: outhouses,
picnic tables, water,
benches, garbage cans
Gov't Topo Map: Port
Mouton 20 P/15

Access: Drive west along Highway 103 from Liverpool toward Yarmouth. Approximately 40 km (25 mi) from Liverpool a large road sign indicates the parking lot and start of the trail.

Introduction: Bowater Mersey Paper Company owns and manages more than 304,000 ha (755,000 a) of land in western Nova Scotia to support its newsprint and lumber manufacturing operations. Nearly 3000 people work directly or indirectly for this company, making it one of the largest employers in the province. Its massive newsprint mill in Brooklyn, Queens County, Nova Scotia, provides much of the paper for New York City's newspapers.

To celebrate their 50th year of operation in 1979, Bowater Mersey constructed a small public nature park near the Atlantic Ocean. This "Pocket Wilderness," as they called it, was so popular with the public that they have built several others throughout southern Nova Scotia. Conservation Areas, containing unusual forest types, rare plants, and old-growth stands, have also been established by Bowater Mersey in several locations throughout the South Shore–Annapolis Valley region.

These sites are all popular and well-used. A quick glance at the guest book in Port L'Hebert this summer showed that tourists from Berlin, Paris, and various lo-

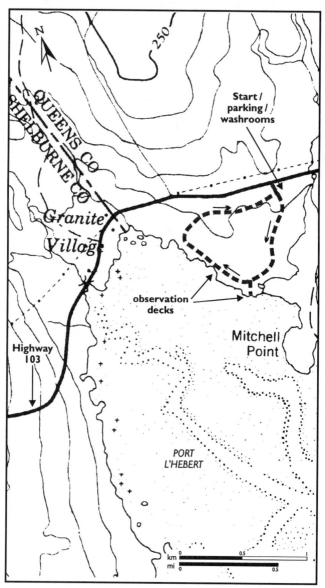

Port L'Hebert Pocket Wilderness

cations in the US had visited. (I remain sceptical about Madonna's signature.) Communities throughout the South Shore were also well represented, but there were very few visitors from the Halifax-Dartmouth area. A shame, because this is a worthwhile place to visit.

Trail Description: The parking lot is right beside the road and is a good size. Wheelchair-accessible outhouses are on the Yarmouth (west) side of the lot; the trail starts on the Liverpool (east) side. At the trailhead are several picnic tables and a water pump as well as the guest book. Make sure you sign it, too!

The path is very easy walking, dry and hard packed. Wet areas are covered by boardwalks, and the standard of maintenance is very high. Although the trail is not wheelchair accessible, everyone else should find it easy going. Designed as a loop, the complete 3 km (2 mi) must be traversed to return to the parking lot. Perhaps 50 m/yd into the walk you come to a junction. There is no sign. This is where the loop begins and either direction will do, although I prefer the left fork. You may notice how well the route is planned. It takes advantage of the shape of the land and obstacles such as rocks and vegetation to vary the view as much as possible. You rarely encounter a long straight section; the path is always curving behind a knoll or dipping into a tiny depression. Gravel fill has covered roots and other obstructions, and the boardwalks keep the path level and dry. There is no significant elevation change on the entire hike.

The first section winds through a hardwood stand filled with huge granite boulders. These massive rocks, called "erratics," were scoured out of the bedrock by the advancing glaciers, then left behind like litter as the ice receded. After about a kilometre, the trail enters into the softwoods of the coastal fringe. There is a view-station by a small freshwater pond. A much larger look-off with seating is available at the end of a boardwalked side trail that takes you to the ocean's edge and your first sight of Port L'Hebert. Canada geese migrating south often winter along the shore, using the eel grass and open, protected water to survive the harsh winter months. Much of the upper end of Port L'Hebert, including the shoreline of the pocket wilderness, has been designated a waterfowl sanctuary by the Canadian Wildlife Service.

The trail now follows the shoreline, mostly inside the tree-line, as it begins its return to the parking lot. Any of the many game trails to the water's edge will provide you with quite a different view. As well, another large viewing station with benches overlooks the bay at the point where the path turns in from the coast. Very quickly you return to mixed hardwoods, where the high leafy canopy keeps the air relatively cool even in the middle of summer. The rolling terrain of this section, the frequent erratics, plus the low undergrowth, provide some wonderful views that remind me of fairy stories my mother used to tell about enchanted forests. You almost expect to see a leprechaun or an elf leaning against a rock in one of the glades. Certainly there is plenty of bird-life, heard rather than seen among the tall trees.

During the last 500 m/yd, where the route parallels the highway, you might hear traffic noises, but they should not intrude overly much, and they pass quickly. All too soon you arrive back at the loop intersection. Turn left for the parking lot. The picnic area, shaded by the same hardwoods you walked under, is a wonderful spot to have a snack before you move on. I just hope you remembered your mosquito repellent.

Cautionary Notes: The coastline around the region is sometimes the winter home of thousands of Canada geese. Visitors during that time of year should try not to disturb the birds. It takes all their energy to survive without human intrusion.

Note that wood ticks can be expected between April and July.

Further Information: Bowater Mersey puts out several free brochures detailing the various conservation areas, pocket wildernesses, and recreational sites on its lands.

Sable River Rail Trail

Length: 52 km
(32.5 mi) return
Time: 12 hrs
Type: abandoned
railway bed
Rating: 5

Uses: hiking, mountain biking, cross-country skiing, snowmobiling, ATV, horseback riding
Facilities: none
Gov't Topo Map:
Shelburne 20 P/14,
Port Mouton 20 P/15

Access: As you approach from the direction of Liverpool, the abandoned rail line crosses Highway 103 in Sable River just before the road crosses the Tidney River. There is no sign for the trail, but there is for the river. Look for a small opening in the low trees on the right; this is the trailhead. Park on a nearby side road.

Introduction: Since 1976, more than 1000 km (625 mi) of railway have been abandoned in Nova Scotia. While it is sad to see the decline of our nation's rail

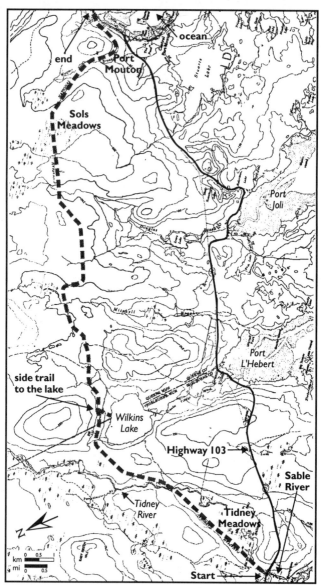

Sable River Rail Trail

heritage, the relinquishment of these routes has presented a unique recreational opportunity. The Department of Natural Resources acquired the section from Liverpool to Yarmouth for recreational purposes, and the portion near Liverpool has formally been declared a rail trail under the provincial Trails Act (see the Liverpool Rail Trail); in other areas, such as between Sable River and Port Mouton, rail trails are used informally, mostly by local residents.

This trail offers one of the few long hikes available in this part of the province that may be legally advertised. Because of its proximity to the Liverpool Rail Trail, Kejimkujik Seaside Adjunct, Thomas Raddall Provincial Park, and several conservancy sites, it offers an interesting option to anyone wanting to make this region a recreation destination. However, this rail trail is completely undeveloped. It leads into a remote area of barrens where help will be far off if needed, and I can recommend it only for those who want a long trek. Bicycling might be the preferred alternative for some, and fall the most pleasant season to attempt it.

Trail Description: For the first 800 m/yd the river follows the track closely on the left. At a small bridge, unmodified since its railway use, the trail crosses the brook, which enters a large boggy area on the right. For the next 4 km (2.5 mi), the route points straight, clearly stretching out ahead of you. In this section the vegetation is mostly hardwood, most of it quite young. The entire length of the hike is without shade, so consider carefully before you venture out on a hot summer day. On the other hand, the fall is spectacular, and the expansive views are best appreciated then.

At the 5 km (3 mi) mark the Tidney River crosses underneath the trail for the last time, and at almost the same point so does a major power line. For the next 3

Sable River Rail Trail. MICHAEL HAYNES

km (2 mi) the scenery remains relatively constant. Then, on your left, you will notice cleared meadows and a small shed. These are new blueberry fields, and more are being added in the same area. The trail continues in a long, gradual curve and decline to the right. At 8.5 km (5.25 mi) a distinct path leads into the woods on the right. Following this less than a kilometre delivers you to the bank of Wilkins Lake and a small sand beach, a great spot for lunch. The lake water is warm and clear and the shoreline deserted. This is Crown land, so access is permitted. If you decide to swim, watch for leeches.

The trail is excellent, in better condition than most dirt roads in the province. The gravel bed has been tightly packed by ATV travel and the trailbed sits higher then the surrounding ground, so it stays dry and well drained. Past Wilkins Lake, you cross another small brook at 10.5 km (6.5 mi) and spot a small shack on the left at 11.5 km (7.25 mi). The first dirt road encountered is North Road at 12 km (7.5 mi) and you cross Mitchell Creek at 13.5 km (8.5 mi). Look for a small beaver dam there. The trail is quite uneventful until reaching Douglas Brook at 18 km (11.25 mi), where it opens up with a small bog to the left. Five hundred m/yd further on, the power line recrosses overhead, and beyond that lies another dirt road. Just 100 m/yd on the left is a whale burial ground. Two whales washed ashore near Hunts Point and Port Joli, and their carcasses were trucked here for disposal. There is nothing to see except bulldozed ground, but if you ever wondered what happens when whales beach themselves, here's your answer.

One kilometre after the road, the trail begins to curve right again as it passes through a region known as Sols Meadows. Trees do not do well in the shallow soil, but blueberries do, and bears have been known to enjoy meals around here in the fall, especially in the clearings beneath power lines. At 22 km (13.75 mi) a different set of power lines cuts above you, and 1 km later a tiny bridge spans Warner Brook. You are almost at your destination. From this point more and more ATV paths connect to the line. The trail curves around the slope of a hill on your left, and you can see the houses of Port Mouton on your right at 25 km (15.5 mi). You meet Highway 103 suddenly, at the 26-km (16.25-mi) mark, emerging beside the large Exit 21 sign. From here either follow Highway 103 right or retrace your route to get back to Sable River. Crossing Highway 103 and continuing along the rail bed another 2.5 km (1.5 mi) leads you to the long bridge crossing Broad River at Summerville Beach. This section is actually quite overgrown, but still it's easily traversable.

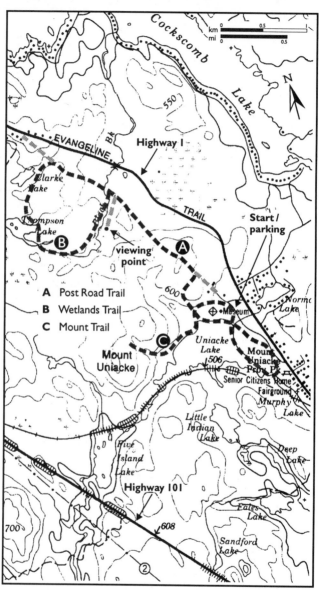

Uniacke Estate

Cautionary Notes: This is an unsupervised area with no population centres anywhere along the route. There are no signs and no services, and the trails are not maintained. Before hiking make certain that you tell someone where you're going and when you'll be back. Be prepared for emergencies.

Expect wood ticks from April to July.

Hunting is permitted on these lands.

Future Plans: 18,800 ha (46,436 a) around the Tidney River area in Shelburne and Queens County have been designated a candidate protected area.

Uniacke Estate

Length: 12 km (7.5 mi) combination
Time: 4 hrs
Type: former road, walking paths
Rating: 3

Uses: hiking, cross-country skiing
Facilities: picnic tables, benches, outhouses
Gov't Topo Map: Middle Sackville 11 D/13

Access: Starting in the Halifax-Dartmouth metro area, take Highway 101 toward Annapolis Valley for 15 km (9.5 mi) until you reach Exit 3. From Exit 3, turn left (west) on Highway 1 and drive 9 km (5.5 mi) through the village of Mount Uniacke. The estate entrance is on the left (south) side of road, well signed. There's parking on the estate grounds after a short drive on a dirt road.

Introduction: Born in Ireland in 1753, Richard John Uniacke established himself as a lawyer in Halifax in 1781, eventually rising to the position of Attorney-General of Nova Scotia in 1797. In 1786, Uniacke acquired his first property, a grant of 305 ha (1000 a); by 1819, his consolidated holdings amounted to 3460 ha (11,340 a). Uniacke developed a working farm and built what has been described as "one of Canada's finest examples of colonial architecture . . . a grand country house in the Georgian tradition." Richard John died in his bed at Mount Uniacke in 1830.

In 1949, the remainder of the estate, approximately 900 ha. (2300 a), was sold by the family to the Province of Nova Scotia, and in 1960 the property became part of the Nova Scotia Museum. Since 1951, the estate has been open to the public, with the main building being the principal attraction. Over the last several years, however, there has been a re-evaluation of use of the extensive property, culminating in a new Landscape Management Plan in 1993. Under this ambitious multi-year strategy, the Uniacke Estate landscape will be restored to a period of 150 years ago and protected as an important cultural resource. Increased access to the property will be encouraged through recreational trail development.

Work began in late 1994, with completion of the first phase, including most of the trails, in June 1995. Uniacke Estate is a great place to visit on a weekend and stretch your legs, and the walking routes are a fine addition to Nova Scotia's trail network.

Trail Description: Various walking opportunities will begin from the interpretive panels located next to the parking lot. These will vary in difficulty, with all fitness levels being accommodated, including a wheelchair-accessible path. One hike will head to Uniacke Lake (Lake Martha) and continue southeasterly along its shore until crossing the brook draining Norman Lake. This portion will feature interpretive panels and benches and will be the easiest walking. A short path will connect to the entrance road, permitting a 500 m/yd loop to the start. Those interested may continue on the path along the lakeshore, passing through mixed forest to return across the top of a drumlin and remains of old fields: total distance 1.5 km (1 mi).

Also from the lakeshore, one may turn northwest and follow a path into the interior toward the hills overlooking Lake Martha. Somewhat more challenging than the drumlin field walk, the Mount Trail features a section passing through a magnificent mature red spruce stand. A return trip of more than 2 km (1.25 mi), this branch returns along the same route to the lake. In the future, however, it may include a connecting trail across a series of fire barrens to the Wetlands Trail.

Leading northeast from the parking lot, a short walk will loop around a small hill to connect to the Old Windsor Road. Along this section just past a barn is a detailed exhibit outlining the entire trail network. One of Nova Scotia's two "Great Roads" required for movement of troops and cattle after the founding of Halifax, the Halifax-Windsor road featured weekly stage service by 1801, with mail and passenger service offered by 1815. Mount Uniacke, located halfway between the communities, made a convenient watering place. On the estate are nearly 5 km (3 mi) of the original alignment, including the #27 milestone. Designated the Post Road Trail, this has been cleared for public use almost to the far end of the property, where the old road rejoins Highway 1, making a 6 km (3.75 mi) return trip.

A final trail, accessible only from the further ends of the Post Road Trail, cuts into the interior of the estate in a loop taking it near two small lakes and a brook. The Wetlands Trail provides several opportunities to sit beside these water features. Perhaps 3 km (2 mi) long, this is the most remote walk on the estate. Combining it with the Post Road Trail produces a hike of at least 8 km (5 mi).

Cautionary Notes: Because of its proximity to swamp, stream, and bog, the Wetlands Trail will often be, well, wet. Be prepared for soggy footings, particularly in spring and after rains.

Future Plans: Over the next few years there may be further changes as the Nova Scotia Museum enacts its plans to utilize the Uniacke property more fully. Expect more trails, further recreation amenities, and the gradual clearing of the lands near Uniacke House to approximate 18th century country estate landscaping. Interpretive panels will inform hikers about the local history and environment, and special events on the estate will be added to an annual calender of activities.

Further Information: The Nova Scotia Museum produces a brochure about Uniacke Estate and its recreational facilities, and it has mounds of research material about the area and about Richard John Uniacke. Contact the Public Information Officer to obtain copies.

Upper Clements Provincial Wildlife Park

Length: 8 km
 (5 mi) return
Time: 3 hrs
Type: logging roads
Rating: 2

Uses: hiking, mountain
 biking, cross-country skiing
Facilities: outhouses,
 garbage cans, picnic
 tables, water, shelter (with
 wood stove and firewood)
Gov't Topo Map: Digby
 21 A/12

Access: From Annapolis Royal, drive 6 km (3.75 mi) west along Highway 1 toward Yarmouth. Road signs indicate the park on the left. The trailhead is at the far end of the parking lot.

Introduction: Annapolis Royal and Upper Clements have become a regional recreation hub. Upper Clements Theme Park, an amusement centre with rides, clowns, and fairground atmosphere, is the only such facility in Nova Scotia. The Historic Gardens and Fort Anne National Historic Site in Annapolis Royal attract thousands of visitors annually, particularly in the summer. Upper Clements Provincial Wildlife Park, in addition to displays of indigenous animals on its 12 ha (30 a) grounds, features a multi-use trail. Originally designed for hiking, the route was later modified to accommodate cross-country ski use. With the increase in popularity of the skating technique, the path system was completely reworked in 1992.

The older route, still visible in places, was abandoned in favour of a 10 km (6.25 mi) chain of three stacked loops constructed on 565 ha (1400 a) of Crown land. Routes of 4 km (2.5 mi), 6 km (3.75 mi), or 8 km (5 mi) are possible on trails a minimum of 3.5 m/yd wide. Directional arrows, signs warning of turns and

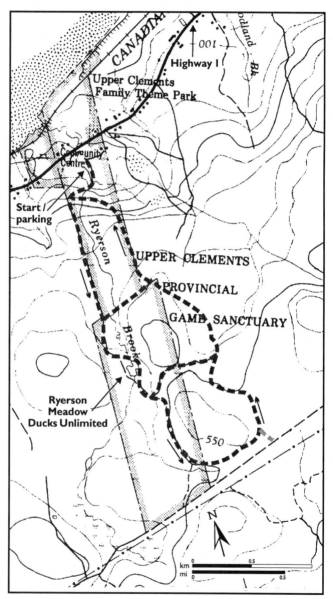

Upper Clements Provincial Wildlife Park

steep grades, and maps are posted at every intersection. In winter the trails are groomed, tracked, and renovated by the park staff, and a trailhead facility was constructed in 1994 for winter use.

This is also a worthwhile warm-weather hike. Beautiful stands of mature spruce and mixed hardwoods enfold the trail in the higher elevations, and an impounded marsh constructed by Ducks Unlimited intersects the route. With the picnic ground as a base, this can be an enjoyable family destination, particularly in the fall.

Trail Description: From the trailhead, walk west a short distance to an old logging road, the first leg of the Prescesky Trail. The first 1.5 km (1 mi) is uphill at a moderate grade. There is no shade along this section, and the route is arrow-straight. The other end of the loop joins from your left. (Hear the roar of the roller coaster in the Theme Park?) As you crest the first knoll, a gravel pit appears just before the cut-over path. Markers and maps provide guidance; turn left to complete the Prescesky Trail, continue straight on to the Ryerson Trail. For the next 500 m/yd enjoy a level, occasionally wet walk. Noticeable cutting makes these woods appear harvested, not the pristine old growth many prefer.

The new route, well signed, curves left and uphill from the original track. Following the old road leads to the middle of Ryerson Meadow, a wetland created by Ducks Unlimited. Unless you are exceptionally curious and do not mind back-tracking, follow the new path to an interpretive station and drier look-off.

Ryerson Meadow was constructed in 1985, a 12 ha (30 a) breeding habitat for black ducks, ring-necked ducks, green-winged teals, and wood ducks, whose nesting boxes are visible on trees in the marsh. The trail crowns the earthen dam and follows the meadow's fringe until the former road reconnects. The next cut-over junction appears on your left 200 m/yd along. Follow it to complete a 6 km (3.75 mi) hike. Continue straight for the Hardwood Trail, which begins to ascend through tall mixed hardwoods. You are finally shaded, and will continue so for most of the remainder of the walk.

The Hardwood Trail circles a large knoll and is the most attractive section for hiking. Leaving the former road finally, the new track loops through an area of splendid birches, curving to reconnect with the Ryerson cut-over path after 3 km (2 mi). The final kilometre is less attractive, with cutting going on, but several spots are still magical. Mostly downhill, Ryerson Trail travels about a kilometre to reconnect with Prescesky loop. Look for a massive crow's nest on a dead tree near the top of a small knoll halfway along. Excavations to provide fill for the track have not healed, nor has vegetation grown in around the new junctions, but the trails passes through lovely woods, including stands of mature spruce.

If you have time, the connecting paths at the top of the Ryerson and Prescesky loops are worth travelling. The Ryerson cut-over (return) will add 1.5 km (1 mi) to your hike, the Prescesky less than a kilometre. I, of course, could not leave a trail unwalked.

The final 1.5 km (1 mi) is downhill and follows a tiny brook on your left for much of its course. Sturdy bridges cross both this stream, as the path cuts left across the hillside, and another brook near the end. Look carefully and you may see the remains of an old stone bridge among the brush in the creek bed. Although steep in a few places, this moderate slope is a pleasant reward for enduring the initial climb. Connecting briefly with the dirt road on which you first started your hike, the trail turns sharply right to follow the fence of the wildlife park the remaining few metres to the parking lot.

Cautionary Notes: This is wood tick territory from April to July.

Further Information: Further information about cross-country skiing, this trail's principal use, may be found in *Nova Scotia Nordic Ski Trails*, published by Nordic Ski Nova Scotia.

Pitcher plant, Spry Bay Trail, Taylor Head Park.
MICHAEL HAYNES

CENTRAL – EASTERN SHORE

Including the Halifax-Dartmouth metropolitan area, this region stretches along the Atlantic coastline from St. Margarets Bay to the Canso Peninsula and inland through the Musquodoboit and Guysborough river valleys. Thinly populated except near the city, the entire region is composed of granites, slates, and greywacke, producing a bleak landscape of poor soils occasionally relieved by intrusions of more fertile drumlins. Scoured by glaciers and shaped by fault lines, the eastern shore features repeated long narrow inlets, created from drowned river valleys, separating jagged rocky headlands.

Many hiking opportunities exist in this area, with the majority on the coast. Several of the provincial beach parks, such as Clam Harbour and Martinique, provide pleasant walks along many kilometres of sandy shore, and Tor Bay in Guysborough County is similar. Inland parks—Dollar Lake, Oakfield, Laurie—have excellent facilities but only short trail systems. All are pleasant, and all are close to Halifax. Metropolitan Halifax-Dartmouth is an area of high usage, and many hiking options are available. Some city parks, such as Hemlock Ravine, are wonderful strolls.

I have not included these in *Hiking Trails of Nova Scotia*, concentrating instead on several hikes long familiar to the outdoor community, despite their being on old roads and exposed headlands and lacking facilities. Duncans Cove, Old St. Margarets Bay Coach Road, and Salmon River are favourites among recreational users, as are Pennant Point and McNabs Island, these last two on park reserve lands. The rail trail near Musquodoboit Harbour is a fragment of an abandoned line more than 100 km (62 miles) long, although some portions have been lost to recreational usage. Taylor Head Provincial Park has a trail system designed for either short or long treks, and its setting is enticing enough to make one happy just to drive there. Middle Musquodoboit, with its educational opportunities, is ideal for families and novices and, located behind the Eastern Shore Granite Ridge in the Musquodoboit River Valley, it offers some variety in landscape. Abrahams Lake is also situated in an area not commonly travelled and also makes a pleasant family day-trip. The Queensport Road, climbing over the Canso Barrens, is more suitable for experienced hikers.

Up the eastern shore and into Guysborough County there are so many wood roads and so much beautiful coastline that local inhabitants can hike from their back yards. The trails here are informal and known only within the community. Groups like the Guysborough County Trails Association are attempting to improve access for visitors, and their work on the former rail-bed between Guysborough and Ferrona Junction is just a start. Perhaps you'll find it in the 8th edition of *Hiking Trails of Nova Scotia*.

Hunting is permitted in the areas of the Old St. Margarets Bay Coach Road, Queensport Road, and Salmon River trails and the Musquodoboit Harbour Rail Trail. Hunting season usually starts around the first of October, but it varies from year to year and according to the species hunted. Contact the Department of Natural Resources for detailed information before going into the woods. Although hunting is not permitted on Sundays, wear hunter orange garb every day in season for safety's sake.

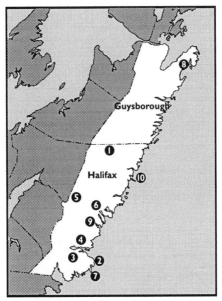

CENTRAL / EASTERN SHORE

1.	Abrahams Lake	*128*
2.	Duncans Cove	*132*
3.	McNabs Island	*138*
4.	Middle Musquodoboit	*142*
5.	Musquodoboit Harbour Rail Trail	*146*
6.	Old St. Margarets Bay Coach Road	*152*
7.	Pennant Point	*156*
8.	Queensport Road	*160*
9.	Salmon River	*164*
10.	Taylor Head Provincial Park	*170*

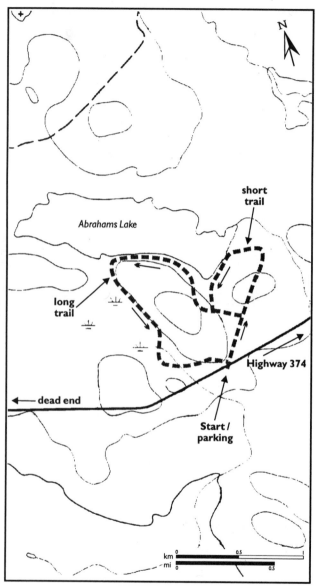

Abrahams Lake

Lands near the Musquodobit Rail Trail and the Queensport Road and Salmon River trails were designated as among 31 candidate protected areas by the Department of Natural Resources in 1994. Over the next several years, the DNR hopes to develop management policies for these areas that may either include or discourage recreational use, depending upon environmental and community concerns. Free copies of the proposed system plan for parks and protected areas may be obtained from the Department of Natural Resources.

Abrahams Lake

Length: 6.5 km (4 mi) return
Time: 2 hrs
Type: walking paths
Rating: 1

Uses: hiking
Facilities: none
Gov't Topo Map: Upper Musquodoboit 11 E/2

Access: From Sheet Harbour, drive 34 km (21.25 mi) toward New Glasgow on Highway 374. Look for a sign on your left stating "Abrahams Lake Road, Built and Maintained by Scott Maritime." (A new sign is to be built by the Nature Conservancy in 1995.) Drive 5 km (3 mi) on a dirt road; a large sign indicates the trailhead on your right. A parking area is provided. From New Glasgow, take Exit 24 off Highway 104 through Stellarton toward Lorne and Trafalgar. Drive 55 km (34 mi) on Highway 374 to Abrahams Lake Road (on your right).

Introduction: In October 1994, the Nature Conservancy of Canada accepted ownership of the 343-ha (846-a) Abrahams Lake Forest Preserve from Scott Maritimes Ltd. Containing one of the few old-growth stands of red spruce, eastern hemlock, and white pine remaining in Nova Scotia, this pocket of pre-European forest has somehow survived centuries of lumber and pulp harvesting as well as the numerous and extensive forest fires that have which devastated this part of Nova Scotia.

The Nature Conservancy of Canada has been purchasing and protecting natural areas for 33 years and maintains a network of 560 sanctuaries containing more than 490,000 ha (1.2 million a) across Canada. They intend to preserve this forest as a "living classroom," dedicated to conservation education. It will become a destination for both schoolchildren and university students. In addition to the area of "Cathedral Forest," so-named for the high cathedral-like canopy of the old growth trees, a 206-ha (511-a) buffer zone has been established surrounding the red spruce forest.

Normally, I would rate any trail longer than 5 km (3 mi) at difficulty level 2. This hike, however, follows a well-marked path through gently rolling terrain, and a shorter option, barely 2.5 km (1.5 mi) long is also available. Suitable for families, this hike instead merits a rating of 1.

Trail Description: From the parking area, the trail immediately heads into the forest under a canopy of young trees. This area bordering the road is part of a buffer zone that protects older trees against the effects of natural disturbances and provides a habitat for animals and birds. Come early in the morning, around dawn, and you may see moose.

At the first junction, just inside the woods, head right. If you do turn left instead, notice that all the trail marking signs are on the reverse side of the trees, and can be seen only from the opposite direction. This trail is designed for one-way traffic.

Soon after this first junction, you head underneath tall spruce. The canopy is so thick that very little undergrowth thrives. Only ferns lift above ground level, and a carpet of rich green moss dominates. The trail here is distinct and easy to follow, moving gently along a hillside to cross the tiny brook and bog draining Abrahams Lake. Now, trail markers, green "Christmas trees" on white rectangles, become more frequent. You will notice them mounted on trees around eye-level. Climbing again, you find another junction, this with a sign pointing right that says, "Short Trail, 15 minutes." This may be the most attractive section of the hike, cresting a tiny hill underneath the 30-m/yd red spruce. It is very still beneath their massive interlocking boughs; wind and sunlight are virtually excluded here.

All too soon the path veers sharply left out of this lovely area and reaches the shore of Abrahams Lake. Loons frequently nest here, so do not be surprised if you hear their call as you approach. A small clearing along the lake's bank is an ideal spot for a picnic, but even though old fire pits may tempt you, please do not light cooking fires. The consequences of an accident here are simply too high. The path continues close to the lake, crosses the brook and follows it inland to another junction. A left turn here returns to the start; the right turn is signed "Long Trail — 1 hour."

The long trail returns to the lake shore, following it for the next 1.5 km (1 mi). At several places the path cuts a swath through the middle of a dense thicket of very young trees, giving a decided tunnel aspect to portions of the walk. Near the lake edge, the trees appear somewhat younger. Turning sharply left, you return to the region of old growth hemlock. In this first portion the path is extremely difficult to follow on the ground, and you must rely upon the posted signs. This lasts only for perhaps 200 m/yd, when a spruce bog on your right

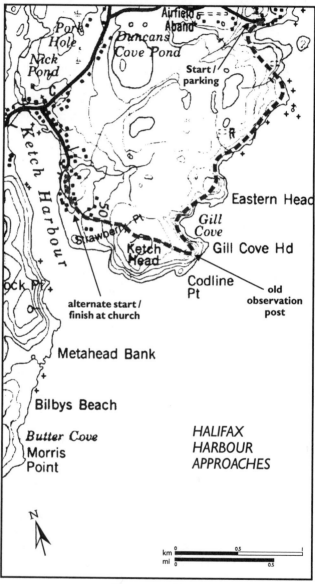

Duncans Cove

and rising ground on your left provide a clearer indication of the route. The final leg continues straight back toward the parking lot, passing through an area of old growth birch and maple along the way. Shortly after crossing another tiny creek, the loop ends at the junction near the parking lot. Turn right for the last 100 m/yd.

Cautionary Notes: This trail is in a somewhat remote location and you should let someone know when you are going in and when you plan to be back. Be cautious during hunting season, even though hunting is not permitted on this property.

Further Information: Abrahams Lake and other areas preserved by the Nature Conservancy of Canada are profiled in their Annual Report.

Duncans Cove

Length: 8 km
(5 mi) return
Time: 3 hrs
Type: former roads,
walking paths
Rating: 3

Uses: hiking
Facilities: none
Gov't Topo Map: Sambro
11 D/5

Access: From the Armdale Rotary in Halifax drive 19 km (12 mi) along Highway 349 toward Sambro. Just after a fire hall, turn left on the Duncans Cove Road. After 1 km (.5 mi), turn right onto a gravel road. The entrance to the trail is a further 500 m/yd, a gravelled track on your right near the water's edge. Park on the road, being careful not to block driveways.

Introduction: Duncans Cove falls under the heading of a "traditional" hike. People have come for generations to walk along this spectacular coastline; my parents told me recently that they brought me here when I was a child. But it is not a legally protected trail, and although much of it is publicly owned, the entrance is private property, as is much of the exit at Ketch Harbour. The growth of Halifax, and the increasing tendency of many to live outside the core area, has seen former fishing communities like Duncans Cove turn into quasi-suburbs. As new buildings go up, access to traditional hikes becomes threatened. That has not yet happened here, thanks to one landowner who permits hikers access. Let us hope that nothing occurs to prevent public passage to this beautiful spot.

Like most of Chebucto Head, Ketch Head, where you will be walking, is exposed granite promontory. Part of the Pennant Barrens, this area features rocky shoreline, high granite knolls, stunted white spruce, and glacial boulders scattered about. The steep cliffs by the water's edge were formed in an early geological age, buried later by softer sedimentary cover, and exposed again when that layer eroded away. The cliffs retain their harsh steepness, which might otherwise have been worn away by wind and rain.

Duncans Cove is a harsh, rugged hike that climbs on narrow, unmaintained footpaths up and down steep, barren hillsides. Several times the trail drops almost to ocean level, only to ascend the next hill. Ketch Head, the highest point, reaches 40 m/yd above the water. But like all coastal trails, this one gives a feeling of closeness to the sea. Beautiful on a warm, sunny day, it is breathtaking during a storm. And really, it should be experienced under both conditions, for two entirely different hikes. Winter is another wonderful time to try this, although you'll need to make special preparations.

Snow, like soil, does not accumulate on these perpetually windswept rocks.

Trail Description: Follow the gravel track past a metal gate and up the hill on the other side of the cove. A sign at the gate says "Private Road, Hikers Welcome, Vehicles Prohibited." Just before the old wartime command post, now a residence, a sign on a power pole stating "Shore Trail" directs you to your right. A distinct track through the brush heads down the other side of the hill to a tiny dam. This is actually one of the most awkward parts of the hike, being quite steep with tricky footing. Many paths seem to head in every direction, but keep along the shoreline route. Once at water level, the path meanders along the hillside past Duncans Reef and Duck Reef. Expect rafts of eiders and scoters in all these little inlets, especially in the fall and winter. There is a ruin of a wartime observation post on the top of the hill above Eastern Cove, but the trail stays below it. Don't worry, there is another ruin on Ketch Head, our destination.

The path climbs Eastern Head at about 2 km (1.25 mi). This elevation affords a magnificent view of Ketch Head in front, and Duncans Cove behind. As you descend into the gully at Gill Cove, the footing becomes difficult again and the path very narrow. Pay attention to your foot placement, at least until you enter a small stand of spruce at the bottom of the ravine. Continue on the coastal route; a trail branching right among the trees circles Ketch Head and leads directly to the village of Ketch Harbour. Continuing on the narrow track, cautiously round Gill Cove and begin the climb to the ruined observation post.

The view at the top is astounding. On the right are Sambro Island and its lighthouse; on the left, Duncans Cove and the eastern shore disappearing into the mists;

dominating the view are the ocean and the approaches to Halifax Harbour. The path takes you directly to the ruined concrete shelter, which actually sits on Gill Cove Head. When I was there last, hundreds of ducks swam below in tiny Codline Cove. The trail continues another kilometre along the former road to Ketch Harbour, but for many this spot is the turning point of their trek. The view inspires silent contemplation, the vastness of the ocean reminiscent of the prairie "big sky." There always seems to be at least one ship around, and sailboats dot the water in the summer. When you are ready, turn around and retrace your route back to Duncans Cove. Or take the road across the top of Ketch Head into the village and follow the pavement back to your car.

Cautionary Notes: Expect harsher weather conditions than in the city, and wind, fog, or rain, if they are to be found anywhere. This is an unsupervised area and the trails are not maintained. Before beginning your hike inform someone where you will be and when you should be back. Be prepared for emergencies. Should you venture out in a storm, beware of getting too close to the water's edge. So-called rogue waves, unpredictable and more powerful than normal breakers, can reach far onto the rocks, and almost every year someone is lost in the ocean.

Further Information: Both the Halifax Hiking Club and the Dartmouth Volksmarch regularly lead group hikes on this trail, as does Halifax City Recreation.

McNabs Island

Length: 7 km
 (4.5 mi) return
Time: 2-3 hrs
Type: old cart tracks,
 walking paths, beaches
Rating: 1

Uses: hiking, mountain
 biking, cross-country skiing
Facilities: outhouses (but
 no toilet paper)
Gov't Topo Map: Halifax
 11 D/12

Access: There is no regularly scheduled year-round access to the island. Starting 1 July, boat service sails daily from Cable Wharf in downtown Halifax. In 1994, the cost was either $8 or $12, depending upon the vendor. The ferry (really a converted fishing boat) departs around 8:00 a.m. and returns from McNabs at either 12:30 or 6:30 p.m. The trip takes about 20 minutes.

Introduction: Few North American cities are blessed with an island wilderness in sight of their business and financial centre. McNabs has been an important part of the metro area for generations. The site of a French fishing station more than a hundred years before the founding of Nova Scotia's capital city, it was frequented by native peoples long before that.

You can reach the island only by boat, and the ferry ride is enjoyable for its own sake. Halifax is one of the busiest ports in Canada, so do not be surprised if a massive container ship glides past. And you will pass close to Georges Island, a tiny rock in the centre of the harbour that was entirely converted into a fortress and is now being reborn as a national park. Remember, the ocean has a far different climate from the land, and even the short distance you travel by boat will expose you to the winds of the Atlantic Ocean in temperatures 5° or 10°C cooler than on the land. Be prepared.

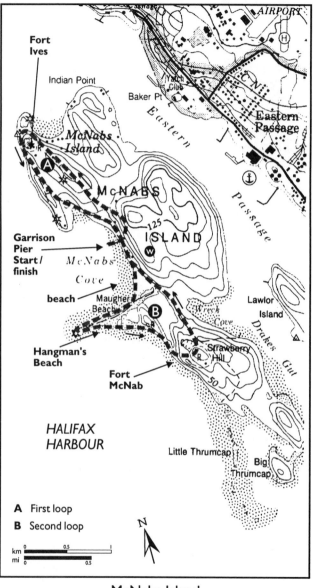

Fort
Ives

Indian Point

*McNabs
Island*

McNABS

ISLAND

Garrison
Pier
Start /
finish

*McNabs
Cove*

beach

Maugher
Beach

Hangman's
Beach

Fort
McNab

HALIFAX
HARBOUR

AIRPORT

Yacht
Club

Baker Pt

Eastern

Eastern
Passage

Passage

Lawlor
Island

Wreck
Cove

Strawberry
Hill

Drakes Gut

Little Thrumcap

Big
Thrumcap

A First loop

B Second loop

km
mi

N

McNabs Island

Trail Description: From the end of Garrison Pier, turn left along the Old Military Road. This dirt track runs the entire length of the island and was the main artery for supplies between the forts. After 100 m/yd turn right onto a small path and walk up a gentle hill to the site of the former McNabs Island Tea House. Once part of a large estate built by Roderick Hugonin when he retired from the British Army in 1851, it has been deserted since the 1930s. However, the grounds are home to a few rare plants, such as a massive copper beech, native to Siberia, which is growing next to the former tea house.

A path north from the tea house leads to the Perrin Road. Turn right up the hill to the Findlay farm site and the remains of an early 20th century soda pop plant. Turn left to return to the Old Military Road, where you turn right and head north. The beautiful mixed-wooded area you pass through was once the location of picnic grounds with a large open-air dance hall, merry-go-round, and carnival games that drew as many as 4,000 revellers playing quoits or cricket. You have less than a kilometre in these woods, the trail gently climbing toward the north end of the island, but in spring you will notice many warblers and other birds. At least 12 osprey pairs nest on McNabs, as well as bald eagles and great blue herons.

Emerging from the trees, you pass a number of buildings, some still privately owned. Stop for a moment and enjoy the view of Ives Cove and Eastern Passage, for it's only 200 m/yd to the ruins of Fort Ives and the northern tip of the island. The fort offers a superb view of both the harbour and the city from the parapet and is a wonderful location to sit and enjoy a snack. An outhouse has been sited near the north end of the fort. Fort Ives, however, has not been maintained for many years, and its masonry and ironwork cannot be trusted. Exercise caution walking around this site.

Exiting the fort, turn right and stroll downhill. A kilometre long, this path, called Garrison Road, leads back towards Garrison Pier. Trees through here are not very old but are full of birds. Surprisingly enough, McNabs Island is home to white-tailed deer and even an occasional visiting moose. Continue down Garrison Road until it ends at the Old Military Road. Turn right and head south past Garrison Pier to the beautiful sand beach beyond it. At its far end is the island's most distinctive landmark, the lighthouse. You can either follow the water line or walk up an old road to reach it. The point juts almost a kilometre into Halifax Harbour, where you end beneath the guns of York Redoubt, another fort in Halifax's defences, on the bluff across the narrows.

You are also now at Hangman's Beach, where the tarred bodies of executed sailors once hung in gibbets as warnings to the crews of Royal Navy ships of the punishment for desertion. Following the south-facing side of the spit, a bouldered breakwater, back toward McNabs Lagoon, you may wish to climb the small hill just east of the pond, through thick alder and beech scrub, to the Strawberry Battery. Its guns and searchlights were part of the harbour's submarine defences during World War II. From here you can continue along the water's edge for about 800 m/yd to Fort McNab. If this seems too challenging, return to the Old Military Road via a small trail at the southern end of the lagoon.

Casual walkers should consider skipping the Strawberry Battery entirely because there is no easy access. Instead follow the Lighthouse Road until it rejoins the Old Military Road, turn right, and walk for about a kilometre. The lagoon will be on your right and Wreck Cove on your left. A four-way intersection 400 m/yd past the pond signals your arrival at Fort McNab. Turn right to see the bomb-proof vaults built right into the hillside. Behind and above these bastions are the gun

Lighthouse at the end of Hangman's Beach, McNab's Island.
MICHAEL HAYNES

emplacements. The concrete blockhouse on the hilltop was their observation and command post, and it is clearly the natural destination of any hiker. From this vantage point are the most spectacular views on the island. Returning to the Garrison Pier and the boat ride home is fairly easy, and less than a 2-km (1.25-mi) walk. Descend the hill and follow the road the way you came. At the intersection, turn left and continue north along the Old Military Road until you reach the pier. If you have time to stop again at the beach, so much the better.

Cautionary Notes: There is no fresh water easily available on McNabs Island. Carry an adequate supply with you, particularly if accompanied by children. The for-

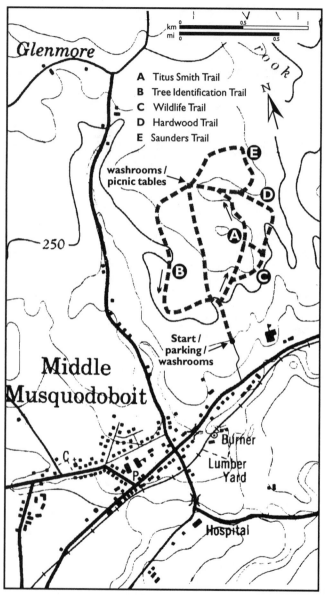

Middle Musquodoboit

tresses are not structurally maintained. Fences, in particular, have decayed, and serious falls are possible. Exercise extreme caution at these sites.

Future Plans: Parks Canada is intending to restore the Fort McNab site over the next five years. Also, the Friends of McNabs Island Society (FOMIS) is working to have the island developed as a full-service provincial park. They will be installing new outhouses, maintaining trails, and erecting signs.

Further Information: FOMIS produces a newsletter, *The Rucksack*, with information on guided walks, beach clean-ups and other activities. FOMIS is also developing a guidebook and eight-panel brochure.

Middle Musquodoboit

Length: 3.5 km (2.25 mi) return
Time: 1-2 hrs
Type: gravel road, walking paths
Rating: 1

Uses: hiking, cross-country skiing
Facilities: outhouses, picnic tables, covered tables
Gov't Topo Map: Shubenacadie 11 E/3

Access: From Highway 102, take Exit 8 at Elmsdale toward Middle Musquodoboit. Follow Highway 277 until it joins Highway 224 and continue north to Middle Musquodoboit. The complex is on the left past the village on the road toward Upper Musquodoboit. A large Department of Natural Resources highway sign marks the complex. A dirt road leads 500 m/yd uphill to the parking lot at the forest edge.

Introduction: The first of its kind in Atlantic Canada, the Musquodoboit Valley Forest Nursery and Educational Complex incorporates a forest nursery, a woodlot, and a visitor centre to provide tours, exhibits, woodlot demonstrations, and a variety of different educational programs. Combining the centre's classrooms with the opportunity for hands-on experience afforded by the adjacent facilities, the complex offers numerous three-to-four-hour school programs for all grades as well as resource people who visit classes with information and activities on more than 20 topics.

This is a wonderful place to learn more about Nova Scotia's flora and fauna while actually being outside. On the various trails are 39 interpretive sites describing everything from common tree species to bird nesting boxes. Free pamphlets are available with accompanying text. Much of the path network is wheelchair accessible with assistance, and the service road through the middle of the lot permits a shorter walk. Picnic tables and outhouses, located at the far end of the property, enable a comfortable break at the halfway mark. The 80 ha (200 a) woodlot with its trail system is open to the public year round.

This is the best walk that I know of for young families and persons of almost any fitness level.

Trail Description: In the parking lot is a large sheltered sign with a map of the trail system of the McCurdy Woodlot. Pamphlets may also be available in protected compartments attached to this display. Start walking along the gravel road behind the parking lot. On your left are outhouses and a cleared area including a small pond, a gazebo, and a botanical garden highlighting the nine main geographic areas of Nova Scotia.

After you've walked perhaps 100 m/yd, the entrance to the Titus Smith Trail appears on your right. Named after one of Nova Scotia's first environmental scientists, it is an easy 1 km (.5 mi) walk with 17 stops featuring examples of silvicultural operations, types of vegetation, and enemies of the forest. Like all the paths, this is wide enough for two to walk side by side and has no difficult grades, and roots and rocks have been hidden by a copious spreading of wood chips.

Continuing up the road another 100 m/yd, you'll see the entrance to the McCurdy Trail (also known as the Tree Identification Trail) on the left. Of the 30 native tree species (10 softwood and 20 hardwood), 11 of the most common are highlighted at stops along the path's 1.5 km (1 mi) route. Site #1, displaying white spruce, is visible from the road. Benches are situated near sites #3 and #6, and this trail is the only one with any hills worth mentioning. Following the road to its end will produce a walk of less than a kilometre but will lead to more outhouses and a picnic area. In addition, the Titus Smith, McCurdy and Saunders trails end here, so several return options are available.

Instead of the road, I recommend starting with the Titus Smith Trail. Its interesting stops are the most valuable component of this hike, and it provides a number of options as well. Just after a bench at site #7, the Fern and Moss Trail supplies a very short diversion. Somewhat longer at 500 m/yd, the Wildlife Trail branches right after site #6 and returns after site #8. It has 11 stops of its own showing ways that different wildlife species can be encouraged and supported by providing extra food and shelter. Splitting from the Wildlife Trail is yet another, the Hardwood Trail, also about 500 m/yd, which does not return to Titus Smith until near site #17.

From the picnic area, return to the start along the Tree Identification Trail. The stops will be in reverse order with #11, red spruce, your first. Also leading from the picnic area is the Saunders Trail, a further 500 m/yd

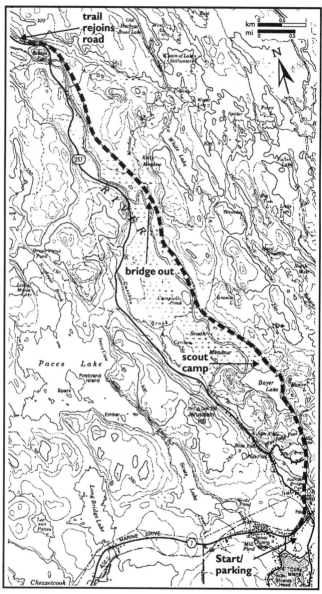

Musquodoboit Harbour Rail Trail

loop that connects to the Hardwood Trail at its other end. At the present time there are no interpretive stops on either the Hardwood or Saunders trails. The pattern of interconnecting trails may seem confusing, but each loop is so short that one cannot remain puzzled for long, and the options they provide permit substantial variety to a hike.

Future Plans: In addition to the McCurdy Woodlot, the complex administers the nearby Chaswood Educational Woodlot. Presently it contains only an access road, but over the next several years new interpretive trails will be constructed.

Further Information: Brochures are available on the Titus Smith Trail, Wildlife Trail, and Tree Identification Trail. Copies can be obtained from the tourist bureau in Middle Musquodoboit, or by writing to the Musquodoboit Valley Forest Nursery and Education Complex.

Musquodoboit Harbour Rail Trail

Length: 25 km
(15.5 mi) return
Time: 7-8 hrs
Type: former rail-bed
Rating: 5

Uses: hiking, mountain
biking, cross-country skiing
Facilities: outhouses,
garbage cans, tables, water
Gov't Topo Map:
Musquodoboit 11 D/14

Access: From Dartmouth, drive east along Highway 107 and then on Highway 7 to the village of Musquodoboit Harbour, approximately 40 km (25 mi). The Railway Museum is on the left side 200 m/yd before the junction with Highway 357.

Introduction: The Musquodoboit Railway Museum commemorates the days of the Intercolonial Railway, and several old railway cars are mounted on 100 m/yd of track that the museum purchased when the line was torn up. Because this is a linear trail, you may decide at any point to return to the start simply by retracing your steps. Like most abandoned railways, this is easy, level, mostly dry walking. This hike has a difficulty rating of 5 because completing 25 km (15.5 mi) in one day is reasonable only for very fit individuals. For a relaxing family walk, I recommend turning back at the far end of Bayer Lake, a 6.5 km (4 mi) return trip.

Trail Description: Starting at the old railway station, turn right and follow the tracks. You soon must cross Highway 357; be cautious because motorists have no warning signs about pedestrians. Another less busy road is a few hundred metres beyond that, and in order to prevent vehicles from driving on the former railway several ditches have been dug across the path. As you will notice, these may have enhanced this section's value to dirt-bikers. Small birch and beech have grown into the soft soil of the embankment, which is quite elevated here, and the small brushes always seem filled with birds.

The bridge over the Musquodoboit River, 500 m/yd further, stands very high over the wide, shallow stream. Once across, you remain in the open for another 500 m/yd before entering mixed softwoods. Frequent paths enter from both sides near the houses of the village, but roads have been barricaded. A small pond on your left signals the end of buildings for the remainder of your walk.

In the decades since this railway last operated, the trees have closed in somewhat, giving the trail a softer appearance than operating sections of track. The footing is hard-packed earth with very little gravel remaining, providing a very good walk. Granite outcroppings and cliffs, visible as you pass the first pond, soon come right down to the trail edge. Less than 2 km (1.25 mi) from the river, Bayer Lake appears on your left. This small, deep, clear pond is surrounded on three sides by steep granite hills. The trail often runs beside a sheer rockface and boulders are scattered throughout. The original bridge over the stream draining Turtle Lake has been burned, but a makeshift foot bridge connects the two banks, so you can continue without getting your feet wet.

At the far end of the lake notice a tiny sandy beach, and just beyond that a distinct path leading left. This is a Boy Scout camp, with benches, garbage can, and fire pit, an ideal spot for casual walkers to stop and rest before returning to the start. Those continuing will find the remainder of the hike open and easy with few exceptions. Shortly past the lake, old fields dominate on the left, with the remains of fences peeking out through tall grasses. Called South Meadow, this open area continues for most of the remainder of the hike. A concrete bridge crosses the brook draining Sparrow and Granite lakes, and the Musquodoboit River flows very close to the trail, its banks supporting several immense maples and oaks.

Moving away from the river, the path narrows to a winding one-person track through the underbrush at several spots, but once again widens as it passes through swampy ground. A burned-out school bus 4 km (2.5 mi) beyond Bayer Lake hints why access roads onto the old rail-bed were cut. Another burnt bridge at Meadow Brook provides a major decision point. This narrow stream must be forded to be crossed, and it is often more than waist deep. The ground on either side of the railway embankment is swampy, and this area, Kelly Meadow, is open for a considerable distance in every direction. Turn back now and you will have enjoyed a 16 km (10 mi) outing. Otherwise, strip down (you do not want wet clothes) and get across.

Kelly Meadow is a beautiful tract of marshy land where you can see almost 2 km (1.25 mi) up Meadow Brook toward the hills surrounding White Lake. That region has long been known for its outstanding wilderness travel opportunities and as a traditional canoing and fishing area. Only 3 km (2 mi) remain, and these are lovely if uneventful. South Meadows gives way in the final kilometre and the river approaches on your left. Traffic noises from Highway 357 become noticeable, and as the trail turns sharply left to avoid the approaching ridge line, railroad and highway converge. If you are fortunate, someone is waiting for you, or you brought two cars, one of which was parked here before you started the walk. Otherwise, about face, and retrace the 12.5 km (7.75 mi) you just walked.

Cautionary Notes: The bridge over the Musquodoboit River has not been prepared for foot traffic. There is no walking deck and there are no guardrails. The drop to the shallow river below is 10 m (33 ft). ATVs and dirt bikes use much of this route, particularly near the village. Be prepared to move to the side of the trail as soon as you hear them approaching. Several bridges have been destroyed and one stream must be forded. In summer, fall, and winter this should be relatively easy. During spring runoff, expect water levels to be much higher.

Hunting is permitted in the woods around here in the fall.

Future Plans: 4558 ha (11,300 a) adjacent to the trail around White Lake are among the candidate protected areas of the Department of Natural Resources. Plans for an extension of Highway 107 show it crossing the trail near the Musquodoboit River. The Nova Scotia Trails

Federation has asked the Department of Transport to incorporate protection of the recreational path into their designs.

Further Information: Historical brochures are available from the Musquodoboit Railway Museum.

Old St. Margarets Bay Coach Road

Length: 40 km (25 mi) return
Time: 10-12 hrs
Type: former road
Rating: 5

Uses: hiking, mountain biking, cross-country skiing, ATV, snowmobiling, horseback riding
Facilities: none
Gov't Topo Map: Halifax 11 D/12

Access: To access the trail near Halifax, drive from Armdale Rotary along Highway 3 for 4 km (2.5 mi) until the junction with Highway 333 at the traffic lights. Turn left on 333 and follow it for 6 km (3.75 mi) to Old Coach Road Estates. The street sign says "Old Coach Road." Turn right off the highway and continue on a gravel road for 200 m/yd. The trail crosses the road, and although it is unsigned it is quite distinct. Park your car here and enter the forest on the left.

Finding the trailhead on St. Margarets Bay is rather difficult. Drive 22 km (13.75 mi) from Halifax on Highway 103 to Exit 5. Turn left and follow Highway 213 for 2.5 km (1.5 mi) to Highway 3. Then turn right and go 500 m/yd to the junction with Highway 333. Follow 333 for 12.5 km (8 mi) until you cross Woodens River, before sighting the "Glen Margaret" road sign. The trail

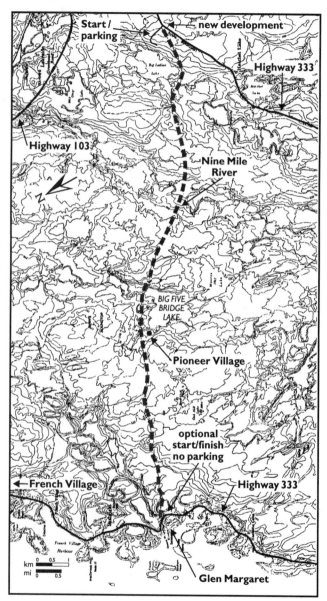

Old St. Margarets Bay Road

is on the left behind house #10697, separating left 50 m/yd up a private driveway. No good parking is available nearby.

Introduction: Coach service for mail and military dispatches was inaugurated in Nova Scotia in 1801 and passenger service was added in 1815. The increasing pace of settlement meant that many roads were constructed and mail coach service was required on most. William MacKay's 1834 map of Nova Scotia shows the St. Margarets Bay Coach Road, running between French Village and Halifax, and it is apparent that features such as Five Mile Pond and Nine Mile River were named because of their location on the journey.

Although not used by vehicles for generations, the road has remained a Crown right-of-way and is a favourite of several recreational groups. It is great for hiking, being long, distinct, and far from population centres. But because of its length, the lack of signage, and the navigation skills required, I recommend the full distance only for experienced hikers. Although it's possible to hike 40 km (25 mi) in one day, only the fittest individuals should attempt that distance. Instead, make this a two-day trip, or arrange for a ride at St. Margarets Bay. A reasonable day hike is the 14-km (8.75-mi) return trip to Nine Mile River.

Trail Description: This trail is unmistakable as an old road. Although it's not officially maintained, ATV users have kept large deadfalls removed and constructed several bridges, most notably across Nine Mile River. Because of its proximity to the city and the numerous connections with other trails, this route is well-used. The first 2 km (1.25 mi) work gradually downhill to Big Indian and Little Indian lakes, both on the right. A good bridge crosses Prospect River, feeding from Little Indian

Lake. Once across, you are outside of Halifax watershed lands and on ground where you may camp. One kilometre (.5 mi) beyond the bridge a well-defined trail joins from the right. Continue straight (left), and do the same 1.5 km (1 mi) later at another junction. You have been climbing since Prospect River, but after you crest the ridge near this second junction you begin to descend toward the Nine Mile River.

At 7 km (4.5 mi) you reach Nine Mile River, where an excellent bridge makes crossing easy. This is a popular campsite on a pretty river. Advanced hikers might wish to follow it 2 km (1.25 mi) upstream to some abandoned farm sites and barrens. For many, the next 5 km (3 mi) are the nicest stretch of the trail, featuring some inland barrens and lovely hardwood stands. The trail initially climbs out of the river valley, then stays mostly level for about 3 km (2 mi). Another intersection before Big Five Bridge Lake might cause confusion. Keep left, despite the high quality of the right-hand path, and you will soon sight the lake. (If you are in doubt, set a north-westerly compass bearing.) Crossing Five Bridge Runs, the path climbs a knoll, giving a good view of the lake.

Continuing straight, the trail passes tiny Five Mile Pond on your right, crossing its creek, and climbs gradually again. Pioneer Village, a wilderness camping site used by various community groups, is found on the shore of Big Five Bridge Lake near here, although in recent years it has fallen into disrepair. Yet another intersection appears, this with a road leading north to Lewis Lake. Make certain you remain on the old post road, continuing left. For the next 5 km (3 mi), the trail continues straight along undulating terrain, staying almost level until falling in the last kilometre as you approach the finish. You may get glimpses of St. Margarets Bay in the distance or of the line of hills to the north along the Woodens River. The final 2 km (1.25 mi)

are as well travelled as the first. Climbing a sma̅
you are suddenly in Glen Margaret and new
border both sides of the trail. If you are doing t,̅
trip, turn around at this point and return along your
route. If you are lucky enough to have a ride waiting,
continue down the hill to Highway 333.

Cautionary Notes: This is an entirely unsupervised
area. There are no signs and no services, and the trails
are not maintained. Before entering the woods make
certain that you make your plans known to someone.
Hunting is permitted on these lands.

Eastern Shore

Pennant Point

Length: 13 km
  (8.25 mi) return
Time: 4 hrs
Type: former roads,
  walking paths, beaches
Rating: 2

Uses: hiking, mountain
  biking, cross-country
  skiing
Facilities: garbage cans
Gov't Topo Map: Sambro
  11 D/5

Access: From the Armdale Rotary in Halifax, take the
Herring Cove Road, Highway 349, until it ends in the
village of Sambro, about 20 km (12.5 mi). Follow the
narrow twisty road until you see signs that clearly indicate the route to follow to reach Crystal Crescent Beach
and the start of the hike. Several junctions must be
navigated correctly in the next 3 km (2 mi), and the last
500 m/yd are along a potholed gravel road. When you
reach the parking lot, leave your car and walk directly
to the beach.

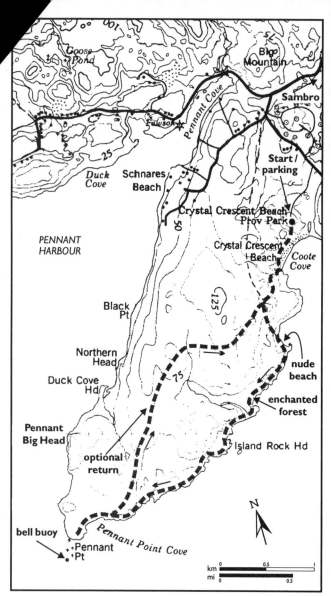

Pennant Point

Introduction: This is one of my favourite walks, and I have been coming here for 20 years. Local hiking clubs, field naturalists, birders, and many other groups have also long recognized the special nature of this tiny finger of exposed coastal headland so close to Halifax, and organized walks along this trail are common. Designated a provincial park in the mid-1970s, Crystal Crescent remained largely untouched. However, interest has grown in recent years and may soon result in the construction of more facilities.

Trail Description: You cannot start a hike with a better view. From the beautiful white sand of Coote Cove, you can look across Sambro Harbour to the rugged and treeless granite islands defining the western boundary of Halifax Harbour. The red-and-white striped lighthouse on Sambro Island looks more imitation than real, but it serves to warn approaching vessels of nearby reefs such as Shag Rock, Mad Rock, and The Sisters, all of which have claimed victims in the past. Expect plenty of company on the beach in the summer. Hundreds flock here on the weekends, filling the parking lots. But the dazzling white sand just cries out for you to walk barefoot and wiggle your toes in it.

Once your wiggling is done, probably at the far end of the beach by a small pond, you have a choice. You may either follow the coast or take an old road up the hill. I recommend the latter, as you get a spectacular view of the area from the top. Just before the crest is a junction. Turn left here and walk toward the high ground 10 m/yd away. From there, continue down the slope to Mackerel Cove and another sandy beach.

A word of warning: this has been a nude beach for more than 20 years, and you may meet naturists anytime during the next kilometre, particularly on hot, sunny days. If this makes you uncomfortable, perhaps you should not continue.

After Mackerel Cove, you leave the Provincial Park but continue on Crown land. Numerous side trails are scattered all through the woods, impossible to describe. Stick close to the vegetation boundary and you should be fine. The coastline also becomes more rugged and difficult, with several sheer rock faces.

About 300 m/yd beyond the beach you will find the place my friend called "the enchanted forest," an exotic sight. About 15 years ago a fire burned most of Pennant Point. Here, the trees were killed but not completely consumed, and their gnarled branches and twisted trunks have been polished by the fog and bleached by the sun. The forest floor plant cover now reaches about waist height, and the contrast between the vibrant green and dead grey is striking.

Shortly afterwards, you turn the corner at Deep Cove and emerge from the cover of the spruce and fir thickets. Many people turn back here, for the remainder of the 3 km (2 mi) to the headland is typical coastal barrens, completely exposed to the wind and often chilly even on an August day. But the footpath is distinct and easy to follow, or you can walk along the massive granite boulders that make up the shoreline. The trail follows the coastline closely, hugging several small coves and points. About a kilometre from the headland, those with better hearing will be able to distinguish the clanging of a buoy located near some submerged rocks from the omnipresent crash of the waves. A freshwater pool just before the point has provided me with surprise sightings of white-tailed deer and otter. A large cairn of rocks a few metres beyond that is your sign that you have reached the southernmost tip of land and the end of the walk.

From here you can see the houses of Lower Prospect and Terence Bay. Sea traffic into Halifax Harbour is often visible on the horizon, and there are almost always fishing or recreational craft in sight during the summer months. This is a pleasant spot to enjoy your lunch. Just remember to pack everything out with you. Return to the parking lot the way you came. Some intrepid hikers tell me that they have hiked down the western side of the point to East Pennant, but the coast is much steeper and I always get lost in the spruce thickets, so I cannot recommend it for the casual hiker.

Cautionary Notes: There is neither fresh water nor an outhouse on site. Make those preparations in advance. The ground is very wet, and the headland is exposed to high, cool winds. Wear appropriate footwear and clothing. Both during and just after a storm, waves can be substantially higher than normal. Be careful near the water's edge.

Although not permitted, ATVs and dirt bikes often use the old roads on the point. If you hear them approaching, step out of the path, and do not assume that they will know you are in their way.

There is a popular *au naturel* beach along your route. If you are offended by nudity you may wish to save this hike for a cold or cloudy day.

Future Plans: A local committee has been assembled to determine future development of Pennant Point.

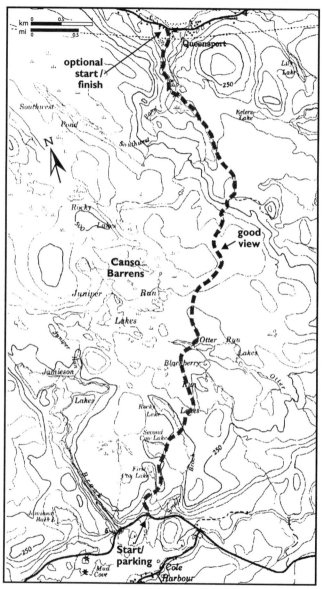

Queensport Road

Queensport Road

Length: 18 km
    (11.25 mi) return
Time: 5-6 hrs
Type: former road
Rating: 4

Uses: hiking, mountain
    biking, ATV, cross-country
    skiing, horseback riding
Facilities: none
Gov't Topo Map:
    Chedabucto Bay 11 F/6

Access: From Highway 104, take Exit 37 toward Canso. Drive on Highway 16 past Guysborough, and take the unnumbered road to Larrys River. At Larrys River, turn left on Highway 316 and drive for 10 km (6.25 mi) to Cole Harbour. The trail is an unmarked dirt track to the left about 500 m/yd beyond the bridge over Jamieson Brook. If you continue to another bridge in the village, you missed the entrance. Back up and look again.

Introduction: The Canso Barrens extend northeastward from New Harbour to Cape Canso, the easternmost tip of the mainland. Composed of granite and forming headlands and knolls with elevations of up to 200 m (650 ft), the barrens are thinly covered by a sandy loam soil that leaves almost 50% of the surface as exposed bedrock. Much of the area looks like a bleak moonscape, with black spruce and balsam fir clustered wherever there is adequate shelter from the winds and sufficient soil. Large boulders deposited by the glaciers litter the landscape.

Around the coast of this inhospitable region, European settlers established communities in order to live closer to the rich fisheries of the New World. Most travel was by boat, with only a few dirt tracks overland. One of these traversed the interior barrens, connecting Cole Harbour on Tor Bay with Queensport on Chedabucto Bay. It fell into disuse after the nearby parallel route from Port Felix to Halfway Cove was paved, and by the 1970s it was no longer maintained by the Department of Highways. Since then the path has gradually grown over, and now it offers a wonderful, wild walk across a remarkable landscape. Bicycling and horseback riding are permitted, but thick growth in some areas may hinder such activity. I recommend this trail only for experienced hikers.

Trail Description: There is ample room to get your car off the highway. In 1994 the owner of an adjacent property used the first 500 m/yd of the public right-of-way to access his woodlot, creating space for parking and a terrible mess. But the direction you walk is clear, the trail climbing a shallow ravine until it reaches First Cow Lake. New beech crowds the trail there, and in summer it becomes cramped. At a trail junction shortly afterward keep right. The left path leads over the barrens to Jamieson Lake and is difficult to follow and very wet; it is also a dead end. By Second Cow Lake, the barrens become visible on your left, although you descend into thick vegetation almost immediately.

Between Rocky Lake and Otter Run Lakes, a distance of 2 km (1.25 mi), the footing gets rougher. Rivulets run down the path and the brush grows so thick that Blackberry Lake is sensed rather than seen, though it's only 100 m/yd on your right. Note numerous sumac trees in this stretch. Nearing Otter Lake, the trail descends into softwood and begins to widen. The remainder of the route is easier walking. One kilometre (.5 mi) beyond Otter Lake, you climb to the spectacular barrens with its clumps of scrubby fir and abundant rocks. Expect the wind to be cooler and harsher. On a clear day you can see across Chedabucto Bay in front of you to the Hadleyville Shore.

Crossing the top of the barrens, the track falls rapidly down the steeper north slope. The climate is much milder here, and, with better soil, the trees are more robust and taller. Keep left at a junction 500 m/yd below the open ground (avoiding the car wrecks), and follow the ravine as it continues 2 km (1.25 mi) downhill to Southwest Pond Brook. ATV users have bridged the river, and the ruins of the original structure remain. This is a lovely spot to take a break. On the other side, the old road follows the ravine 1.5 km (1 mi) further past a gravel pit and under a power line to emerge on Highway 316 across from St. Pauls Cemetery in Queensport. Unless there is someone to pick you up, turn around, and back you go to the other side. The return walk will be steeper, but you get to see the barrens one more time, and that will be worth the effort.

Cautionary Notes: This is a completely unsupervised path over one of the most rugged and isolated regions of Nova Scotia. Weather on the barrens is both highly changeable and severe. Much of the area is without significant tree cover because of the extreme conditions. Be prepared for anything, particularly strong, cool winds. There are no signs or facilities, and there are not likely to be too many other people. Make certain that you notify someone of your location and intended time of return.

This is not park land, so hunting is permitted in the fall.

Future Plans: The Guysborough County Trails Association wants to see this former road protected under the Trails Act and is working with government agencies to accomplish this. They hope to have trail markers up in the next few years.

Much of the land this trail passes through is part of the proposed 10,846-ha (27,000-a) Bonnet Lake Barrens Candidate Protected Area.

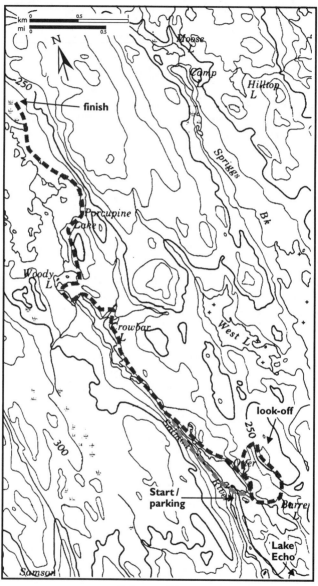

Salmon River

Salmon River

Length: 12 km
   (7.5 mi) return
Time: 4-5 hrs
Type: walking paths,
   former road
Rating: 4

Uses: hiking
Facilities: none
Gov't Topo Map:
   Musquodoboit 11 D/14

Access: From the Angus L. MacDonald Bridge in Dartmouth, drive 17 km (10.5 mi) to Exit 18 off Highway 107. Turn left 1 for (.5 mi) on Mineville Road to Highway 7, and turn right for 3 km (2 mi). Crossing the river, turn left off Highway 7 onto Circle Drive. At the next intersection, turn left onto River Drive and follow the dirt road for 3 km (2 mi) to its end by an iron bridge. Park here.

Introduction: This trail was created, not by recreational hikers, but by hunters and anglers following the waters to the interior in search of game. Listed in the first *Hiking Trails of Nova Scotia* almost 30 years ago, the path has probably been in existence along the Salmon River since shortly after the first European settlers arrived around modern-day Lake Echo. And most likely the colonists followed a path created by the Native peoples even before that. It is rough, narrow, and winding, always following the waterway, and it is heavily used during hunting and fishing seasons. The land here forms part of the Eastern Shore Granite Ridge Landscape, a prominent feature about 80 km (50 mi) long and 8-10 km (5-6 mi) wide in the interior behind the Atlantic Coast Region. Rising sharply to elevations of 100 m (350 ft), frequently in cliffs, the large areas of exposed bedrock and the frequent glacial boulders make for a rugged and forbidding appearance.

This is not a walk for the average family. Unlike the carefully maintained trails in provincial and national parks, Salmon River is simply a beaten path. Nowadays, flagging tape is used to mark the route, but no one monitors its use or performs repairs. Brooks have no bridges and bogs no boardwalks, and I found it easy to wander off the track. But if you want to imagine what it might have been like to wander in the wilderness along an authentic ancient trail, this is the hike you should undertake. It is also a marvellous place to camp, with many excellent spots along the river.

Trail Description: You may choose to cross the iron bridge, which someone has planked to ease foot traffic, and follow the old road along the south bank of Otter Lake for about 1 km (.5 mi). The road veers left up the hill (to I know not where), but a marked path drops to hug the Salmon River for another 500 m/yd. This ends where a bridge once crossed the river, but the easy crossing is long gone. When conditions permit, you can ford the stream to rejoin the main trail on the other side. Once across, turn left to continue the main hike, right to complete the loop of Otter Lake and a 3 km (2 mi) hike. In times of high water, you have no choice but to turn back.

The main footpath and look-off trail head away from the iron bridge. Turn and walk back along the road 25 m/yd. The trail follows the south shore of Otter Lake through the woods, emerging in a clearing next to the hospital camp. Follow the vegetation boundary left past the camp's lake deck. The path re-enters the woods just past it and descends to a makeshift bridge over a brook. Crossing here puts you on the main trail, but I recommend including the look-off loop, so turn right instead. This path follows the brook and crosses a few hundred metres later near Barren Lake. Immediately after, it begins a steep climb to the look-off. Yellow and orange flagging tape provides guidance as you ascend to an exposed granite outcropping with a magnificent view of the river valley, the fire-ravaged slopes on the far side of the ravine, and even the Atlantic Ocean. Note the jack pine around you, an uncommon feature in Nova Scotia. Watch also for bald eagles patrolling the valley; they are becoming more frequent every year and now even overwinter.

Descending on the other side of the ridge, through a second stand of jack pine, complete the 2 km (1.25 mi) loop by joining the main trail not far from the camp. Turn right, and follow the stony path as it skirts the lake and traces the river upstream. For the next 4-5 km (2.5-3 mi) you will enjoy the trek alongside this gorgeous stream, passing through frequent stands of mature pine, spruce, and hemlock forest. You will sight several semi-permanent campsites, too often with their usual litter of beer cans and broken glass, and find other spots that invite you to establish your own. Tiny Crowbar Lake, Woody Lake, and Porcupine Lake are all lovely, and there is a particularly nice old-growth hemlock stand between Crowbar and Woody. The trail eventually disappears in a messy bog near Salmon River Long Lake. Advanced navigators and woodsy types may wish to continue upstream, but there is no longer any path, and the nearest road is one by Halifax Airport more than 10 km (6.25 mi) further away. I recommend that all hikers end their trip at this point and retrace their steps to their car.

Cautionary Notes: Hunting is common in these woods.

This is an entirely unsupervised area. There are no signs and no services, and the trails are not maintained. Tell someone where you will be and when you'll be back.

Future Plans: 9278 ha (23,000 a) in the Waverly– Salmon River – Long Lake area have been designated a candidate protected area.

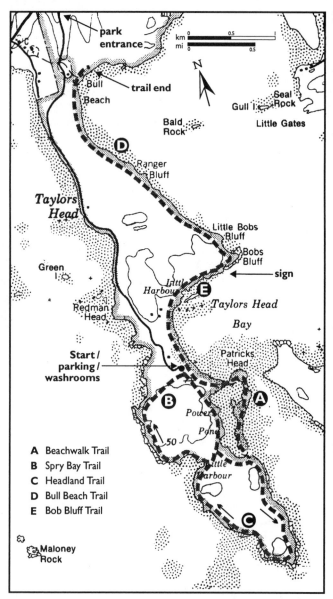

Taylor Head Provincial Park

Taylor Head Provincial Park

Length: 18 km
  (11.25 mi) return
Time: 6-7 hrs
Type: walking paths,
  beaches, former road
Rating: 3

Uses: hiking
Facilities: outhouses,
  picnic tables, change
  houses, interpretive kiosk
Gov't Topo Map: Tangier
  11 D/15

Access: The park is in Spry Bay on Highway 7, 100 km (62.5 mi) from Halifax and 11 km (7 mi) from Sheet Harbour. A very large road sign marks the entrance; turn onto a dirt road and drive 5 km (3 mi) to the parking lot. Most hikers should continue to the final (4th) parking area; wheelchair access to the beach is available from the first lot.

Introduction: This is a wonderful spot to hike for several reasons. With more than 18 km (11.25 mi) of walking possible, avid trekkers should be able to enjoy a challenging excursion. Because of the layout of the trails, which radiate from a central starting point, several shorter distances are possible for the less ambitious. Finally, the place is simply gorgeous.

Situated on the rugged eastern shore, Taylor Head is a narrow granite finger jutting more than 6.5 km (4 mi) into the Atlantic Ocean. With more than 16 km (10 mi) of coastline, of which more than 1 km (.5 mi) is magnificent white-sand beach, the granite headland has been scoured by glaciers that deposited erratics throughout the peninsula.

Taylor Head was granted to Loyalists fleeing the American Revolution. The poor soil thinly covering the granite was insufficient to support the families who arrived, so, like most settlers in this area, the pioneers here depended upon a mix of fishing, farming, and lumbering to survive. This lifestyle lasted until the 1950s, and members of some of the original families rest in a cemetery near the trailhead.

Trail Description: There are really three hikes possible in the park, all starting from the 4th parking area and all heading in different directions. In order to complete everything, a hiker must return to the starting area after finishing each walk. Since this is adjacent to the beach and the picnic area, there's ample reason on a sunny summer day to shuck the pack and relax.

The shortest trail is the Beachwalk. A 2 km (1.25 mi) return trip, this begins on the sand on Psyche Cove and follows the coastline as it heads onto a barrier beach system separating a sheltered pond from Mushaboom Harbour. At the end of the beach, either retrace your steps or return on the Spry Bay Trail. This easy walk is ideal for bird watching and several species of duck are commonly seen in the pond.

Next are the Spry Bay and Headland trails. In the form of a stacked loop, these can be hiked either as a 3.5 km (2.25 mi) or 7 km (4.5 mi) circle. My favourite, this path takes you to the very tip of Taylor Head with its rocky coastline and windswept barrens. I recommend following the eastern boundary, crossing the remnants of the abandoned fields cleared by the settlers and hugging the inside of the pond.

After 1 km (.5 mi) a junction permits cutting across the narrow peninsula to the western coast and following the shorter loop back to the start area. Frequent look-offs facing Spry Bay may be found, and although the trail is rough walking at times, stairs and bridges enable most people to complete this trail comfortably. Turning left adds 3.5 km (2.25 mi) to the walk but is well worth the extra effort. Once past the pond, the

Bob Bluff, Taylor Head. MICHAEL HAYNES

trail hugs the rocky shore, protected by the stunted coastal forest. On the headland, even the krumholz gives way to the barrens. Only stunted spruce and larch, juniper and lichens resist the high winds and fog. The trail almost disappears here and on the rocky, cobble beaches on the western shore. Rugged and rough, this is a wonderfully scenic hike.

The final trails, Bob Bluff and Bull Beach, will give you the longest walk in the park, almost 9.5 km (6 mi). Turn left on the beach and follow it to its northern end, where a sign and map indicate the start of the path. Narrow and windy, rising and falling as it hugs the uneven coast, this is a hiker's dream. Frequent viewing spots on high bluffs afford vistas of Taylor Head Bay.

Flowers on the beach, Taylor Head Park. MICHAEL HAYNES

Watch out for seals at Bob Bluff; I always notice at least one.

The 3 km (2 mi) path to Bull Beach, opened in 1994 to extend the previously existing trail beyond Bob Bluff, follows the eastern shore as it gently curves to the slender neck at the base of Taylor Head. There is a spectacular view of the islands across Mushaboom Harbour and an inland-facing look-off surveys an excellent example of a raised bog with peaty soil. Reaching tiny (but beautiful) Bull Beach and the end of the trail, retrace your route to return to the start area. You are less than 200 m/yd from the road, and when the park is closed this may make an alternative return route.

Cautionary Notes: Taylor Head, extending far into the Atlantic, is exposed to high winds and extreme conditions much of the year. Users of the Headland Trail should expect lower temperatures and should avoid the ocean's edge in stormy and high water conditions.

Future Plans: Originally intended to include a campground, Taylor Head now appears to be simply a day-park. Current government finances preclude immediate development of the large area between Mushaboom Harbour and Highway 7, but planning staff are prepared should the fiscal climate ever change.

Further Information: A brochure about the park, printed by the Department of Natural Resources, is available from the Parks and Recreation Division.

Eastern Shore

North River Falls. MICHAEL HAYNES

CAPE BRETON ISLAND

Cape Breton is the perfect venue for hiking: beautiful and interesting scenery can be found virtually everywhere on the island and the massive hills, deep ravines, and magnificent coastline positively encourage exploration. Three of the four counties publish brochures or booklets listing more than 40 trails, and several superior provincial parks trail systems are available. Private trail networks exist or are being developed, and Louisbourg National Historic Site includes several former roads in its backcountry and is currently adding specifically constructed recreational paths. New trails seem to become available almost every week.

Hiking Trails of Nova Scotia includes trails from all four counties in Cape Breton — coastal hikes, particularly along the wonderful till plain of the eastern seaboard; the waterfalls at North River and Usige Ban; Cape Smokey, as well as the exciting Mabou Highlands; and Meat Cove — all are unique. Whycocomagh Provincial Park offers a marvellous climb over a short distance that most people can complete.

There is great potential for many more trails in Cape Breton. Snowmobile clubs already have a massive network on the highland plateau in Inverness and Victoria Counties. A particularly scenic 100 km (62 mi) section of abandoned railway from Port Hastings to Inverness is under consideration for development. Private landowners, such as Maxie MacNeil at Highland Hill, are discovering that recreational use is not incompatible with silviculture. The recreation department of Victoria County inaugurated an annual hiking festival in the summer of 1994, and a trail construction workshop held at the Gaelic College in St. Anns in October 1994 attracted more than 100 participants when only 35 had been anticipated. As an outdoor recreation destination, Cape Breton may be farther ahead than some other areas of the province in capitalizing on it natural bounty and taking advantage of the current ecotourism trend.

In 1994, the Department of Natural Resources designated the areas around the Gull Cove and Meat Cove trails and North River Provincial Park as candidate protected areas. Over the next several years, the department hopes to develop a management policy for the various recreational and economic uses of these lands. The proposed system plan for parks and protected areas can be obtained at no charge from the Department of Natural Resources.

Hunting is permitted on the lands crossed by the Cape Breton, Gull Cove, Highland Hill, Mabou Highlands, and Pringle Mountain trails. The season usually starts around the beginning of October and varies from year to year and according to the game hunted. Contact the Department of Natural Resources for detailed information before going into the woods. Wear hunter orange for safety, even on Sundays, when hunting is prohibited.

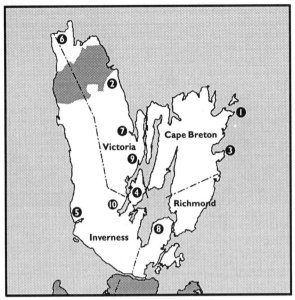

CAPE BRETON ISLAND

1.	Cape Breton	*178*
2.	Cape Smokey Provincial Park	*182*
3.	Gulll Cove	*188*
4.	Highland Hill	*192*
5.	Mabou Highlands	*196*
6.	Meat Cove	*200*
7.	North River Provincial Park	*206*
8.	Pringle Mountain	*210*
9.	Usige Ban Falls	*214*
10.	Whycocomagh Provincial Park	*218*

Cape Breton Island

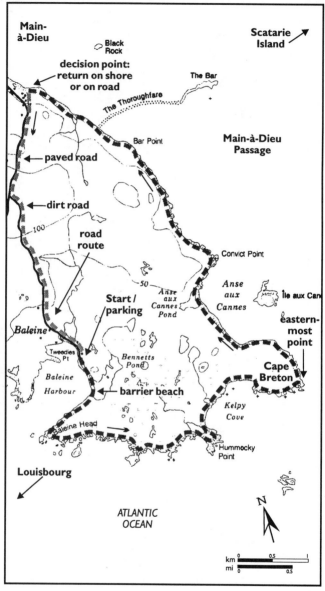

Cape Breton

Cape Breton

Length: 15 km
  (9.5 mi) return
Time: 5 hrs
Type: walking paths,
  sand beaches, cobble
  beaches, dirt road,
  highway
Rating: 4

Uses: hiking
Facilities: none
Gov't Topo Map:
  Louisbourg 11 G/13

Access: From Sydney, drive on Highway 22 toward Louisbourg approximately 25 km (15.5 mi). At Catalone, turn left on an unnumbered road toward Main-à-Dieu. After 5 km (3.25 mi), you reach the ocean at Bateston; turn right. At Main-à-Dieu, turn right at the intersection at the water's edge and drive south toward Louisbourg for 4.5 km (2.75 mi). The dirt road to Baleine is on the left near the summit of the hill. Follow it until it ends, 3 km (2 mi) later, on small hill overlooking a barrier beach.

Introduction: The easternmost tip of Cape Breton, this exposed headland gives its name to the entire island. Almost flat, the highly eroded bedrock surface is thickly covered in glacial till, sand, and gravel. Bogs and swamps dominate the poorly drained landscape, and balsam fir, larch, and black spruce cling to the thin sustenance found in the poor soil. Around Baleine, rare arctic-alpine plants such as rose-root and fir club moss survive in the harsh, cool conditions.

Spanish fishermen were coming to Baleine in the 16th century, but it was the English who first built a fort here in 1629. It was destroyed that same year, and there was no permanent habitation until French settlers arrived in 1714. These in turn were supplanted by English colonists after the destruction of Louisbourg in 1758. Main-à-Dieu, French for "hand of god," actually derived its name from the Mi'kmaq word "mendoo," or "spirit of evil." This village, too, became English after French military power was destroyed in 1763.

Trail Description: The hike starts on a small rise above a rocky barrier beach separating Bennetts Pond from Baleine Harbour. The few houses in the tiny village seem fragile protection when the surf is pounding and the wind blustering, which is often. Walking along the cobbled beach, watch for ducks sheltering in the fresh water on your left. In winter, the lack of snow makes this area an excellent wintering spot for deer. Reaching the other end of the beach, you'll see a distinct track continuing along the shore. Actually, this entire hike requires few navigation skills; just follow the water's edge. From Baleine Head, on a clear day you might be able to sight Fortress Louisbourg to the south. In 1725, the ship *Le Chameau*, arriving from France, went down on this rugged, rocky point with a loss of 310 lives and the pay for the garrison of New France. The wreck and most of the treasure were rediscovered in 1965.

Most people like to hike on sunny days, but I think that for Atlantic coastline walks raw, blustery days are best. Only then does the overwhelming and intoxicating power of the sea become apparent, the grey waves pounding the rocks with a deafening roar. On a sunny, calm day, the ocean is deceptive, beautiful and benign. For the next 5 km (3 mi) your hike continues along this bleak headland. Every twist and turn reveals tiny inlets, sometimes cobble beaches and other times cliff walls, each spectacular and exciting. At Hummocky Point, a large bracken pond is protected behind its rocky projection. Stay close to the ocean's edge; trying to bypass the pond inland leads you into muddy, thick underbrush.

From Hummocky Point you first sight Cape Breton, a barren headland on the other side of Kelpy Cove. Crossing the cobble and sand covering Kelpy Beach, you reach the easternmost tip of Nova Scotia (excepting a few islands).

As the trail turns west into Anse aux Cannes, low hills supply protection from the wind and the trees start growing taller. Instead of barrens and brush, the woods come right to the beach's edge. Only Ile aux Cannes sits bereft of trees, the guano from seabirds having killed them. Waves are far less ferocious along this stretch, and it is warmer. Reaching Convict Point, you gain a better view of Scatarie Island. Home to 12 fishing families as late as 1942, today it is a provincial wildlife sanctuary. Arctic hare and rock ptarmigan have been introduced, the only location for these species in the Maritimes, and they do quite well. Seabirds such as northern gannet are commonly sighted.

From Convict Point, perhaps 4 km (2.5 mi) of wooded walking remain. Main-à-Dieu Passage, often busy with little boats, lies between you and Scatarie. A clear path runs along the forest's edge, and the coastline is now all high jagged cliff until you round Bar Point. Here you will also find some old foundation sites and abandoned fields. The houses of Main-à-Dieu are quite clear now, and the trail actually ends by an abandoned house on a road at the water's edge. From here, either turn around and go back along the coast, making a 20 km (12.5 mi) hike, or follow the road uphill to the pavement, and then on to the Baleine Road and your car, 4.5 km (2.75 mi) away.

Cautionary Notes: Expect variable weather conditions, usually wind, fog, or rain, particularly on the Baleine side. This is an entirely unsupervised area with no signs and no services, and the trails are not maintained. Be-

Cape Breton Island

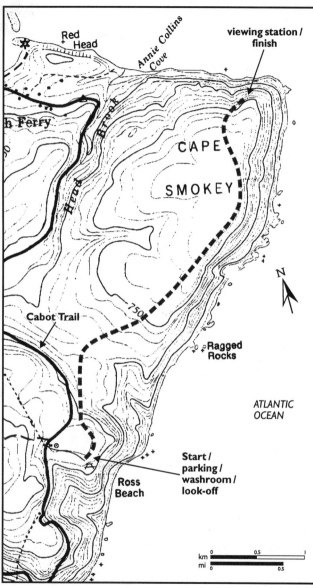

Cape Smokey

fore beginning your hike make certain that you tell someone where you're going and when you plan to return. Be prepared for emergencies.

Hunting is permitted on these lands.

Further Information: Large boardwalks have been built in Main-à-Dieu Bay, and a trail north of that village has been developed. The Cape Breton Trail is listed in a booklet produced by the County of Cape Breton.

Cape Smokey Provincial Park

Length: 11 km
(7 mi) return
Time: 3-4 hrs
Type: walking paths
Rating: 3

Uses: hiking, cross-country skiing
Facilities: outhouses, picnic tables, garbage cans
Gov't Topo Map: Ingonish 11 K/9

Access: On the Cabot Trail and at the top of the most famous hill in Nova Scotia, this hike can be found easily by anybody. It is 13 km (8 mi) from Ingonish Beach and the entrance to the Cape Breton Highlands National Park. A large sign at the highest point of the road directs you into the picnic park toward the shoreline. The trail starts at the north side of the parking lot.

Introduction: If there is one spot along the Cabot Trail that everybody seems to remember, it is Cape Smokey. Perhaps it is the unbelievably steep climb to the summit, or maybe it is the awesome panorama of the Atlantic Ocean spreading out beyond and below as you ascend, or possibly it is the spectacular view of the lowlands of Wreck Cove, Birch Plaini Birch Plain, and Skir

Dhu stretching south until they disappear in the mists. Whatever the reason, this place has a magical effect on people's imaginations.

The park is opposite the road's highest point, on the edge of the shoreline cliff. The communities of industrial Cape Breton — Glace Bay, New Waterford, Sydney Mines — are visible on clear days despite being more than 50 km (31 mi) distant, and the massive smoke stacks of the coal-fired electric generator at Point Aconi are unmistakeable. At night the lights to the south pattern a vast arc seemingly appearing out of the water.

Picnic tables and outhouses are located beside the parking lot, and many people hike no further than the nearest empty seat. After all, the magnificent view is the big attraction. But if you want an interesting walk and the chance for a completely different vista, make for the trailhead.

Trail Description: The first 500 m/yd of the path are wide, open, and gravelled. Most of the area covered by the park was devastated by huge fires in 1968, and the poor soil and exposed location have made regrowth slow and patchy. At the beginning, only a few scrawny birch and cherry trees break the wind. As the trail curves left back toward the highway, the shelter created by the hill permits more healthy growth.

Virtually the only wet areas of the hike are found in the first kilometre, and none of these areas are particularly bad. The granite rocks here date from the Late Ordovician Period of 450 million years ago, and although traces of sandstone overlay may be found on the north-side incline, most has long since eroded away. Like most granite districts, especially those with frequent high winds, only a thin soil gathers in hollows and protected spots, resulting in limited vegetation and poor drainage.

Turning away from the road, the trail descends rapidly into a fairly open barren. An area of richer soil at the lowest elevation supports white spruce and balsam fir, and a bench may be found beside the small bridge over a brook.

Climbing out of the sheltered ground, you see the first look-off on your right at the cliff edge above open terrain. There are several similar stations along the ridge top, all with comparable views and with benches in case you need a rest. Climbing 105 m (350 ft) over the next 1.5 km (1 mi), the trail continues through areas devastated by fire. Because of the lack of tall trees, many of the red rectangular markers designating the path are mounted at the top of stakes positioned beside the trail. Yellow markers, for the return route, are affixed on the other side.

Your route takes you over the top of Cape Smokey, higher than the parking area. Expect to find fresh moose scat (if not a fresh moose) everywhere, and notice how their browsing has damaged many of the trees. Look for evidence of bobcat and coyote through this area, as well as their dinner, snowshoe hare. The vegetation along the top is far more rugged than on the protected slopes.

The final kilometre of the trail descends about 90 m (300 ft) to a look-off on South Bay Ingonish. You have rounded the headland of Cape Smokey, as the sound of the buoy off Stanley Point indicates. These woods are much more lush than any you have been through on this hike; the trees, including a 200-year-old yellow birch, are some of the few survivors of the fire. You can imagine what the original forest of birch, spruce, and fir must have looked like.

Instead of facing east, your view is directed north and west toward new sights. Keltic Lodge, one of Nova Scotia's most famous resorts, gleams white against the greens of Middle Head, the thin peninsula dominating the huge bay. Ingonish Beach, more than 2 km (1.25 mi) long, draws a golden line to your left dividing land and sea. Beyond the lowlands you should be able to see the fire tower on top of Franey Mountain, another essential hiking destination. Do not attempt to proceed beyond the barrier because it guards the edge of a 180 m (600 ft) cliff. Instead, rest on the bench, take a few photographs, and prepare for the hike back. This is a linear trail, so you must return the way you hiked in.

Cautionary Notes: Some of the viewing points are at the top of a 275 m (900 ft) cliff. Do not go beyond the barriers. Do not venture along the ridge line at the south end of the park, despite the appearance of paths. This is not part of the trail system, and the footing is very uncertain.

There is no water available on the hike; take your own.

Weather conditions on the exposed cape are more extreme than normal. Pay attention to cloud and fog conditions, expect high winds, and be prepared for rapid changes.

Further Information: A brochure, *Provincial Hiking Trails of Victoria County*, can be obtained by contacting the Department of Natural Resources.

Gull Cove

Length: 12 km
    (7.5 mi) return
Time: 3-4 hrs
Type: former road,
    walking paths,
    rock beaches
Rating: 2

Uses: hiking, mountain
    biking, cross-country
    skiing, snowmobiling,
    horseback riding, ATV
Facilities: none
Gov't Topo Map: Mira
    River 11 F/16

Access: From Sydney, follow Highway 327 to Gabarus, about 35 km (22 mi). Drive through the village until the pavement ends by the breakwater, and turn right on the dirt road, following it until it ends in a parking lot beside a cemetery. The trail starts on the far side of the parking lot, a former road no longer maintained.

Introduction: This is a lovely coastal walk. On a clear day the coastline of Louisbourg National Historic Site can be seen across the bay. There are numerous spectacular camping opportunities along the route, and your chance of seeing wildlife is high. The barrier beach system beyond Gull Cove is one of the most extensive in the province, permitting the experienced to extend this hike into an excursion of several days.

    The last residents left Gull Cove in the early part of this century, leaving behind numerous foundations, stone walls, old fields, and the road connecting it to Gabarus. You can find the names of the families who lived there in the graveyard by the church at the start of the hike.

Trail Description: Your route, starting on the far side of the parking lot, is the former cart track connecting Gabarus and Gull Cove. Now used by ATVs, it offers quite easy walking despite numerous wet areas. Even the quickest glance at the map shows extensive

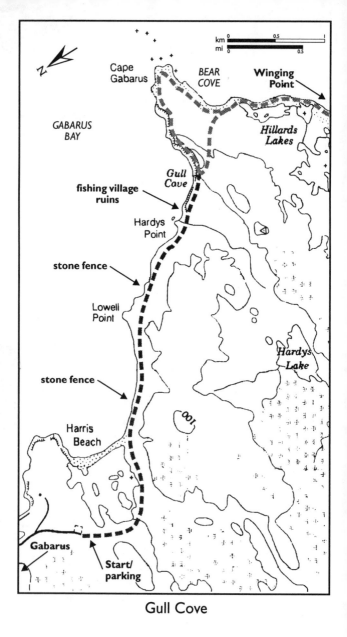

Gull Cove

swampy ground. Comprised entirely of granite till chewed by glacier action, this region is relatively flat, has practically no soil cover, and is poorly drained.

You will find the first 2.5 km (1.5 mi) very wet throughout the year. The trail skirts Harris Lake through an extensive bog. Fortunately, the ATV people have built a bridge over the brook from Rush Lake, although you may wish they had also ditched the road. But your difficulties will be forgotten when you reach the coast. You emerge at the far end of Harris Beach, a typical barrier beach of rock and till separating ocean and freshwater. The lake, though small, is deep enough for swimming and can be quite warm, and loons nest there. It is a gorgeous spot, and I have camped on the grassy headland near where the trail comes out of the woods.

For the next 2.5 km (1.5 mi) the trail follows the coastline closely. Between Harris Beach and Lowell Point you find a stone fence on your right near an old field, and there is another just past Lowell Point as well. In such harsh weather conditions, the forest takes a long time to reclaim these clearings. You may notice that almost all the trees are white spruce. Although black spruce and larch are common in wet depressions, and balsam fir dominate inland, only white spruce can survive the constant exposure of facing the Altantic Ocean. After 5 km (3 mi) of walking, you arrive at Hardys Point and Gull Cove. The woods give way to a substantial expanse of cleared land climbing up Bull Hill, and on the far side of the cove is a chain of sea cliffs, the only ones along this entire coast.

This is where the amateur archaeologist can poke around and set up camp. Numerous stone walls and house foundations may be found in the tall grasses. The area is also fairly sheltered from the wind and a good spot for a picnic. Because of the low snowfall, this is valuable winter habitat for deer. Expect to see at least one somewhere around here. During migratory season, numerous birds use Fourchu Bay as a staging area, and this coastline is an important breeding territory for seabirds. On Green Island, visible from Cape Gabarus, is the only nesting colony of black-legged kittiwakes known in the Maritimes.

For most people, this is the best place to turn back. However, the shore is available for an extension of the hike for the next 25 km (15.5 mi) (50 km [31 mi] return). The ATV trails cut across Cape Gabarus and emerge at Bear Cove. From there, a continuous cobble and till beach system stretches all the way to Belfry Gut on Fourchu Bay. This is a spectacular area of barrachois ponds enclosed by barrier beaches, and Winging Point, 10 km (6.25 mi) beyond Gull Cove, is extraordinary.

Past Gull Cove conditions become harsher and more variable. In stormy weather, some of the barrier beaches are swept by waves and provide no protection. The further you travel along this route, the more isolated from assistance you become. Only very experienced backpackers should attempt this trip, and only after notifying authorities of their intentions. Once finished your picnic at Gull Cove, retrace your route back to the parking lot in Gabarus.

Cautionary Notes: There is no signage anywhere along this hike, although the trail is quite distinct. Nor are any services, such as water, available. Remember that exposed coastline is usually cooler and windier than the interior. Following the coastline will extend the hike to more than 40 km, but you must return the way you hiked in.

Hunting is permitted on these lands.

Future Plans: 4413 ha (10,900 a) in the Gabarus area have been designated as a candidate protected area.

Further Information: This trail is listed in a booklet produced by the County of Cape Breton.

Highland Hill

Length: 7.5 km
(4.75 mi) return
Time: 2-3 hrs
Type: dirt roads, former roads
Rating: 1

Uses: hiking, mountain biking, cross-country skiing
Facilities: interpretive panel, garbage cans
Gov't Topo Map: Grand Narrows 11 F/15

Access: From the Trans-Canada Highway, take Exit 6 near Whycocomagh toward Little Narrows. A 25¢ ferry ride takes you across St. Patricks Channel, where you turn right and follow Highway 223 toward Iona and Grand Narrows. Drive approximately 15 km (9.5 mi) until you reach McKinnons Harbour. A road sign advises that a hiking and skiing trail is within 3 km (2 mi) and directs you left up the unpaved Barra Glen Road. At the Highland Hill Road, another signs directs you left again, notifying you that the trail is only 1 km (.5 mi) away. Continue uphill past Maxie MacNeil's house and sawmill. Keep right at the next junction; just past it on your left is a large gravelled parking lot and interpretive panel.

From Sydney, take Exit 3 on Highway 125 at Leitches Creek Station toward Grand Narrows. Follow Highway 223 and the train tracks down the length of St. Andrews Channel and cross over the new bridge to Iona. A further 5 km (3 mi) takes you to Jamesville West and the sign warning you of the upcoming right turn onto the Barra Glen Road.

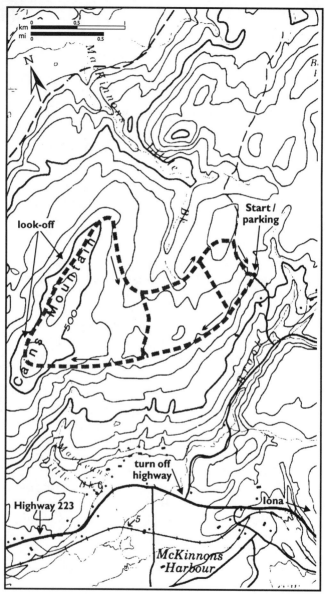

Highland Hill

Introduction: Most trails in Nova Scotia have been developed on reserved land by government. What makes the Highland Hill Trail special is that it is primarily on private land and in the middle of working woods. This trail begins and ends on a 106 ha (262 a) property belonging to Maxie MacNeil, who was named Woodlot Owner of the Year in 1994 for integrating educational and recreational opportunities with his forestry operation.

An interpretive sign in the parking lot explains the nature of the work going on in these woods today and the history of settlement and logging activity in this area. Nine kilometres (5.5 mi) of trails work through 570 ha (1,400 a) of upland forest that sustain forestry practises involving shelterwood, weeding, planting, and thinning. Keep in mind that these lands were clear-cut in the 1920s and devastated by spruce budworm in the 1970s; there are no untouched woods remaining, and you are going to observe modern integrated resource management silviculture.

Established and maintained by the Clan Nordic Ski Club, the trails are wide enough for skating-technique cross-country skiing and are intermittently groomed in winter. These trails are used for both mountain bike and ski races and are open for a wide range of recreational and educational activities.

Trail Description: Start on the left road, route #1, Peadair Custie's Trail. This is a wide, open wood road, as are most of these trails. You will notice a number of small yellow signs posted along the trail. These tell you what forestry practise is being used on that particular patch of woods, the species involved, and the date of the work. After 300 m/yd you come to your first junction, with route #5 on your right. This system is organized as a stacked loop, with a small initial circular path having a second loop added on to it, and a third loop added on to the second trail. Your hike can be 2.5 km (1.5 mi), 4 km (2.5 mi), or 7.5 km (4.75 mi) depending upon your fitness level or interest. The total network includes 9 km (5.5 mi) of trails.

If you want to do the full loop, continue straight. Shortly afterward, on your left you will come across the clearing that has been put aside for Rankin Memorial School's commemorative tree plantation. Each year since 1994 the graduating class has planted a block of different species of trees. A little more than 1 km (.5 mi) from the start is the turnoff right for route #3. Just past there is a section where the new trees are coming up through the remains of the old, providing an arresting contrast. Former homestead sites can be identified by the presence of old apple trees.

When you cross a small brook after about 2 km (1.25 mi), you'll know that you are beginning your ascent to the top of Cains Mountain. You are now on route #2, and you can see all four counties of Cape Breton from the scenic lookouts. These are not signed, but I think you can guess where they are. The woods in which you are walking are now mostly sugar maple and yellow birch, except for a large area of Norway spruce.

You may notice other, older wood roads, but your trail is marked with yellow rectangular symbols nailed onto trees. You may also notice a fair amount of wildlife. I scared up numbers of grouse, as well as a very annoyed red-tailed hawk, and deer tracks were fresh and everywhere, particularly near MacKinnons Little Brook. Two solid bridges cross the brook, and just after the second, on the steepest hill you will face, the turn to route #4 is almost hidden. You have travelled more than 5 km (3 mi), and about 2 km (1.25 mi) remain no matter what path you select.

Route #4 is only 500 m/yd long and is named Bottom's Up. This could be because it immediately descends to a small creek, then climbs the other side to the next junction. Route #6, Rabbit Run, on your left, takes you to Maxie's Road through the only wet section. Tiny log bridges cross frequent seasonal streams. Just before you reach the road, a planted area of white pine and fir provides warning. Turn right to return to the parking lot, less than a kilometre away.

Cautionary Notes: Hunting is permitted on these lands with permission.

There is neither water nor an outhouse.

Further Information: The growers' association has produced an attractive free full-colour brochure of the hiking trail.

An excellent reference to accompany this walk is *Trees of Nova Scotia: A Guide to Native and Exotic Species*, by Gary L. Saunders. It can be ordered from the Government Bookstore in Halifax.

Cape Breton Island

Mabou Highlands

Length: 14 km
(8.75 mi) return
Time: 6-7 hrs
Type: old cart tracks, walking paths, dirt roads
Rating: 5

Uses: hiking
Facilities: none
Gov't Topo Map:
Lake Ainslie 11 K/3

Access: From the Canso causeway drive north on Highway 19 to Mabou. In town, turn left on the unnumbered paved road toward Mabou Harbour. Drive 5 km (3 mi), turning right on the dirt road to MacDonalds Glen. Continue 7 km (4.5 mi) to the bridge at Mill Brook just

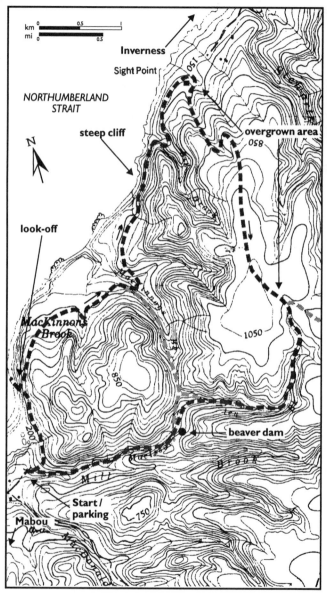

Mabou Highlands

past the last house and clearing. Park here without blocking the road.

Introduction: The rugged hills of the beautiful Mabou Highlands, once the home of many industrious Scottish immigrants, now lie mostly deserted, save only for a few cottages. The old roads connecting their farms have become a network of rough but exciting trails, courtesy of a volunteer association, the Cape Mabou Trail Club. I have not described the entire network; many options are available, but I have combined three of their trails into a loop that should occupy a full day.

When I last hiked this area, in July 1994, several of the trails, in particular the stretch from Sight Point to the TV towers, were almost completely obscured by new growth. Advanced navigation skills were required to follow some segments with confidence. Since then, I have been told, volunteers from the Cape Mabou Trails Association have performed substantial maintenance work. However, because I have not seen these improvements, I have based this description on my own recent experiences. Should the trails be cleared and well-signed, then the difficulty factor of the hike I have mentioned can be reduced to 4.

Trail Description: The trail starts on the hillside directly ahead of you, and a sign directs you up the open slope heading left toward the ocean. On the way up the hill, the path turns in to a shallow ravine, crosses a tiny brook, and swings onto an open rocky area. A look-off on a small side-trail to the left provides a wonderful vista looking south: Finlay Point, Mabou Mines, and MacDonalds Glen lie beneath this very steep hillside. Please be careful: there is no railing. Continuing north, the main trail follows the route of an old road through dense white spruce that is reclaiming former farmlands.

Note the many piles of stones and old fences. Unmarked side trails will guide the adventurous to stone foundations, but there are no signs, so please be cautious. At the base of the hill, the trail intersects a dirt road; turn right and follow the road past a house to a metal gate.

The road is your trail for nearly a kilometre until you reach MacKinnons Brook. A sign directs you into the woods, and after a brief descent you cross the brook. This is a lovely spot to camp. The trail turns sharply left and follows the curve of the hill toward the ocean. As you near the water, the spruce woods give way to spacious meadows. In July, these fields are alive with fireflies. Turning right again to follow the coast, the trail climbs continuously and the hillside becomes steeper. On your right, almost undetectable when I was last there, is the entrance to the Beinn Bhiorach Trail, which climbs 1 km (.5 mi) to the top of this peak. The main trail climbs to nearly 150 m (500 ft) above the water and narrows to less than 1 m/yd wide, hugging the cliff above a straight drop to the ocean. If you are not afraid of heights, this is one of the best views in Nova Scotia. There are even ropes for assistance at some of the most difficult spots.

After crossing Big Brook, where the Oak Ridge Trail connects on your right, the path becomes easier for the last kilometre to Sight Point. There the path joins a dirt road once again; turn right and walk inland until the road bends almost 180° crossing a creek. The South Highlands Trail leaves the road and follows the creek left and upward on the toughest walk you will face. After first following a narrow, steep ravine, then crossing the top of the plateau, this trail climbs to 320 m (1,050 ft) in 3 km (2 mi). The route is clear hiking at first, though it is poorly signed at the entrance. After moving away from the creek the path eventually disappears,

Beaver Dam, MacIsaacs Glen Brook, Cape Mabou.
MICHAEL HAYNES

crossed so thickly with deadfall that you'll sometimes want to hike in the forest. Even if this route has been cleared, expect a tough trek but a beautiful walk.

Less than 500 m/yd after South Highlands starts downhill, the junction with Bear Trap Trail appears. Turn right and follow this path as it parallels MacIsaacs Glen Brook's increasingly steep fall. A wonderful 3 km (2 mi) stroll down the middle of a curving, steep-sided ravine follows, ending at a dirt road in a clearing. Note several large beaver dams making impressive pools. To return to your car, turn left and continue downhill on the road a further 2 km (1.25 mi).

Cautionary Notes: The path on the sheer cliff at Sight Point is very narrow and lacks a railing; further on, a rope assists scrambling over a particularly rough spot.

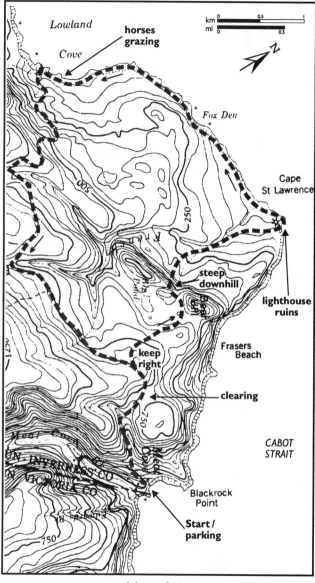

Meat Cove

Small children and pets should not be taken through here, nor anyone afraid of heights.

Hunting is permitted on these lands.

Future Plans: Continuing improvement of the existing network is planned over the next several years, including better signage, benches, and possibly tent sites. New trails, utilizing other abandoned roads, will also be cleared for hikers.

Further Information: A brochure called *Trails of Inverness County*, mapping recognized hiking, cross-country skiing, mountain biking, and equestrian routes is available from the Inverness County Tourism Department. The snowmobile clubs of Inverness and Victoria counties have produced a waterproof map of their extensive groomed and signed trail system throughout this half of Cape Breton Island.

Meat Cove

Length: 16 km
(10 mi) return
Time: 6 hrs
Type: former roads,
animal trails
Rating: 4

Uses: hiking, mountain
biking, ATV, cross-country
skiing, snowmobiling
Facilities: camping, tables,
water, outhouses
Gov't Topo Map: Cape St.
Lawrence 11 N/2

Access: From Cape North on the Cabot Trail, turn onto the unnumbered road toward Bay St. Lawrence. After driving about 14 km (8.75 mi) north, look for the turn-off to Capstick and Meat Cove on your left. For the first 6 km (3.75 mi) this road is paved, but the last 7 km (4.5

mi) is aq narrow dirt road. Follow until it ends in McLellan's Campground. Parking is available, with a $2 charge.

Introduction: This is the trail at the end of the earth, or so you may think as you drive toward it. The sheer cliffs hugged by the narrow dirt track seem invulnerable to human habitation, and Meat Cove, when you finally see it, appears hopelessly fragile, dwarfed by the rugged hills surrounding it. Meat Cove is an amazingly fertile area for orchids, some found nowhere else in the province; no one seems to know why, exactly. Flower-lovers flock here regularly to find unique plants.

There are several hiking options available, and I am describing only two: the Lighthouse and the Lowland Cove trails. These can be put together as either a challenging one-day loop or a more relaxed two-day campout. Considering the splendour of Lowland Cove, I recommend taking the time and spending the extra day. I know few more beautiful places to camp anywhere.

Trail Description: Start uphill along a continuation of the dirt road behind the McLellan picnic site. Expect a long climb as the road switches back and forth up the hillside. A gate 500 m/yd along restricts vehicular traffic but not hikers, and the unmarked and overgrown Old Fraser Road joins on the left. There are no signs anywhere along this section, but do not panic. The trail to Cape St. Lawrence is clearly indicated and does not diverge until you crest this elevation and start downhill.

After nearly a kilometre, an apparent junction at an old field might fool you into turning right, but this path disappears on the far side of the clearing. The real trail turns sharply left, continuing to climb. Shortly afterward, it levels then starts downhill. A distinct intersection with an old road forking to the right is the turning point to the lighthouse. Flagging tape and yellow rectangular metal markers signal this branch.

For the first time since you started, the trees provide cover overhead. While there is still room for two to walk side by side, the woods crowd this path more closely. Watch for the yellow markers as you pass numerous side-paths on your gradual descent down Bear Hill. After a kilometre, the trail bears left and plunges downward. This section is exceptionally steep and rocky, and bicyclists are advised to check their brakes before this point. The trees suddenly end, revealing the grassy fields of Cape St. Lawrence. The tip of the point is littered with the ruins of former lighthouses, and only a small automated signal remains. To the right, on a clear day, you can see St. Paul Island, the northernmost place in Nova Scotia.

The trail continues left along the open shoreline. There are no trees for markers here, but the area has long been used as a free range for cattle, and their path along the coast becomes yours. The small deep gully cut by French Brook is a popular camping site, providing shelter from the restless winds, but you continue past it and the Fox Den, a rocky cliff-lined gorge. Watch for minke whales and pilot whales, common off this coast.

As you round Tittle Point, breathtaking Lowland Cove gradually reveals itself. The forested hills of Lowland Point enclose the grassy fields of the cove in a sheltered bowl that is ideal for camping. Look for horses grazing on the tough grasses clinging to the gentle slopes. The best location for an overnight is at the far end of the field close by a small hollow near Lowland Brook. This is also the end of the trail. It will be difficult to leave this beauty and return to your car. You can return the way you walked in, thus ensuring the maximum amount of coastal hiking. Or you can follow a different route over the hillside behind the open ground of the cove, which is marked by red rectangular metal signs. Either choice involves steep climbs, although the trail behind Lowland Cove does break them up.

After a tough climb up this trail from behind the cove, you return to the intersection with the Lighthouse Trail, completing the loop. Perhaps only 2 km (1.25 mi) remain, and only 300 m/yd of this is uphill. Trekking down the hill into Meat Cove, you'll be dazzled by more spectacular views of cliffs and ocean, and so ends a hike you will not soon forget.

Cautionary Notes: Although some signage has been installed, there are several areas where mistakes can be made. Anyone planning to hike these trails should obtain the topographical map for the area. This is an isolated territory, and accurate navigation is essential.

There are no services after the start of the hike. Pack adequate water (and other essentials) in with you.

Future Plans: The Meat Cove–Pollett Cove–Pleasant Bay trail is slated for improvement. At present it is extremely difficult to follow in the bogs between Meat Cove and Pollett Cove and can only completed by advanced navigators and backpackers.

27,566 ha (68,360 a) north of Cape Breton Highlands National Park, including most of the land over which you hiked, has been designated a candidate protected area by the Department of Natural Resources.

Further Information: A brochure showing the hiking trails in the Cape North area is available from Tourism Nova Scotia.

North River Provincial Park

Length: 18 km (11.25 mi) return

Time: 7-10 hrs

Type: former road, walking paths, steep slopes

Rating: 4

Uses: hiking, cross-country skiing

Facilities: outhouses, water, garbage cans, picnic tables, benches

Gov't Topo Map: St. Anns Harbour 11 K/7

Access: The road leading to the park turns off the Cabot Trail in the village of North River Bridge, 16 km (10 mi) from Highway 105 and 35 km (22 mi) from Baddeck. There are signs on both sides of the road. The park is 5 km (3 mi) up the dirt road, which ends at the trailhead. A large sign with a map is located at the entrance to the woods.

Introduction: In the mid-1880s, this valley was home to several families of Highland Scots, who attempted to farm and raise livestock on the unrewarding soil. McLean, McKenzie, McLeod, and McAskill are still familiar names in Cape Breton, but the homesteads of the North River Valley have long been abandoned. Remnants of their presence may still be found along the trail, and the park is located on the former site of a school house and tannery.

Everyone has favourite trails, and this is one of mine. This is an extremely demanding hike, long and with numerous scrambles up narrow paths clinging to steep slopes, but your reward, should you continue to the end, is an unparalleled view of the highest waterfall in Nova Scotia, 32 m (104 ft). I think it's worth the effort.

Trail Description: From the parking lot, the trail starts just past the large sign containing a map of the path sys-

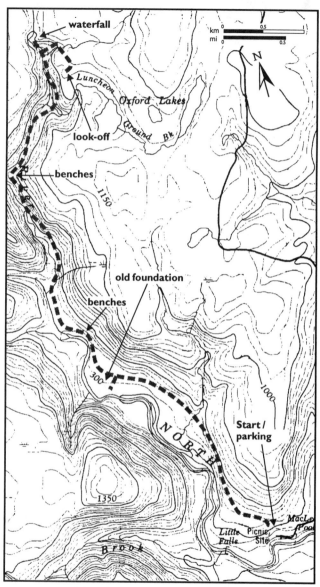

waterfall

Luncheon

Oxford Lakes

Ground Bk.

look-off

benches

1150

old foundation

benches

300

NORTH

Start / parking

1000

1350

MacLe... ...Pool

Little Falls

Picnic Site

Brook

km
mi

N

North River Provincial Park

tem. For the first 100 m/yd you hike uphill to connect to the former road. Beware of the numerous side-trails cut by fishermen on their way to salmon pools; the route you want is marked by rectangular red metal strips affixed to trees. For casual hikers, the first 5 km (3 mi) will make an enjoyable excursion. The trail follows the course of the old road along the steep slopes of the gorge, ascending and descending between the intervales that sheltered the early settlers. Except for a few wet patches, however, it is comfortable walking for two side by side, with numerous sturdy bridges crossing the roughest ravines. North River can be heard rather than seen for much of this section, and the hills towering overhead are particularly spectacular in late October when the leaves change colour.

After crossing a quite large bridge, the trail gradually descends toward river level. A junction at a small clearing provides the opportunity for a diversion. Turn left and stroll for perhaps 200 m/yd to arrive at a salmon pool underneath one of the highest hills in the area. This is a wonderful spot to rest and enjoy the surroundings, and it's the place where casual walkers may wish to turn around and return.

Turn right, however, for the main trail. Notice house foundations and stone walls below their white spruce covering. The path starts to narrow as you move beyond the sites of the original homesteads and into more rugged terrain. A few hundred metres further on a bench provides a resting spot where the river loops back. A sign there features a map, and you can see that the remaining few kilometres will be far more challenging. After this bench, roots and rocks frequently invade the trail, which begins to zigzag along the slope of the hill as the stream crowds to the edge of the steep slopes on either side. Handrails become more common now both as safety features and as an assist in climbing. The

bridges over the little feeder streams take on a decid-
edly homemade appearance.

The North River shrinks as you pass the various
tributaries spilling from their own canyons on the far
side. The trail follows the East Branch the remaining 3
km (2 mi) to the waterfall. Opposite the confluence
with John MacLeods Brook, in a small level area about
1.5 km (1 mi) from the end of the hike, two benches invite the weary traveller, and just past here you cross the
river and walk on the other side for a short stretch.
There are well-constructed bridges at both ends, but for
a section in between the trail consists of the rocks of the
river bank. In summer that is adequate, but during
spring runoff this is a very dangerous spot. Guardrails
become fewer and slopes steeper, and you may be for-
given if you think that the route was designed by a
mountain goat.

The last kilometre seems to be continuous steep
climbs and drops, but any fatigue you feel will disappear when you sight the magnificent waterfall. The
main trail leads to a small pool nearly underneath the
cascade, and a 1 km (.5 mi) extremely challenging side
trip climbs to a dramatic look-off above the falls. Near
the summit you encounter an unsigned junction with a
connecting trail cut by snowmobilers. Turn right; the
look-off is perhaps 75 m/yd away. You must return
along the same route you hiked in. This trail should be
planned as a full day's activity to be really appreciated.

Cautionary Notes: Rugged and rocky, this trail will require adequate hiking books. There is no water supply
after the start, and you should not attempt this walk
without some food.

Weather is highly variable, and showers can occur
anytime; flurries in May or October are not uncommon.
Runoff from the late melting snow of the Highlands

makes this walk potentially dangerous in March and April. In the summer, expect high humidity in the ravine.

Future Plans: The Department of Natural Resources hopes to eventually construct a loop trail system including several no-service wilderness camping sites within the confines of North River Park. 4334 ha (10,750 a) around and including the park form a candidate protected area.

Further Information: See *Provincial Hiking Trails of Victoria County*, obtained from the Department of Natural Resources.

Pringle Mountain

Length: 12 km
(7.5 mi) return
Time: 4 hrs
Type: former road, ATV trails
Rating: 3

Uses: hiking, mountain biking, cross-country skiing, horseback riding, snowmobiling, ATV
Facilities: none
Gov't Topo Map: St. Peters 11 F/10

Access: From the Canso Causeway, drive 53 km (33 mi) along Highway 104 and #4 to St. Peter's. From Sydney, drive 88 km (55 mi) along Highway 4 to St. Peters. Turn off Highway 4 in the village on the paved road leading toward Oban, French Cove, and The Points, and follow it for 25 km (15.5 mi). Reaching The Points West Bay, look for a small unnamed bridge crossing Pringle Brook. The entrance to the old road is 100 m/yd before the bridge, on the left between the bridge and the MacLean residence. In 1994 this entrance was hidden by vegetation, but ask around; the people here are friendly and

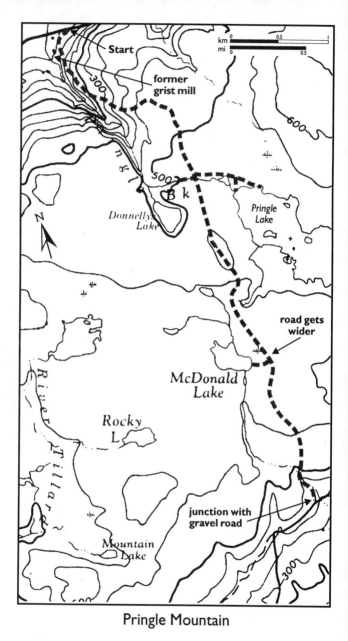

Start

former
grist mill

km
mi

300

600

500

Donnelly
Lake

B k

Pringle
Lake

N

road gets
wider

McDonald
Lake

Rocky
L

River Tillar

junction with
gravel road

Mountain
Lake

300

Pringle Mountain

helpful. Park your car by the side of the road, making sure the wheels are off the pavement.

Introduction: Of the four Cape Breton counties, Richmond County is probably the least well known to outsiders. Inverness and Victoria counties have the Cabot Trail, Highlands National Park, and the Trans-Canada Highway. Cape Breton County has industrial and urban centres and Fortress Louisbourg. Visitors tend to hurry to these more famous locations, neglecting Richmond County. I have to confess to this myself, never having hiked on any of the trails there until 1994. Yet I found the scenery in Richmond just as exciting as anywhere else on Cape Breton.

The Points West Bay was first settled in 1851 by James Pringle. (This explains why you will find Pringle Harbour, Pringle Brook, Pringle Island, Pringle Mountain, and Pringle Lake in the immediate area.) Alexander MacLeod (MacLeods Point, MacLeods Pond, and MacLeods Brook) was the next settler, granted land in 1857. The area had long been used by the Native peoples in their seasonal migrations; Indian Beach at the mouth of Pringle Brook is so named because it was the site of their encampment. The area prospered for a time, combining agriculture, forestry, and livestock, and in 1904 it possessed a carding mill, a sawmill, and a grist mill. But, for Richmond County as well as for the rest of rural Nova Scotia, the 20th century has been a time of significant out-migration and population decline. Fewer live here now than in 1904, although the names Pringle and MacLeod are still common.

Trail Description: Starting from the highway, the path leads uphill immediately. Offering clear walking under a softwood canopy, the trail, still a provincial road into the 1940s, runs near the ruins of the grist mill on the bank of Pringle Brook within 200 m/yd of the pavement. The two-storey mill was made of stone, and some of the milling wheels remain inside. (Please do not disturb anything. This is private property.) You find the mill by turning right at a junction shortly after the start of the hike. Reaching a deserted house, walk behind it and locate a path to the mill. Retrace your steps to rejoin the main trail.

Continuing uphill, the path quickly gets rocky and rugged, climbing more than 150 m (500 ft) in the first 2 km (1.25 mi). Several areas in the first kilometre resemble a creek bed, with deep washouts down the centre. Houses you see across the ravine belong to local historian Will Pringle and other descendants of the original settler. Turning away from the brook, the path begins to grow in, young beech and birch crowding the centre. As the trail levels out, it also gets wetter, with large puddles filling it from side to side. The forest shows signs of logging and succession, with young spruce and pine growing in the shade provided by the older hardwoods.

Reaching Pringle Brook, 2.5 km (1.5 mi) from the start, you have two options. Turn left and follow the new ATV trail for 500 m/yd for a view of Pringle Lake, or cross over the bridge, turn right, and find a delightful spot for a picnic on a grassy knoll overlooking the brook. Although you will notice several fire pits, remember that this is private property. Do not camp here without asking permission, and do not light a fire. For some, this might be the point to turn back. I suggest continuing another 3 km (2 mi) to McDonald Lake. The trail is much easier walking, suitable for two side by side (when it's dry) and with little elevation change. McDonald Lake is on your right in an area of open bog and clear-cut, an ATV trail running to its shore and another peaceful rest site. The path continues downhill another 2 km (1.25 mi) to a dirt road still in use, but it has been widened for logging use and is not especially enjoyable. Instead, return to The Points West Bay along the same route you hiked in.

Cautionary Notes: This trail is in a somewhat remote location and you should let someone know when you are going in and when to expect you back. In 1994 there were no signs or markers; carry a map and compass. There are no services; carry water and emergency supplies.

Hunting is permitted on these lands.

Future Plans: The Recreation Department of Richmond County is embarking on a trail signage and maintenance program starting in the summer of 1995. Pringle Mountain is near the first on their list for this work.

Further Information: A brochure outlining 11 hikes and more than 90 km (55 mi) of walking opportunities in Richmond County is available from the Department of Tourism, at local tourist bureaus or by contacting the recreation department.

Cape Breton Island

Usige Ban Falls

Length: 7 km
  (4.5 mi) return
Time: 2-3 hrs
Type: walking paths
Rating: 1

Uses: hiking, cross-country skiing
Facilities: outhouses, tables, covered tables, garbage cans
Gov't Topo Map: Baddeck 11 K/2

Access: From Highway 105, take Exit 9. Signs indicating the park direct you north toward Forks Baddeck, where

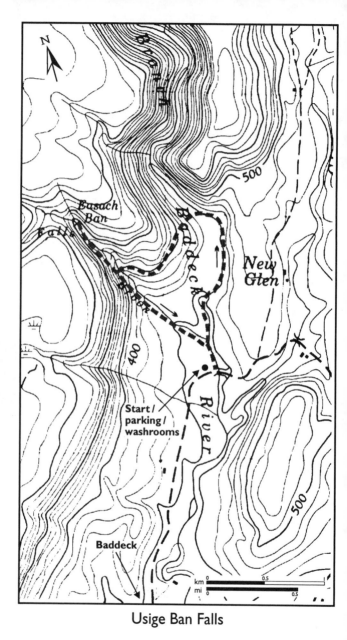

Usige Ban Falls

the falls are 15 km (9.25 mi) from Baddeck. Turn right on a dirt road just after crossing Baddeck River. Follow the dirt road 3 km (2 mi) to the park, which is on your left.

Introduction: At the end of the Mesozoic Era, 65 million years ago, all the land in the Maritimes was near sea-level. The area now called the Cape Breton Highlands was suddenly (in geological terms) uplifted 500 m/yd, separated from neighbouring landforms by precipitous cliffs. Over the millennia, these cliffs have become deeply eroded, cut by narrow steep-sided ravines that provide drainage for the soil-poor heights. Waterfalls are common at the edge of the scarp slopes, and drainage valleys are often covered with talus (rocky debris) produced by freeze-thaw action. High rainfall, 1400-1600 mm (56-64 in) annually, and frequent low-level clouds or fog ensure relatively high humidity. Snowfall in most of the highlands area is 400 cm (160 in) annually, and the spring thaw occurs later than in other parts of the province.

Usige (pronounced "ush-ka") Ban is Gaelic for "white water," and if you make the walk to the base of this 15 m (50 ft) waterfall, especially after a heavy rain, you will understand why it received this name. At the southern edge of the Cape Breton Highlands, Falls Brook is one of the many small streams permitting runoff from the plateau to escape. March and April are the months of the greatest flow, and the amount will shock anyone who has seen the brook only in August.

This trail is similar in many respects to the much longer and more challenging North River hike. However, because of its proximity to a road, this walk can be successfully negotiated by people of most fitness levels. Although smaller than the North River Falls, Usige Ban is no less beautiful and makes a worthwhile addition to any itinerary. Trail construction was a cooperative venture between Stora Industries, which leases these Crown lands, and the Department of Natural Resources.

Trail Description: A large sign is located at the head of the trail with a map showing all the distances of each segment of the walk. The path starts out well gravelled and wide enough for two people to walk side by side. All roots and rocks have been covered by a thick tread of crushed stone. For the first 250 m/yd there is only one path, high on the bluffs above the North Branch Baddeck River on your right. Reaching Falls Brook you are given a choice of directions, and I recommend turning right and following the River Trail.

The path descends a small hill, and a new sign directs you across a bridge. Climbing a small spur on the other side, the trail follows the river for almost a kilometre, often at water level but at times ascending as much as 10 m (33 ft) above the river. Generally, this is fairly easy walking, except for one steep switchback at the head of a bend in the river. Fortunately, a guardrail is provided for assistance.

The woods throughout this section are extraordinary, mixed at first, but mostly hardwoods once the trail turns inland. Many maples and birches are more than 100 years old, which is not all that common in Nova Scotia. The canopy they spread ensures a sheltered walk even on the hottest day. With the frequent cascades in the river and the numerous benches, this pleasant stroll is ideal for families. Turning almost 180° as it moves inland, the trail follows the ridge-line back toward Falls Brook. With good views in all directions thanks to low undergrowth, this 700 m/yd stretch is the hike's easiest walking.

The River Trail connects to the Falls Trail perhaps 500 m/yd beneath the cataract, crossing the creek over a newly constructed and sturdy bridge. This final distance demands a bit more effort, with more than 100 m/yd of climbing required, and most of that in the final

Indian Island, view from Salt Mountain. MICHAEL HAYNES

300 m/yd. As you approach the falls, its noise becomes deafening. Crossing again to the north bank, round one more hill and you are suddenly at the base of the waterfall. A small bench is available should you need a rest or simply wish to enjoy the impressive view. Resist any temptation to climb above the trail limits as there is no safe route from this point.

To return to the parking lot, retrace the route as far as the junction with the River Trail, but remain on the south side of Falls Brook. This path will follow the watercourse through lovely hardwoods until it reaches North Branch Baddeck River, where both trails combine to climb the bluffs for the final 250 m/yd of the hike. Once again, expect to find frequent benches along a level, easy path.

Cautionary Notes: After heavy rains, water flow in the brook can increase dramatically and suddenly. Be careful approaching the foot of the falls and do not yield to the temptation to scale the slippery surrounding rocks. There is no path there for good reason.

Further Information: See *Provincial Hiking Trails of Victoria County*.

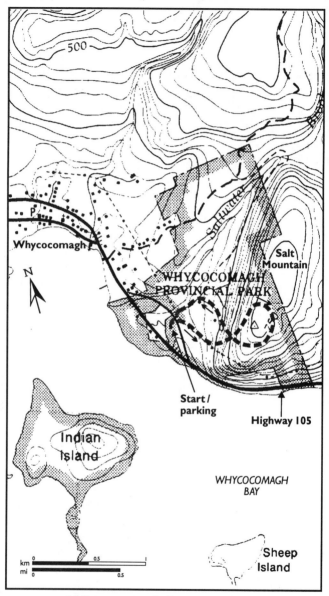

Whycocomagh Provincial Park

Whycocomagh Provincial Park

Length: 2.5 km
(1.5 mi) return
Time: 1-1.5 hours
Type: walking paths
Rating: 2

Uses: hiking
Facilities: outhouses, water,
picnic tables, benches,
camping, firewood
Gov't Topo Map:
Whycocomagh 11 F/14

Access: From the Canso Causeway, drive 50 km (31 mi) toward Sydney on Highway 105. Continue through Whycocomagh; the park entrance is on the far side. Turn left off the highway; the trailhead is just before the campground entrance opposite the Department of Natural Resources district office.

Introduction: Although it is the shortest hike in *Hiking Trails of Nova Scotia*, this is a walk that no one should overlook because of the extraordinary view of Whycocomagh Bay and St. Patricks Channel from Salt Mountain. Do not be deceived by its short length, however, for the summit is 230 m (750 ft) above Bras d'Or Lake, requiring a steep climb indeed. Another attractive feature of the trail is the abundance of bald eagles in the Skye River Valley and Whycocomagh Bay. Good nesting locations and plentiful fish in the lake mean that visitors often will sight an eagle soaring on the updraughts near the mountain or perching on a tree near the lakeshore.

Meaning "Head of the Waters," Whycocomagh is the Mi'kmaq word for the area surrounding Salt Mountain, and a large community of Native people lives across the bay from the park. Settled in 1812 by Highland Scots, the new community retained its original name despite the colonists' nostalgic fondness for reminders of their past, as Cape Breton place-names such

Cape Breton Island

as Glencoe, Skir Dhu, and Loch Lomond attest. The 204 ha (507 a) park contains 75 campsites, a picnic area, and a boat launch. The property was donated to the Province of Nova Scotia in 1959 by Isabelle Stewart Farley, of Boston, in memory of her brother, Hugh McLellan, of Sydney, killed in World War I.

The entire family may be able to complete this short but challenging walk. It's an ideal outing for those camping at the park, and its proximity to the main road makes it a pleasant diversion for those passing by who want to stretch their legs and enjoy a marvellous view. Expect to earn it, however.

Trail Description: The trail starts broad and grassy with a wide entrance. Wooden arrows point the way along a well-defined path that begins to climb immediately, getting a little rough over rocky ground. Notice the old stone wall on your right, evidence of former farming in the crofter style. The trail climbs fairly steeply, and soon Whycocomagh Bay becomes visible on your right through the leaves. The slope is so precipitous that you are soon higher than the tops of most trees on the hillside.

Switching back to the left, the route levels for a short distance. Note the stone work underfoot; this is a beautifully maintained trail. At a junction, a sign stating "exit" points down the hill, while arrows continue to point up. A bench is provided for the undecided or the plain weary. Those who have found the climb exhausting to this point should consider returning down the hill after a brief rest. More strenuous activity is required on the remaining hike to the summit.

A second intersection soon afterward is also clearly marked, arrows directing left. A series of short switchbacks takes you through another rough section, but the trail soon starts to become less steep. Near the top, numerous side paths branch out, but the main trail remains quite distinct. The reward for your hard climb is a grassy clearing covering a rocky outcrop facing west overlooking Whycocomagh and the campground, a tremendous sight. Continuing on, climb a little more and loop around to the south side of Salt Mountain, where a fence keeps hikers from falling over the high cliff. Here your view is of Orangedale and Marble Mountain. After you have spent enough time enjoying the panorama, follow the trail as it returns downhill. Just past this second look-off is a bronze plaque set in granite commemorating the donation of the park. After that, a final look-off is situated on your left just before the path starts steeply downhill.

Quickly you return to the intersections you passed on the way up. Amazing how easy the trip downhill is, don't you think? Following the exit sign leads you down a short, steep slope into the campground behind sites #82 and #83. You will notice that there are signs telling campers where to find the trailhead, but the entrance here is somewhat camouflaged by thick foliage. The camping area is a gorgeous site on the gentle slope of Salt Mountain with a view of the surrounding hills. To return to the car, follow the road downhill through the park to the administration building at the entrance. The parking area for the trail is to your left about 100 m/yd.

Cautionary Notes: Although short, the hike is quite steep with extended climbs. Take it easy on the way up, especially if you are a novice. People with mobility problems will find this hike extremely difficult, if not impossible.

Further Information: A brochure about the park is printed by the Department of Natural Resources and is available from the Parks and Recreation Division.

View of the Cabot Trail climbing French Mountain, seen from the Skyline Trail. MICHAEL HAYNES

CAPE BRETON HIGHLANDS NATIONAL PARK

The Cape Breton Highlands were an obvious choice for the first national park in Nova Scotia. Cut by innumerable little bays and inlets, the land rises steeply out of the ocean to create a plateau more than 450 m (1500 ft) high. It also features the only taiga region in the Maritimes. The coastline itself consists of spectacular sandy beaches, rocky capes, and rugged headlands jutting into the Atlantic. In 1936, 1186 km² (741 mi²) of land in the northern parts of Inverness and Victoria counties were incorporated into the Cape Breton Highlands National Park. Subsequent reductions have brought the present size to 950.5 km² (594 mi²), the losses being mostly in the interior.

Offering both summer and winter recreation possibilities, the park boasts three large and three small campgrounds and two wilderness camping areas. Almost 200 km (125 mi) of hiking is available on 27 different signed and maintained trails, and mountain biking is permitted on the Clyburn Valley, Lake of Islands, and Trous de Saumon paths. In winter, the extremely high snowfall permits cross-country skiing almost everywhere. In addition to these more rugged activities, the park also maintains an 18-hole golf course near Keltic Lodge at Ingonish Beach.

Main park entrances are at Ingonish on the east coast and Cheticamp on the west, and information centres with nature bookstores can be found at either side.

Park entry fees are charged to drive through on the Cabot Trail; in 1995 the full season rate is $30 per party. This may change in future years as the national park system experiments with different fee structures. Camping charges in 1995 are $13-$17 per day in campgrounds and $11 per day for wilderness camping. Contact the Cape Breton Highlands National Park, Ingonish Beach NS B0C 1L0, or telephone (902) 285-2691, (902) 224-3403 or 1-800-565-9464 for a complete list of up-to-date fee schedules.

This park contains some of the most stunning scenery in the province, and it justly is a primary destination for many tourists. The hikes in *Hiking Trails of Nova Scotia* include a portion of every landscape—coastline, mountain, valley, headland, and plateau—but many more options are available. This is also one of the least populated areas of Nova Scotia, far from large towns. Your chances of meeting wildlife such as moose are greater in this park than anywhere else. Be prepared for the wild and the rugged.

Parks Canada produces several brochures about the flora and fauna of the highlands, a park map with hikers' information in the back, and a special topographical map showing the hiking trails. These, plus books on the natural history of the region, can be obtained at Les Amis du Plein Air bookstores in the information centres at Cheticamp and Ingonish.

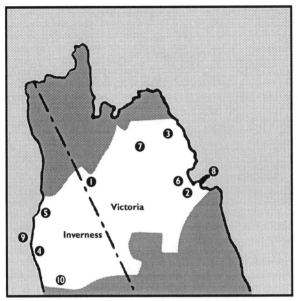

CAPE BRETON HIGHLANDS NATIONAL PARK

1.	Aspy	*226*
2.	Clyburn Valley	*230*
3.	Coastal Trail	*234*
4.	Corney Brook	*240*
5.	Fishing Cove	*244*
6.	Franey Mountain	*248*
7.	Glasgow Lakes	*252*
8.	Middle Head	*256*
9.	Skyline	*260*
10.	Trous de Saumon	*264*

Cape Breton Highlands

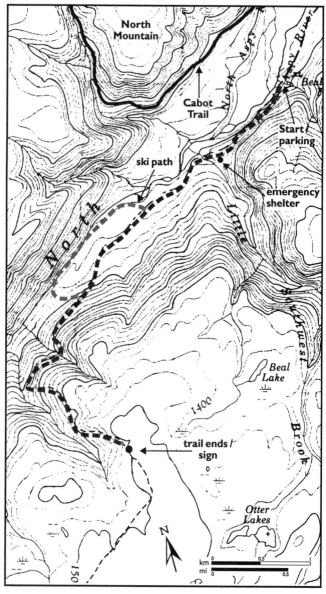

Aspy

Aspy

Length: 9.5 km
  (6 mi) return
Time: 3 hrs
Type: former road,
  walking path
Rating: 3

Uses: hiking
Facilities: outhouses,
  picnic table, garbage
  cans at trail head
Gov't Topo Map: Pleasant
  Bay 11 K/15

Access: Drive about 12 km (7.5 mi) west of the village of Cape North along the Cabot Trail. This takes you to Big Intervale, a Parks Canada campground on the Aspy River at the base of North Mountain. On the hill just above the campground, a sign directs you onto the gravel road to Beulach Ban Falls. Continue for 2 km (1.25 mi) until this road ends at the falls parking lot. The Aspy Trail starts across the creek.

Introduction: The Aspy fault has produced the most striking escarpment in the Maritimes. Stretching from Cape North to deep into the highlands, this 45 km (28 mi) ridge divides the older granites of the uplands from the softer sedimentary rocks of the valley like a fence separating neighbouring backyards.

Beulach Ban Falls illustrates another geological oddity. Glaciers scoured away the softer rocks in the valley, leaving the canyons previously carved by erosion through the harder rock of the South Mountain suspended high above the new valley floor. Falls like Beulack Ban resulted, thin trickles of water falling over exposed rock.

This is a good starting location for a hike. The waterfalls are gentle and relaxing, the area is sheltered, and picnic tables are available for meals. This trail can easily be partitioned into three different levels of difficulty. Walking as far as the shelter and back rates a 1. Continuing to the point where the cross-country ski trail joins the hiking trail the second time makes for a 2. Following the path up the steep slopes to its end earns a rating of 3.

Trail Description: Head over the bridge and up the hill on the other side. A small sign on your right, almost hidden by brush, announces that you have begun the Aspy Trail. A gate prevents vehicular access, and a second sign confirms your route. The first kilometre gently ambles along the wide, hard-packed former road through lovely hardwoods, including a large number of oak trees. The Aspy River, slightly below to your right, is visible occasionally through the vegetation. At Little Southwest Brook a sturdy vehicle bridge connects with the far bank, and an outhouse and emergency shelter, not marked on the park's map, sit on the near side.

Past the brook, the trail climbs slightly before levelling off again. Brush growing in the thoroughfare gets thicker and the sides close in, but the trail is still recognizable as a road. The Aspy moves towards the far side of the valley, and a beautiful hardwood plateau opens on your right. The blue-flagged trail heading into it is a ski route; the hiking path continues straight. Just beyond this junction notice the perpendicular slash left by the spring runoff. Completely dry in the summer, these rocky courses teem during late April and May as the snow melts on the highland plateau.

The next 2 km (1.25 mi) are gorgeous. The high hardwood canopy keeps you cool and shaded, and the lack of underbrush enables an unobstructed view of several hundred meters. Expect small hawks or even owls on dark days hunting beneath the leafy roof. Warblers, vireos and thrushes abound in this environment, and the springtime air resonates with their melodies.

From here the hike changes dramatically as the path starts its ascent toward the summit. The remaining 2 km (1.25 mi) will seem like 20 as you climb nonstop up the steep slope of South Mountain. The trail narrows to a slender footpath, particularly as it veers into a deep ravine gouged out by a tiny brook. Hills on the other side, mostly hidden by vegetation to this point, loom prominently across the valley. No bench relieves your "grunt" to the top. Spruce and fir surround you now, tougher species more resistant to the harsher weather of the highlands than the oaks below.

Round one more hillside, this one apparently deforested by fire, and the trail turns back inland toward another gorge. You are almost level with the escarpment across the valley. The hillside is so steep here that the tops of the trees are lower than the trail. The birds have changed too: chickadees, juncos, and kinglets flit through the softwoods.

Suddenly, the trail ends. A sign (missing in September 1994) simply states that you have reached the end of the hike. You are facing inland, away from the valley, 450 m (1500 ft) high, at the edge of the highlands. Although the path once continued further inland, it is no longer maintained and degrades rapidly past the sign. An exposed rock supplies adequate seating from which you may enjoy the scenery. It is a fantastic panorama, with the Aspy fault extending far into the distance. Look below, and you may see hawks riding the winds in their endless pursuit of prey. When you have recovered, and I expect even the fittest will work up a healthy sweat during this climb, return along the same path. Considering that it is all downhill, it should take somewhat less time than the approach.

Cautionary Notes: As you climb up from the river valley, particularly in the spring and fall, chances are good that the weather will be more extreme. Near the top, the trail hugs a very steep slope; people with children should be particularly attentive.

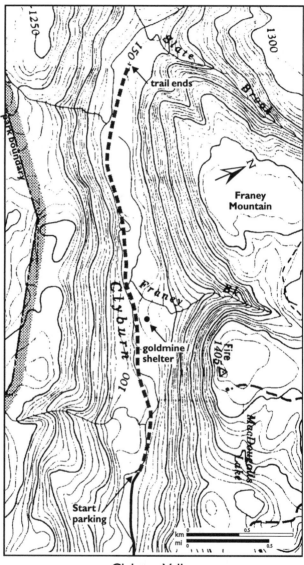

Clyburn Valley

This trail follows an old fire trail that led into the interior. Although a sign indicates the end of the public portion, when I was there in September 1994 this was missing. Once the vegetation begins to interfere with walking, that is your sign that you have come to the end of your walk.

Clyburn Valley

Length: 9 km
(5.5 mi) return
Time: 2-3 hrs
Type: former road
Rating: 2

Uses: hiking, mountain biking, cross-country skiing
Facilities: outhouse, shelter (with stove and wood), garbage cans
Gov't Topo Map: Ingonish 11 K/9

Access: Drive 1.5 km (1 mi) north along the Cabot Trail from the park's Ingonish campground. Just after you cross Clyburn Brook, signs direct you left off the paved road. Follow a dirt road 3 km (2 mi) to its end at a small parking area. A metal gate prevents further driving.

Introduction: Gold was discovered in this valley around the turn of the century, and the remains of the old mine is the hike's principal attraction. In 1911 exploratory work was undertaken to determine the richness of the claim, but the site was abandoned after less than two years' digging. In addition to the entrance to the mine, the concrete ruins of the buildings which housed the workers endure, but the forest is gradually reclaiming the abandoned grounds.

Although the park's recommended hiking trail begins 3 km (2 mi) from the paved Cabot Trail, I found this first section to be an enjoyable walk or jog, and I suggest that you consider starting from the parking lot by the highway if you have the time. But whether you drive or hike, this road is a pleasure to travel. On your left for almost the entire distance are the fairways and greens of the magnificent Highlands Links golf course. Opened in 1940, the 18-hole course stretches from Keltic Lodge on Middle Head far up the Clyburn Valley. One of the most scenic locations to golf in North America, it makes wonderful viewing as you progress up the Clyburn River.

The trail is a former road and offers easy walking without much change in elevation. Almost anyone can complete this hike with little difficulty, although expect to do some fording beyond the gold mine site.

Trail Description: A small information sign is in the parking lot, as well as a notice that this is hike #24. A garbage can is located by the gate. The road initially follows the river bank very closely. Notice how shallow and broad the creek is and how fast running. Note also the number of trees uprooted and strewn along its banks, substantial evidence this can be a ferocious torrent during heavy rainfall or runoff. You will find several places deeply etched by the current where it runs high. The bare granite cliff of Franey Mountain dominates the skyline on your right, the fire tower marking the summit. Boulders are strewn in their thousands up the hillside, at times making the trees look out of place.

The trail is mostly on the floodplain and often needs repair from washout. When the route moves inland a bit, after perhaps a kilometre, the path becomes quite stable and grass-covered. Boulders persist, at times seeming like gateposts, forcing the road to dodge between them as the trail climbs gently through an area of young maple and birch, particularly spectacular in late October.

Gold mine shelter, Clyburn Valley. MICHAEL HAYNES

Near the top of the rise is a wonderful little shelter hut. Labelled "Gold Mine" on the door, this emergency shack contains benches, a wood stove, and a guest book. Beside the hut is a brand new outhouse. Look in the woods behind the building to see concrete foundations hidden among the trees. These are the ruins of the lodgings that housed the workers.

Franey Brook cuts across 150 m/yd past the gold mine, and this turbulent little creek is spanned by a sturdy bridge, although suspicious gravel gouges on the far side suggest that the stream occasionally prefers alternative channels. Beyond this point, the trail returns to river level, continuing another 2.5 km (1.5 mi) through lovely woods to end in a clearing beside Clyburn Brook at the base of Klondike Mountain. Several times branches of the brook cut the path, but there are no more bridges, so fording is necessary. Once at trail's end, rest a moment and enjoy your view of towering

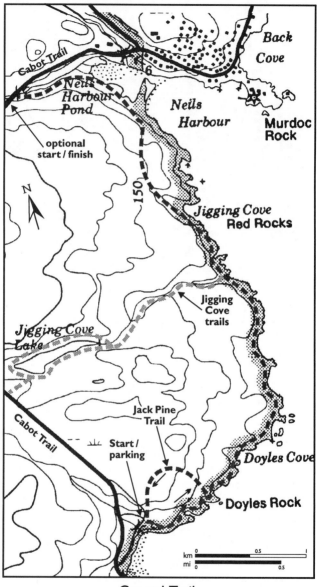

Coastal Trail

hills surrounding you, then return along the previous route to the parking lot.

Cautionary Notes: In spring, Clyburn Brook often overflows its banks and runs through lower sections of the trail. Check conditions with park staff before attempting this hike in March, April, and early May. Past the Gold Mine, expect new rivulets to cut the trail almost anywhere. These will not be bridged, and after a rainfall some will be knee-deep.

Future Plans: Because of increasing conflict with other trail users, the risk of harm to wildlife, and the fragility of some of the trails, mountain bikers are restricted to only three trails in Cape Breton Highlands National Park. Clyburn Valley is one of the three.

Coastal Trail

Length: 11 km
   (7 mi) return
Time: 4 hrs
Type: walking paths
Rating: 3

Uses: hiking
Facilities: garbage cans
Gov't Topo Map: Dingwall
   11 K/16 or CBHRP topo
   map

Access: The Coastal Trail can be picked up either at Halfway Brook, near Neils Harbour, from a parking lot next to the Cabot Trail, or at Black Brook, which I will be using as the start. Drive 20 km (12.5 mi) from the Ingonish information centre; the entrance to the beach and picnic site at Black Brook is on your right, and it is well signed. Once off the highway, turn left at an intersection 100 m/yd in; the road ends in the parking lot.

Introduction: In July 1921, an out-of-control campfire started a blaze that devastated this area, destroying more than 1500 ha (3700 a) of forest. The situation was so serious that the communities of Neils Harbour and New Haven had to be evacuated by sea, and one ship was wrecked in the attempt. A contemporary report statees that "on the blackened coast, not a blade of grass remained." But the trees and plants returned quickly, in particular the usually scarce jack pine.

Jack pine is one of only three native pines found in Nova Scotia, and the rarest. Only two large stands are found inside the park, and they are also uncommon elsewhere in Cape Breton. Able to grow on very poor soil, jack pines usually develop in pure stands. Their cones require very high temperatures to open, 44°C (116°F), so a forest fire where seed trees are present can result in the land's regenerating beneath a pure forest of jack pine. The woods along the Jack Pine Trail have been designated as a Heritage Tree Stand.

The Coastal Trail starts near the Black Brook beach and picnic area. Although only garbage cans are located at the trailhead, picnic tables and outhouses can be found by the beach. Because of the presence of the Jack Pine and Jigging Cove trails, and the option of using the highway, this trail can be walked in either 3 km (2 mi), 7 km (4.5 mi), or 11 km (7 mi) circuits. The Coastal Trail will provide some diversity to your highland itinerary.

Trail Description: The Coastal Trail enters the woods on the ocean side at the lower (Ingonish) end of the parking lot, while the Jack Pine Trail starts at the upper end. Immediately descending into a deep ravine cut by a brook, the Coastal Trail presents you with the chance to sidetrack to a look-off viewing Black Brook Beach.

The narrow main trail keeps left and winds through young softwoods, rising and falling as it accommodates the rugged rocks near the coast. At several places in this first kilometre you will notice that flat stones have been arranged to create stairs. This enables people of most fitness levels to complete this portion of Coastal and return to the parking area along the Jack Pine Trail in 3 km (2 mi).

The junction with the Jack Pine Trail occurs just beyond Squeaker Hole, a narrow cove that produces distinctive noises when waves hit it just right. Well signed, Jack Pine heads uphill and turns inland, but our route follows the ocean for now. For the next 1.5 km (1 mi) the well-defined trail continues to trace the waterline, occasionally dropping lower to cross sections of cobble beach. These segments are well marked with red-tipped stakes 2 m (6 ft) tall positioned along the route until the trail re-enters an area of vegetation. As you round a gently curving point, the first sight of Neils Harbour in the distance alerts you to the impending junction with the Jigging Cove trails.

As you cross the stones of Victoria Beach, the Jigging Cove Brook Trail joins from the woods on your left. Following it inland, then back to the starting point, results in a shorter walk of about 7 km (4.5 mi), although the final 2 km (1.25 mi) will be along the highway. Continuing along the coast, you'll find the terrain getting rougher, which forces the trail to head into the woods. The coastline becomes more vertical, and when you reach Jigging Cove the path must leave the shore and cut inland behind the roughest sections.

This is the toughest part of the hike, climbing straight up more than 30 m (100 ft) from near water level, then descending to the sandbar separating Neils Harbour Pond from the ocean. You can walk along this sandy beach if you wish. A further kilometre remains as the trail follows the pond edge and Halfway Brook, crossing underneath the highway and ending in a parking lot about 2 km (1.25 mi) from the community of Neils Harbour.

From here your choices are to return along the same path, hike along the Cabot Trail back to Black Brook, or have someone pick you up. I recommend returning along the path. Even though this involves retracing the same ground, this is a beautiful walk and one of the very few coastal excursions available in the park. When you arrive at the junction with the Jack Pine Trail, follow it inland. Interpretive signs tell a fascinating story about nature and human intervention. It is worth the extra kilometre, if you have the energy.

Cautionary Notes: There are several exposed fingers of land that jut into the ocean. Rogue waves, undetectable to most of us and most common during or just after a storm, can scour those points. Every year they catch an unwary victim somewhere in Nova Scotia. Resist the temptation to stand at the very edge of the land with your toes in the water, except on calm days.

Further Information: The park brochures and David Lawley's book *A Nature and Hiking Guide to Cape Breton's Cabot Trail* provide more information.

Corney Brook

Length: 8 km
(5 mi) return
Time: 2 hrs
Type: former road,
walking path
Rating: 2

Uses: hiking, cross-country
skiing
Facilities: outhouses, water,
campsites, firewood,
garbage cans, benches
Gov't Topo Map:
Cheticamp River 11 K/10

Access: From the information centre at the west park entrance, drive 9 km (5.5 mi) north along the Cabot Trail. The parking lot for the trail is on the left (the ocean side) near the Corney Brook campground.

Introduction: An American hiker I met described Corney Brook as "the I-95 of trails." (For those unfamiliar with US road terminology, the I-95 is the multi-lane interstate highway running the length of the east coast of the United States.) In the case of Corney Brook, the broad, well-maintained path, almost always comfortable for side-by-side walking, is an easy hike, suitable for almost anyone. The bridges crossing the tiny stream are so sturdy that people unfamiliar with the violence of the spring runoff might question their construction. And the benches along the route, providing frequent rest breaks for those challenged by the gentle (but steady) climb, make this walk seem more appropriate to a city park than to the edge of a wilderness.

This trail conducts you to one of the many small waterfalls in Cape Breton. The massive upthrusting 65 million years ago of highly erosion-resistant granite created escarpments that were ideal for cascades. But over time, the action of water and glaciers carved deep furrows into the hard rocks of these sheer cliffs. Rapids, cataracts, and waterfalls are now common but not al-

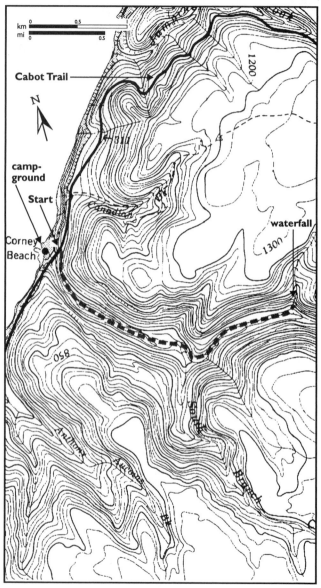

Corney Brook

ways easy to reach. The park features four, two accessible by car and one by an easy 3 km (2 mi) walk. Corney Brook, located deep in a gorge at the foot of French Mountain, lies at the end of a modest hike.

This is a good family excursion. Water and outhouses are available in the campground. The trail offers easy walking, and it is almost impossible to get lost. At 8 km (5 mi), even fit walkers can work up a sweat if they try. Corney Brook campground is also a great place to spend the night. Next to the ocean, it is often windy, but the growl of the surf makes sweet music to lull you to sleep after a tough day of hiking. Try it.

Trail Description: From the parking lot, cross the highway to the trailhead. The path follows the north bank of Corney Brook as it heads into the deep ravine. It starts with a little bit of a climb, but it soon descends toward water level as it enters the woods. This well-established trail is covered in grass for much of the early part of the route, and a substantial amount of stone work has been done to build up and level the path.

Like all trails following these deep gorges, the path climbs the hillside whenever the stream runs near and descends when the brook flows close to the far bank. But in the first 2 km (1.25 mi), these are gentle grades and not very taxing. In fact, the elevation at the end of the hike is only 75 m (250 ft) above the start. The vegetation throughout the valley is predominantly hardwood — birch, beech, and maple — and the canopy they provide shades most of the walk, a welcome feature on a hot summer day.

When the valley divides, with the South Branch creating a deep gorge that is clearly visible in the far range of hills, the trail turns almost 90° and becomes slightly more challenging. The ravine compresses rapidly, and the path similarly constricts to one lane. The massive concrete foundations of the two bridges that cross Corney Brook attest to the fierce power of the spring runoff. And above the second bridge you will find places where the trail has been almost obliterated by the brook spilling over its banks.

The climb continues to get steeper and the lane narrower as you climb toward the falls. When you spot a bench, you are 150 m/yd from the end of the hike. Round one more corner and you are there. Another bench is situated at the very end of the path above a small pool. A small path climbs the steep hillside closer to the falls, but it is not as easy to traverse, and, since it is not actually part of the trail, park authorities do not encourage its use.

Rest a moment beside the small waterfall and enjoy the tranquillity of this sheltered spot. When you are ready, return along the same path to the start. This time, watch closely for animals and birds. There is abundant wildlife in this valley, and apparently more bobcats are seen here than anywhere else in the park. For some reason I always spot four or five garter snakes (all snakes in Nova Scotia are harmless), but I have yet to see a bobcat. Perhaps you will have better luck.

Cautionary Notes: The most dangerous aspect of this hike is the fact that, to reach the trailhead from the parking area, you must cross the highway. Do not forget: in the summer this is a very busy stretch of road, so watch for traffic.

During the spring runoff and heavy rains, the brook might wash out the trail. Check at the information centre about conditions before starting your hike, especially in May and early June. The trail is not maintained before the May long weekend.

Fishing Cove

Length: 16 km
   (10 mi) return
Time: 6 hrs
Type: former road,
   walking path
Rating: 4

Uses: hiking
Facilities: outhouses,
   campsites, garbage cans,
   firewood, benches
Gov't Topo Map: Pleasant
   Bay 11 K/15

Access: From the Cheticamp park entrance, drive 22 km (13.75 mi) north along the Cabot Trail. From Pleasant Bay, drive 10 km (6.25 mi) south. A road sign indicates the turnoff to the parking lot, which is just off the highway on the ocean side. The trail begins at the far end of the lot.

Introduction: Once the site of a lobster cannery, Fishing cove was abandoned by the last residents in 1915. The Frasiers, Hinkleys, MacKinnons, and MacRaes who originally settled the deep ravine left for other parts of Cape Breton Island looking for a better life than the precarious existence afforded in their remote refuge. After you have visited there, you may find it difficult to believe people chose to live in such isolation, despite the striking beauty of the surrounding landscape.

Fishing Cove, one of two designated wilderness camping areas in the park, has eight tenting sites, and people who stay there once almost always return. Falling asleep to the sound of the surf, swimming in the sheltered cove in either salt or fresh water, and experiencing the remoteness from human activity makes this a special place for many who visit. The walk is challenging and the terrain rugged, but the rewards are incomparable. And although it is possible to complete the trail in one day, the difficulty of the terrain encourages spreading the hike over two days and taking

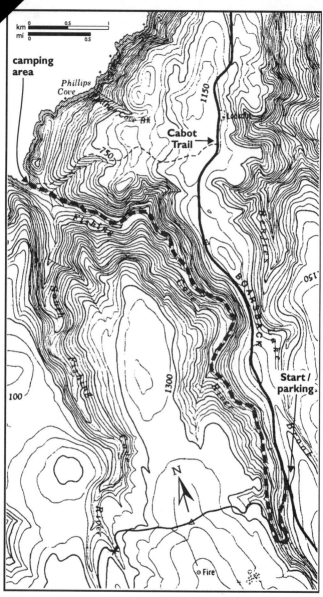

Fishing Cove

advantage of the camping in the cove area. You must get a wilderness camping permit at a park information centre. The use of camp stoves is recommended, and you must also pack out all of your litter.

From its start on the ridge-line above, the trail loses 335 m (1100 ft) in its descent to the ocean. With several climbs in the middle of the hike, more than 500 m (1600 ft) of uphill walking is required on the round trip. This is not a hike to be attempted casually. I do not recommend it for young children or novice hikers. Always carry extra water and food, and be prepared for changing weather conditions.

Trail Description: A sign at the trailhead says the walk is 7 km (4.5 mi), but park literature says 8 km (5 mi). When in doubt, I plan for the longer distance, and I will accept being pleasantly surprised if wrong. The path is initially a continuation of the former route of the main highway, now considerably overgrown. A metal gate prevents vehicles from going further. The pleasant but deceiving aspect of this walk is that the route in is predominantly downhill, and in the first few kilometres the drop is substantial. The old road descends the hillside rather briskly until it reaches Fishing Cove Creek. Spare a moment to examine the bridge, labelled "unsafe," that spans the ravine, then turn sharply to the right and enter the woods on the narrow footpath. The constricted, steep-sided ravine the path follows is wonderful. The trail hangs onto the slope above the creek like a goat track because there is no room at the bottom of the V-shaped valley for anything but stream. At times you are quite high above the cascading water with nothing to stop you from falling if you are careless. The trail is distinct and well maintained, and the woods in the ravine are magnificent. Small bridges span places where rainwater falls down the steep hillside, and numerous benches provide much needed rest areas for the return climb. Views are scarce because the valley is so narrow and winding, and tree cover in summer and fall is quite thick.

There are one or two areas where tough climbing is required on the trip down, and the trail has several switchbacks at the steepest sections. Fortunately, you will find benches near the top of the toughest climbs from either direction, offering a valuable respite. You catch your first glimpse of the ocean at the top of the worst stretch, and at the bottom of this hill you rejoin the brook. The trail broadens and becomes surfaced with spruce needles. The hills recede as you near the cove, and the final kilometre is almost level, gently rolling along the brook's bank. Advancing through a spruce thicket, you abruptly emerge onto the large grassy field at the stream's mouth.

Once there, explore the headlands or just lie on the grass and eat lunch. If you are staying overnight, select your site and set up camp; firewood is usually available, brought in by boat and thrown onto the beach. There are outhouses as well. Should you plan on hiking back out, a short rest is in order in any case. On the way out, make sure you follow the correct trail. A much steeper track joins the trail in the spruce thicket. Used by park wardens and not open to the public, it climbs 230 m (750 ft) in less than 1 km (.5 mi). You do not wish to hike this one, trust me. The official trail is difficult enough without asking for more, and the 8 km (5 miles) you must still navigate is mostly uphill throughout.

Cautionary Notes: This is a rugged trail, following a steep ravine to the ocean. You are often on a narrow track carved into a steep slope, so do not stumble. As there is no safe water source on this hike, be sure to carry an adequate supply.

A backcountry use permit is required for ove[r]
camping, and reservations are not accepted.

Mountain biking is not allowed on the Fishing Cove
path.

Franey Mountain

Length: 6.5 km
  (4 mi) return
Time: 3 hrs
Type: walking path,
  former road, dirt road
Rating: 3

Uses: hiking
Facilities: outhouse,
  garbage cans
Gov't Topo Map: Ingonish
  11 K/9

Access: From the national park's Ingonish campground, drive 1.5 km (1 mi) north. A large road sign
across from the beach at Ingonish Centre instructs you
to turn left off the main highway. Continue to follow this
road as it changes from pavement to dirt and climbs 1.1
km (.75 mi) to the trailhead. Continuing up this road
another kilometre will take you to a small parking lot in
front of a gate. Those wishing an easier ascent may follow the former road from here to the tower.

Introduction: This may well be my favourite hike in all
Nova Scotia. Certainly it takes you to the best hilltop
view in the province. But to get to this special site requires uncommon effort. Although short, this trail is
particularly challenging. Within 2.5 km (1.75 mi) you
must climb 366 m (1200 ft). Though this is not unusual
in other areas, such an elevation change is almost
unique among Nova Scotia hiking trails and is certain to
surprise both the novice and the imprudent. I have
rated this trail a 3, requiring some level of fitness to

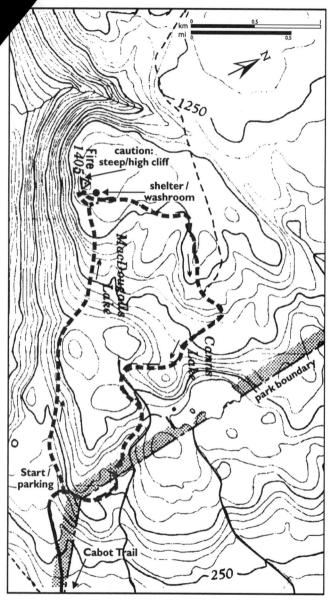

km 0 | 0.5 | 1
mi 0 | 0.5

Z

1250

Fire ▽ 1405
caution:
steep/high cliff

shelter /
washroom

MacDougalls Lake

Canns Lake

park boundary

Start /
parking

Cabot Trail

250

Franey Mountain

complete, but anyone approaching the fire tower from the direction of the former road will have a somewhat easier time. Watch for moose, and in the spring you may see bear.

Trail Description: I recommend starting the hike at the lower parking area and climbing, rather than descending, the steep section of this trail. This route is easier on your muscles and joints, as walking uphill is less wearing than going downhill. If you have knee problems, I suggest parking at the upper lot and both ascending and descending on the former road.

From the lower lot, the trail enters the woods and climbs gradually. The approach road has already shaved 120 m (400 ft) from your climb, leaving only about 300 m (1000 ft) remaining to the top. You also start on a small plateau between steep elevation changes, permitting some warm-up before the tough climbing. The trail is very well constructed and maintained, gravel surfaced at the start with logs set diagonally at intervals to divert runoff. It is also wide enough for two to walk abreast, at least at the beginning. On your right you see the ridge line that will be your first objective. It is about 120 m (400 ft) above the start, and there is another small plateau there.

Within a kilometre you come to the first steep section. The trail becomes narrower and rockier, and it starts to hug the hillside more. As you climb, your view looks across at the hills on the opposite side of the Clyburn Valley. They are higher than you are now, but by the end of the hike you will be looking over them. A small viewing spot provides an unobstructed view up the Clyburn Brook and also of the fire tower. You get a brief respite just beyond that point where the trail descends a tiny bit to follow the side of the hill into a little ravine. At the back of the gully a beautifully clear brook

CAPE BRETON HIGHLANDS NATIONAL PARK   249

bubbles down the hill. Drinking untreated water is not recommended, but I find it hard to resist this inviting fountain.

Unfortunately, just on the other side of the brook is a very steep climb, with an elaborate series of stairs constructed into the hill. At least you have a lovely little creek on your right during this ascent. You may appreciate its gurgling noises, which will mask the groans emerging from you and your travelling companions. Portions of this section are heavily eroded and very rocky, but you should find good traction for your boots and the stairways invaluable. As you start along the second set of stairs you should be able to see MacDougalls Lake to your right and below. You will also get a good view of South Bay Ingonish and Cape Smokey.

After an eternity (really not much more than a kilometre), you crest a knoll and sight the fire tower at almost the same elevation. On your right is a small open bog, another demonstration of the poor drainage in the miserable soil of the highlands. Look for moose droppings, or even for moose. A sometimes-steep 30 m (100 ft) remains to be climbed, but the views are wonderful and the horizon is opening up.

Finally, you are there. Expect higher winds and lower temperatures at the summit. Also expect to spend quite a bit of time sitting on the cliff, which is about 100 m/yd from the tower, enjoying the view. It is a fair reward for a demanding walk. Many hikers climb the fire tower, though you're not supposed to. The shelter at the top is locked, as is a small cabin nearby. You'll find outhouses next to the cabin. To return to your car, follow the former road down the hill and make a loop out of the trail. This route is slightly longer than the hill slope but far easier. There is one short uphill about a kilometre from the tower, but generally the 4 km (2.5 mi) of this path is all down.

At the lake there is a short side trail that takes you to the water's edge; continuing past that the road descends steeply, with a boisterous brook accompanying you on your left. You reach the gate and upper parking lot within another 500 m/yd, and the road curves gently right around the hill, affording further superb views of Ingonish Bay. Very quickly, no doubt because of the steepness of the grade, you arrive at the lower parking lot.

Cautionary Notes: The trail takes you to the top of a 400 m (1300 ft) cliff with no safety barriers. The climb is a steep, difficult effort, so take it easy and rest often. Wear layers so that you may adjust your clothing as your body temperature rises during the climb and falls at the summit.

Further Information: See David Lawley's book on the Cabot Trail as well as the park brochures.

Glasgow Lakes

Length: 8 km
(5 mi) return
Time: 2-3 hrs
Type: former road, walking paths
Rating: 2

Uses: hiking, cross-country skiing
Facilities: garbage cans
Gov't Topo Map: Dingwall 11 K/16

Access: From Neils Harbour, drive 9 km (5.5 mi) along the Cabot Trail toward Cape North and Dingwall. Road signs indicate the turnoff on the left shortly after the highway begins to descend toward the ocean. A dirt road continues inland for 2 km (1.25 mi), ending at a parking lot by Paquets (Paquette) Lake.

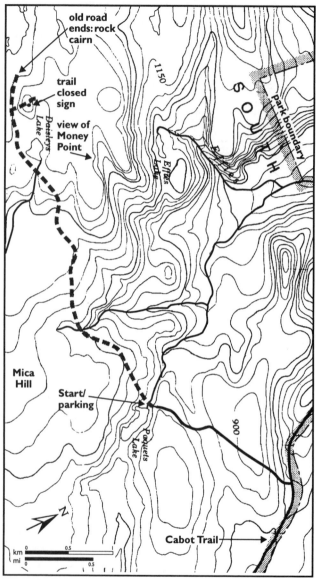

old road
ends: rock
cairn

trail
closed
sign

view of
Money
Point

Bartleys Lake

1150

S O U T H

park boundary

Effies Lake

Mica
Hill

Start/
parking

Paquets Lake

900

N

Cabot Trail

km
mi

0   0.5
0   0.5

Glasgow Lakes Trail

Introduction: The Glasgow Lakes Trail climbs from 200 m (850 ft) to 440 m (1450 ft.) and takes you onto the highlands plateau. Formerly a fire road, the path climbs almost steadily from its start to the windswept barrens of the look-off at the end of the trail. From there, views of Aspy Bay and Money Point far to the north are possible on clear days.

This is the highest elevation reached by any hike in this book, and environmental conditions here are vastly different from almost any other spot in the province. Check with the information centre before attempting the hike, especially in May (when there may still be snow), September and October, and expect it to be cooler and windier near Glasgow Lake than at the start. However, because of its relatively short distance and reasonably good track, Glasgow Lakes offers the best opportunity for most people to experience the highland plateau.

Trail Description: From the parking lot, continue along the former road as it crosses the brook leading from Paquets Lake. This turns right, away from the lake, and heads uphill toward the highland plateau. Its track is wide and provides comfortable walking for two, although in wet weather (which I have encountered every time I have attempted this walk) many puddles and streams must be sidestepped. Rocks intrude throughout the path, the thin soil here being inadequate to cover the massive granite block constituting the entire highlands.

Within minutes the hardwoods growing in the sheltered area around Paquets Lake disappear, unable to survive the brutal conditions of the exposed north-facing slope. The tiny trees around you, many barely a metre high, are not new growth, but 50 to 75 years old. In winter, high winds drive ice crystals into exposed branches, killing them. Only those parts of the tree covered by snow are able to survive. Like carefully tended shrubs, the spruce, firs, and larch are pruned back year after year by the unforgiving climate.

Less than a kilometre from the start, the view north opens up as the trail climbs the slope above Effies Brook. (I am told that you can see Cape North in the distance, but my four hikes on this trail have all been in fog.) Halfway to Daisleys Lake, you see Mica Hill dominating to your left. Although the ground to it seems open and easy walking, I recommend staying on the path. In addition to the usual safety reasons, the land is quite sensitive to intrusion, and repeated human use will damage it beyond repair.

Crossing the brook draining Daisleys Lake may be a challenge. The ground up here is almost always wet, but during or after a rainfall water runs everywhere. The path makes a detour from its original route, which is now a pond, to connect with a bridge. Even this does not guarantee dry feet, however, so be prepared. Sheltered somewhat, taller trees are present during the final steep climb toward the lake. Approaching the pond on your right, note that the bark on most of the trees has been stripped by browsing moose. Access to the water's edge can be gained by following one of the many broad trails moose have cleared through the undergrowth.

Beyond Daisleys Lake you come to several apparent junctions, all unsigned. Wrong turns are possible, and the former trail to Long Lake is the most tempting. It is on your left and heads downhill, but it rapidly degrades. Continue along the most travelled-looking path, but remember that you should find a sign pointing to the look-off on your right within a kilometre of Daisleys Lake. Do not continue along the road beyond this sign, but climb the narrow path leading to the knoll.

Once on top, you are treated to the view for which you have worked so hard. A "Closed" sign has been posted across the path. Please turn around here and retrace your route back.

Cautionary Notes: Up on the highland plateau the weather is the most variable and harsh of any in the Maritimes. It is easy to get lost on the barrens, particularly in fog. Because the old road continues beyond the turnoff to the knoll, some people mistake it for the trail. Also, the map produced by Parks Canada inadvertently shows the trail continuing along the road and avoiding the hill, increasing the potential for confusion. Should you take the wrong turn, turn back when you find a cairn of rocks at the road's end, 300 m/yd beyond the knoll. It is extremely easy to get lost on the bog beyond the cairn, particularly in poor visibility. I know; I have done it more than once.

Some recent books and maps show the trail continuing beyond the knoll between Glasgow and Daisleys Lake. This extended section has recently been closed by Parks Canada because of the negative environmental impact of high use and is no longer being maintained. Although the trail appears well defined beyond the sign, please venture no further.

Further Information: See David Lawley's book about the Cabot Trail as well as the Parks Canada brochures.

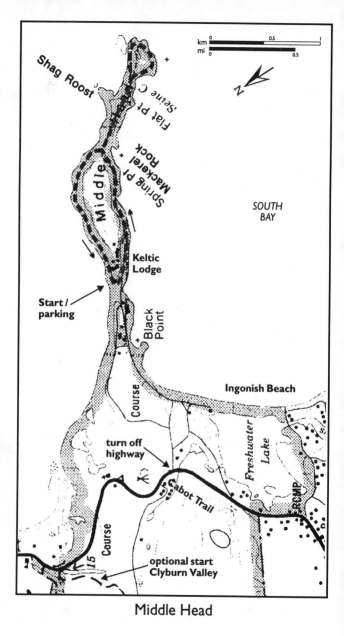

Middle Head

Middle Head

Length: 4 km
  (2.5 mi) return
Time: 1-2 hrs
Type: former road,
  walking path
Rating: 1

Uses: hiking, cross-country
  skiing
Facilities: garbage cans,
  benches
Gov't Topo Map: Ingonish
  11 K/9

Access: From the Cabot Trail, signs clearly indicate the road to Keltic Lodge and the trail. The turn is less than a kilometre from the park entrance, and a further 2 km (1.25 mi) must be driven to reach the parking lot and trailhead located behind the resort. Should the gate be closed, as it periodically is, the trailhead is an additional kilometre on foot (each way).

Introduction: Dividing Ingonish Bay almost equally in two, Middle Head, a narrow granite finger stretching into the ocean and flanked by magnificent sandy beaches, is one of the most recognizable sights in Nova Scotia. It is home of the renowned Keltic Lodge resort. Called "Geganisg," "remarkable place," by the Mi'kmaq, it was once a worksite for both Native and European fishers. Much of the hiking trail was once the carriage road connecting a summer estate, where the lodge now stands, with the fishing village. This walk is in a stacked loop arrangement. After 1 km (.5 mi), a branch loops back to the lodge on the other side of the point. This is recommended for some, because scaling a fairly steep hill is required in the second half of the walk. Fortunately, several benches along the route permit rest for the weary.

Experienced hikers may overlook this walk because it is so short, but perhaps they should reconsider. With the sea stacks at the point, the fishing settlement ruins, and the spectacular views, this walk is well worth the little time required to complete it.

Trail Description: From the parking lot, climb the stairs and turn right. Numerous interpretive signs describe the history of the area. Pass between the concrete pillars that were the estate's gate and go by the drinking trough and benches (unless you wish to sit and enjoy the view). The track is wide, and it stays level until a short uphill section just before the junction. Turn left to return to Keltic Lodge, right to continue the full hike to the end of Middle Head.

The trail descends fairly steeply (passing four benches) until it reaches a grassy field at a very narrow point of the peninsula. This was the location of the fishing village, which was active into the early 1900s. Climbing up the far side of the field, you will notice that almost no hardwoods remain. Farther out on the point, the salt spray kills almost every species of tree. Only the white spruce, growing densely together for protection and gnarled by wind into stunted stands called krumholz, can live here.

The trail remains sheltered by the trees for most of this last kilometre, although views of Cape Smokey and Ingonish Beach are frequent. The footing becomes a carpet of roots and spruce needles instead of grass, and as you approach the headland the cart-track trail narrows to a footpath. Overlooking Seine Cove is another bench and an interpretive panel. An unmarked junction permits the option of a short jaunt left to the north side of the point and an observation site viewing Mink Cove. Continue to the right to reach the headland, only 200 m/yd away.

You emerge suddenly from the shelter of the trees onto the exposed and barren point. The grassy area is crisscrossed with paths made by generations of tourists.

To the south are several foundations of abandoned fishing shelters and a splendid view of Cape Smokey. To the north, Ingonish Island is the prominent landmark. Tiny Ingonish Island is crisscrossed with a grid of thin ropes about a foot above ground level. This net allows terns to land and nest there, but it keeps out the larger gulls, which would eat the tern eggs and chicks if they could. Guillemots, cormorants, and several species of gull are frequently sighted from this location. Expect it to be much cooler here than at Keltic Lodge.

To return to the start, retrace your steps, at least as far as the junction at the top of the long hill. For a different route, turn right here and follow the track as it works its way around the hill to the north side of Middle Head. The views of North Bay Ingonish are superb, and the broad, level trail is marvellous walking. Note the old stone work and its excellent condition; several cuttings of trees have been made to permit clear views, and benches have been placed to take advantage of them.

After 750 m/yd the path cuts back left, climbing higher ground to complete the loop. It rejoins the old carriage road closer to the resort than your starting position but in sight of the parking lot. A short hike perhaps, but definitely a good one.

Cautionary Notes: Be mindful of steep cliffs near the trail border at several places, particularly if you are accompanied by children. The very tip of Middle Head is exposed to high winds and waves. Be careful near the water's edge.

Steering Island, at the tip of Middle Head, is home to a colony of common and arctic terns. At certain times of the year this end of the trail will be closed for their protection.

Cape Breton Highlands

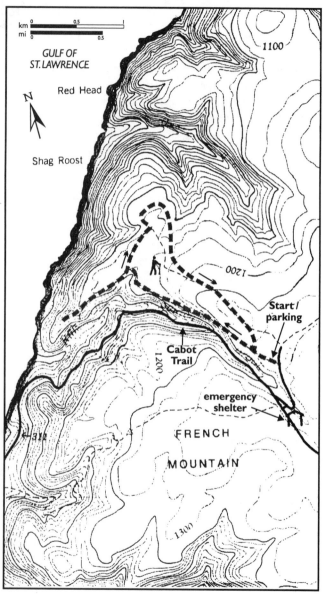

km 0   0.5   1
mi 0   0.5

GULF OF
ST. LAWRENCE

Red Head

N

Shag Roost

1100

1200

Start /
parking

Cabot
Trail

1200

emergency
shelter

FRENCH

MOUNTAIN

1300

Skyline

Skyline

Length: 7 km
(4.5 mi) return
Time: 2 hrs
Type: walking path
Rating: 2

Uses: hiking, cross-country
skiing
Facilities: outhouses,
garbage cans
Gov't Topo Map: Pleasant
Bay 11 K/15, Cheticamp
River 11 K/10

Access: From the west park entrance north of Cheti-camp, drive 15 km (9.5 mi) north on the Cabot Trail. Near the summit of French Mountain, a sign directs you left off the pavement onto a gravel road. Continue along this for 1 km (.5 mi) to a parking lot.

Introduction: Skyline Trail is a 7 km (4.5 mi) loop that leads to the steep headland cliff overlooking the Gulf of St. Lawrence. This relatively easy hike along the high plateau is a very popular day hike. Increased use means that on summer weekends you may expect to meet 30 or 40 people along here. But, like most Nova Scotia trails, it is less thickly populated in the spring and fall, which are usually the best times for walking anyway.

This trail is well maintained from start to finish with all the deadfall speedily removed during the summer season. A visit in November or April can be quite in-structive, showing how quickly a trail can begin to close in and demonstrating how much maintenance is per-formed by park staff.

Trail Description: The trailhead is found at the parking lot, behind the outhouses. The trail begins quite gently, gradually descending toward the water through ragged patches of tamarack, black spruce, and balsam fir. For the first 500 m/yd both entrance and exit are along the same route, but at a well-signed junction you must choose your approach to the cliffs. The attraction for most people is the point where the long barren spur follows Jumping Brook as it winds toward the ocean. To get there the quickest, turn left. For the next 2 km (1.25 mi) your route parallels the ravine on your left, and occasionally you catch glimpses of the sea off French Mountain through the spotty vegetation.

A forest fire ravaged these slopes in 1951, and even though many of the trees are almost 40 years old, they are only 2.5-3 m (8-10 ft) high. The poor soil and extreme weather conditions combine to prevent healthy growth. Only in sheltered areas do you find more vigorous trees. Notice also the damage done by browsing moose. They will strip the bark as high as they can reach, and this almost kills, and definitely scars, many trees.

As you approach the water's edge your vista begins to expand. Another junction with benches marks the location where you follow the remainder of the loop, but keep left. Just beyond that the view opens on to one of the most thrilling sights available: the Gulf of St. Lawrence, stretching across the entire horizon. French Mountain, to your left and below, dominates the south, and the deep ravine containing Jumping Brook is directly beneath you. The path continues, descending steeply down the spur nearly 100 m (325 ft) in only 300 m (100 ft). This part of the trail is open and visible from the rocks above, and people at the lower level are readily discernible.

From this lower elevation there is nowhere else to go. On all sides save your approach, steep cliffs fall precipitously. The crumbling, twisted metamorphic rocks are too unstable to permit climbing. But this is such a fantastic spot that you may wish to linger. Observe the birds take flight. Perched on the sheer hillsides, they

Skyline Trail. MICHAEL HAYNES

merely open their wings. They don't need to flap, they are instantly airborne. Watch closely: sometimes eagles mix among the gulls. For most people, the visit to this spot is enough, and they return they way they hiked in. But a further 3 km (2 mi) of trail exists, and it provides your best chance of seeing wildlife. As you climb back up from the spur and re-enter the trees, you return to a junction. Turn left, and follow the path along the coastline as it takes you another kilometre further toward Georges Brook and above Shag Roost. The woods are thicker with far more hardwoods flourishing, including some beech.

From this section, before it turns inland and climbs back to the parking lot, you get a view of the land toward Fishing Cove. And, on a clear day, you can sit on one of the benches and detect the Magdalen Islands, nearly 100 km (62 mi) away. At dusk its lights are often visible from this high vantage point. The trail begins to circle inland and rise slowly as you climb back to the top of the highlands. Pay attention for moose grazing in

Cape Breton Highlands

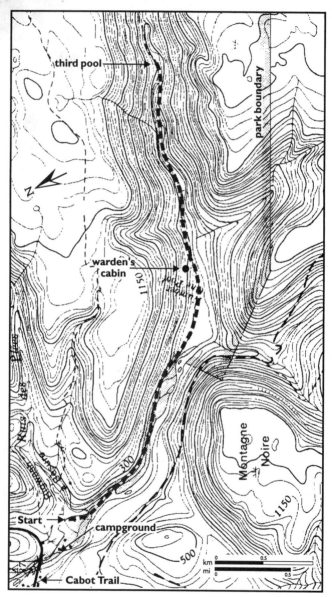

Trous de Saumon

this area. A visiting friend from the United ⟨
walked around a patch of krumholtz and almost ⟨
lided with a 450 kg (1000 lb) bull. Needless to say, h
found another way past that point. The trail steers back
to the first junction you encountered. Keep left, and
500 m/yd more walking puts you back in your car.

Cautionary Notes: Much of the trail follows a cliff
edge, and some of that is hidden by vegetation. There
are no guardrails, so keep children in sight at all times.
The winds at the water's edge will be high and cool;
gale-force winds are not uncommon, particularly in late
fall and winter. Expect temperatures lower than inland.

Moose are common and black bear infrequent visitors. Ask at the information centre about recent
sightings.

Trous de Saumon

Length: 13 km
(8 mi) return
Time: 5 hrs
Type: former road,
walking paths
Rating: 3

Uses: hiking, mountain
biking, cross-country skiing
Facilities: outhouses, water,
campsite, firewood,
showers, shelters, picnic
tables, garbage cans
Gov't Topo Map:
Cheticamp River 11 K/10

Access: Enter the park, crossing over the Cheticamp
River. The information centre, including Les Amis du
Plein Air bookstore, is situated between the bridge and
the entrance kiosk. Park your car in its lot and continue
on foot through the campground toward the group
camping area. The road nearest the river is the trail, al-

though the sign is difficult to see, being just a tiny marker perhaps 20 m/yd past the large "Department vehicles only beyond this point" notice. Do not follow the road heading sharply left up the hill.

Introduction: Looking at a topographical map of the Cape Breton Highlands, you will immediately notice the path of the Cheticamp River. With its mouth at the park's western border, the steep-sided valley cuts deeply into the highlands, reaching almost halfway across the island like a moat protecting the park's southern boundaries. In the upper reaches, the slopes of the ravine are sheer cliffs, falling vertically nearly 200 m (650 ft).

Cheticamp River is known for its fishing; the name of this hike is French for "salmon pools," and you will often find anglers at the deep lagoons beneath the several cataracts along the route. In fact, the trail was developed to encourage anglers to visit the park by making access to the best spots easier. If you wish to try your luck, remember that you must use a tied fly and have a licence.

This hike can be enjoyed by the novice. As far as the first pool and the warden's cabin, the trail is road-width and well graded, suitable for almost anyone. If you turned back here, the trail would have a difficulty rating of 2. Beyond this point, however, the trail becomes progressively more difficult and should be attempted only by more experienced walkers.

Trail Description: A metal gate prevents vehicular access and the path is broad and well graded, wide enough for two. Initially climbing a small hill, the trail rapidly descends to near river level. At first it does not follow close to the water, instead staying near the northern slope. Ample evidence exists of the flooding that occurs in this narrow valley during spring runoff. But there are several lovely hardwood glades with pin cherry and striped maple in the understory and larger maple, beech, and oak overhead. Benches are available for those who wish to sit and enjoy the shade.

In this first portion of the hike, massive Montaigne Noire dominates the southern side of the valley. Do not be surprised if you hear the occasional sound of a motor, as a road from the community of La Prairie parallels the river on the other bank just outside the park's boundaries. After nearly 3 km (2 mi), you will notice the broad valley cut by Faribault Creek dividing the southern skyline. Soon the canyon walls of the Cheticamp River Valley will begin to constrict.

Shortly after crossing two bridges, you reach the first salmon pool. The path divides, with anglers heading to the water and hikers heading uphill. Signs reminds anglers of proper fishing etiquette. An observation area permits the sharp-sighted to discern Atlantic salmon swimming in the deep pool below, if the time of year is right. Just past this spot on the left, at the crest of a small hill, is a warden's cabin. Up to this point, the hike can be completed by almost anyone, and returning to the start now constitutes a respectable 7 km (4.5 mi) amble.

If you continue your hike, you find that both valley and trail narrow considerably. Whenever the river strays northward the trail is forced to climb up the steep slope; when the stream is near the south the path descends again. Chance's Pool is only a few hundred metres beyond the cabin, and the second pool less than a kilometre beyond that. Here there is a small emergency shelter, and a sign says that bicycles may proceed no further.

Now the trail definitely becomes more challenging, climbing steeply to pass over the cataract above the second pool and following a narrow ravine deep into the hillside before crossing a brook on a plank bridge (with handrail). The path becomes much narrower and far rougher walking, and talus shed from the enveloping slopes occasionally intrudes. The views of the steep-sided and V-shaped valley beyond, however, are magnificent.

All too soon, it seems, the path abruptly ends at the third pool, opening up into a small clearing. With plenty of bare rock by the river's edge, this is a lovely spot to have a snack. Steep cliff walls prevent further impromptu trekking. After that, unless you plan to fish, retrace your steps back to the parking lot and the information centre. Fortunately, you will find that most of the return trip is downhill, with the exception of the final climb before you reach the campground.

Cautionary Notes: During the spring melt the Cheticamp River runs very fast and often overflows its banks. Inquire about conditions before hiking in April and early May. Remember, weather conditions change very quickly in the highlands. Always carry some warm clothing, even in summer.

KEJIMKUJIK NATIONAL PARK

With more than 120 km (75 mi) of marked trail, Kejimkujik National Park is the largest centre of hiking opportunities in mainland Nova Scotia. In 1994 more than 60,000 people visited the park, with 11,000 camping in the backcountry and 17,500 staying at the large Jeremys Bay Campground. In fact, every year since its opening, the number of visitors to Kejimkujik has increased, so much so that, on summer weekends, it may not be possible to find an open backcountry site, and, in winter, Mason's Cabin is always full.

Canoeing is even more popular than hiking and cross-country skiing. At least 23 of the 40 backcountry sites are accessible to canoes only (nine are on islands). The Mersey River, running through Kejimkujik Lake, can be followed more than 50 km (31 mi) to the ocean at Liverpool, and the Shelburne River, the first in Nova Scotia to be nominated a Heritage River, comes within 500 m/yd of the park's southern boundary.

Opened in 1967, Kejimkujik is the province's second national park. 381 km² (238 mi²) in size, Kejimkujik was selected in order to preserve a representative sampling of Nova Scotia's Atlantic Coast Uplands natural region, a zone encompassing nearly half the province. Distinguished by a profusion of lakes and rivers and diverse glacial landforms, this is one of the few wildernesses remaining in the province. In 1988, the 22 km² (13.74 mi²) Seaside Adjunct, located on the Atlantic Ocean near Port Mouton, was added to the park in order to preserve significant coastal headlands and protect crucial nesting sites for the endangered piping plover.

No better site exists to experience the interior forests of Nova Scotia. Every backcountry campsite contains an outhouse, fire grill, firewood, and flat tent pads. The trails are kept clear, and most streams and wet areas are bridged and boardwalked. Kejimkujik is a wonderful place for novice hikers and your first overnight trip. The Liberty Lake Trail (described in three sections in this book), is the only long distance loop trail in Nova Scotia.

Be sure to pick up brochures on the park and its plants and animals at the visitor centre at the park entrance. There's also a very useful map with brief descriptions of day walks in the park. Get the brochure about the park's Seaside Adjunct and the piping plovers found there at Kejimkujik, because the Adjunct has no visitor centre.

Wood ticks may be a problem throughout Kejimkujik National Park and the Seaside Adjunct from April to July.

Kejimkujik is one of several national parks testing a trial entry fee schedule in 1995 (and possibly beyond), so park entrance and camping charges will be changing significantly from previous years. For a complete list of rates contact Kejimkujik National Park, telephone (902) 682-2772, or fax (902) 682-3367.

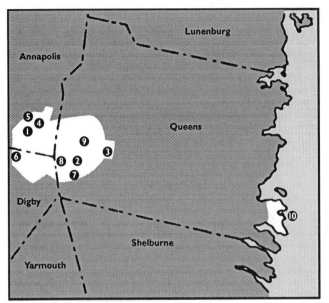

KEJIMKUJIK NATIONAL PARK

1.	Channel Lake	272
2.	Fire Tower	276
3.	Gold Mines	282
4.	Hemlocks and Hardwoods	286
5.	Liberty Lake: Big Dam - Campsite #43	290
6.	Liberty Lake: Campsite #43 - #37	294
7.	Liberty Lake: Campsite #37 - Mersey River	298
8.	Luxton Lake	302
9.	Peter Point	308
10.	Seaside Adjunct	312

kejimkujik

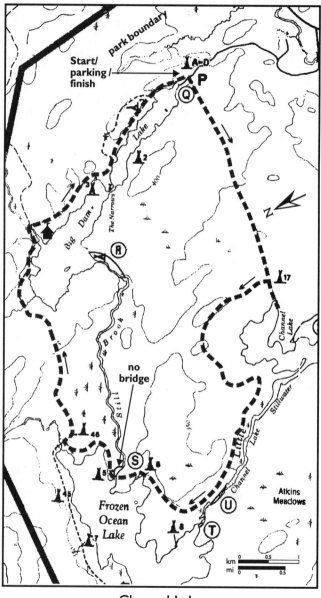

Channel Lake

Channel Lake

Length: 26 km
(16 mi) return
Time: 8-9 hrs
Type: walking path,
former road, dirt road
Rating: 5

Uses: hiking, cross-country
skiing
Facilities: outhouses,
campsites, firewood,
garbage cans
Gov't Topo Map:
Kejimkujik 21 A/6

Access: From the park entrance, drive along the pavement 5 km (3 mi) until you reach the turnoff for Jeremys Bay Campground. Turn right and follow the road over the Mersey River. On the far side of the bridge the road divides, with a dirt road going right. Follow this 3 km (2 mi) to its end, a parking lot. The trail starts at the far end.

Introduction: For those who want a challenging day hike or an overnight experience without undertaking the rigours of the loop trail, Channel Lake is a good choice. At 26 km (16 mi), it will challenge even the fittest hiker. Spending two days on the trail can make this a pleasant venture for a family and drop the rating to 3.

The Channel Lake Trail can be an excellent selection for an outdoors weekend. Arriving in the park Friday, camp in Sites A-D at Big Dam Lake. Hike about 14 km (8.75 mi) on Saturday past Channel Lake to Site #6 on Frozen Ocean Lake. On Sunday, finish the remaining 12 km (7.5 mi), including a visit to the old-growth hemlocks.

Trail Description: I recommend heading directly toward Channel Lake and Site #17, because this is the route least travelled. Most hikers follow the banks of Big Dam Lake, so you should encounter fewer people your

Kejimkujik

first day in the woods and more on the second day as you return. The path is easily found, just inside the woods at the end of the Big Dam parking lot. Trails to the canoe landing and other routes go straight; a small sign indicates where you turn left instead.

The first 6 km (3.75 mi), with few exceptions, passes through beautiful mature hardwoods. You'll face one or two wet portions, including a lengthy boardwalked stretch, fairly early, but the trail is generally easy walking. It seems that the path turns more and is hillier than is shown in the *Backcountry Guide*, but there is never any doubt about the route, so no harm is done. Nor is there confusion at junctions; these are always well signed.

Your first diversion is the side-trail to campsite #17. This will take you more than 500 m/yd off the main trail to the shores of Channel Lake, providing you with your only opportunity to see this body of water. If you are lucky, you may see a family of loons or sight the barn swallows that nest on one of the small rocky islands.

From the turnoff, the main trail takes a wide, almost circular diversion for the next several kilometres. The ground here is prone to flooding, and you'll have to detour to keep your feet ensure reasonably dry. There are stands of gorgeous softwoods through this area, but in 1994 many of the boardwalks desperately needed replacement.

The walk paralleling Channel Lake Stillwater follows the brook for more than 2 km (1.25 mi) although you may not actually see it. Only when you approach Portage U and a small open swamp are you certain to sight the river, approximately the halfway point of the hike. Turning almost 90°, the trail follows high ground until it reaches the shore of Frozen Ocean Lake a kilometre later. Shortly, campsite #6, situated in a magnificent hemlock stand, comes into view, and 500 m/yd beyond that is Still Brook. There is no bridge here. At low water, you can cross without getting wet if the season is very dry. If you are not prepared to ford, make certain you enquire about conditions from park staff before you start.

On the other side of Still Brook is campsite #5, and from here the trail follows the top of the small ridge paralleling the lake for another kilometre. Not far from campsite #46, the path leaves the ridge, and you'll cross a long boardwalk immediately before the campsite. An important junction is 50 m/yd beyond. The trail that continues straight heads toward Liberty Lake, so turn right (east) up the former road and start heading home. You will be able to walk side by side through this section. During the next 4 km (2.5 mi), note the large piles of granite boulders deposited by glaciers.

Just past the second large bridge, Thomas Meadow Brook, on top of the next hill, your path merges with another road; turn right here. The trail then branches to the left 100 m/yd later. (A warden's cabin is at the end of the road.) You now move through a Special Preservation Area, so designated because this is one of the few fragments of original, unlogged forest in Nova Scotia. Continue through magnificent softwoods alongside Big Dam Lake, and less than a kilometre later you'll arrive at Campsite #3 on your right.

Shortly you reach another junction, and the direct route is straight ahead. Turning left onto the Hemlocks and Hardwoods Trail will add less than a kilometre to your hike, and you will pass beneath 300-year-old hemlocks, a very rare treat. By either route, you have no more than 3 km (2 mi) remaining. Less than a kilometre from the finish, the Hemlock and Hardwoods Trail connects again from the left, and side-tracks to campsites A, B, and D join on the right. Finally, just before the parking lot, you will reach your starting point.

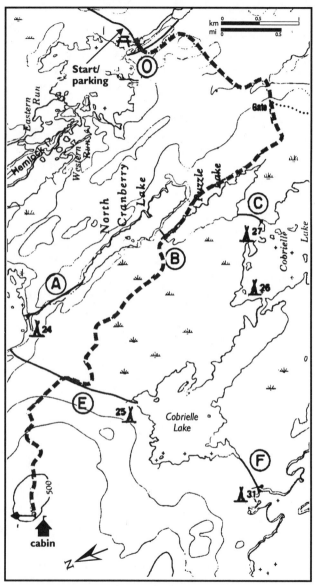

Fire Tower

Cautionary Notes: Still Brook must be forded, and if the water is high this can be done only by getting wet up to the waist. Before starting this hike ask park officials about conditions. July and August are good, but September and October are the best months to hike this trail. Flooding in other parts of the trail can be a problem, particularly in the spring.

Future Plans: The 1994 Management Plan suggested that a solution to the spring flooding problem be sought. This may include changing the trail's route substantially.

Half of campsite #5, at Still Brook, will be closed for the next few years to allow the area to recover.

Fire Tower

Length: 12.5 km
   (7.5 mi) return
Time: 5 hrs
Type: gravel road,
   dirt road
Rating: 3

Uses: hiking, mountain
   biking, cross-country skiing
Facilities: outhouses, tables,
   garbage cans, shelter with
   stove, firewood
Gov't Topo Map:
   Kejimkujik 21 A/6

Access: Follow the paved road from the park entrance to its end, approximately 11 km (7 mi). Follow the gravel road another 8 km. (5 mi) to the gate at the Mersey River. Park your car in the lot there and start your hike on the far side of the bridge.

Introduction: There are not many places in Kejimkujik where you can get a good view. The rolling, gentle hills of inland Nova Scotia do not present many vistas, and I don't think there is a single cliff in the entire park.

Kejimkujik

However, there is the fire tower. Perched on a 170-m (500-ft) knoll, it's 24 m (80 ft) tall, and from it you can see large areas of the south and east portions of the park and beyond.

Trail Description: Your trek starts at the parking lot on the Mersey River. Although the gravel road continues another 8 km (5 mi) to Peskowesk Lake, from mid-June to Labour Day there is a gate at the Mersey restricting vehicular access. This is a popular jumping-off centre for canoeing, hiking, and bicycling, and it is where people leave a vehicle to find when they complete the Liberty Lake Loop Trail. Accordingly there is a large parking lot with picnic facilities nearby. In the winter, park officials erect a winterized tent with stove as a warm-up and emergency overnight shelter.

Portage O, connecting George and Loon lakes, stretches for nearly a kilometre on the far side of the river. There were major settlements of Native peoples at both ends of this section of the Mersey River, and artifacts such as ceramic pots, arrowheads, and scrapers indicate 4,000 years of their activity. The remains of V-shaped rock walls in the water, used for eel weirs, are still easily recognized and give this site its Mi'kmaq name. Walk along the portage to get a better view of these structures.

Once across the bridge, your trail climbs slightly to the top of a long drumlin-like ridge on the far side, which it follows for most of the next kilometre. Turning west again, the road continues through rolling terrain and attractive hardwood stands until it reaches a small bridge over Square Camp Brook 2.5 km (1.5 mi) later. A few hundred metres beyond that is the Fire Tower Trail turnoff, clearly signed.

The trail becomes a dirt road from this point, and the trees provide far less shade than they did earlier. On hot summer days, the next few kilometres will be unbearable without a hat. Within a kilometre you come to a small clearing at the south end of Puzzle Lake. The trail turns north now, with the lake on your left, and shortly afterward you will see another small north-south body of water, North Cranberry Lake, on your right. The trail runs on the top of a narrow ridge separating the lakes, and at the top of Puzzle Lake is Portage B, only 150 m/yd long, but a stiff climb from either direction if you're carrying a canoe. Past this area the trail meanders gradually upward for nearly 3 km (2 mi) through mixed woods and occasional open bogs.

At more than 2 km (1.25 mi), Portage E is the longest in the park. It is the only one with a name — Big Hardwood Carry — and it may also be the most beautiful. The trail cuts across the portage at about its middle, so taking either direction is good for a diversion. I recommend turning right and following the narrow, well-beaten path to Minards Bay on Kejimkujik Lake. There is a bit of a steep descent to the water, but your reward is passing through old-growth hardwoods for most of the distance.

Back on the main trail, the Fire Tower Road now begins its climb to the summit. A little more than 2 km (1.25 mi) remain, all uphill. Nevertheless, the higher elevation does not provide any distant views, because you are also heading into a region of splendid old-growth sugar maple and yellow birch. These are quite tall, your way is finally shaded again. The end of the trail arrives suddenly. You round a gradual corner and find the fire tower and warden's cabin in a small clearing surrounded by trees. The cabin is unlocked in the winter and has a table and chairs, counter, bench, sleeping pallets, and a wood stove with firewood.

The fire tower is a thin metal frame with a tiny one-person cage at the top. A sign at the bottom of the ladder says that it is unsafe in high winds, so be sensible about deciding to climb up. You will probably want to ascend a few rungs, because even at the top of the knoll there is no view. Trees block it in every direction, and if you want to see anything, you must climb.

Once you have finished here (and the cabin does make a nice spot for a lunch), you return to your car via the same route. You will probably find this somewhat faster, because it is almost all downhill.

Cautionary Notes: The Native peoples settlement area is one of the most important cultural sites in the park. Even though extensive disturbance has already taken place, please resist the temptation to play amateur archaeologist. Stay on the paths, and if you discover an artifact please turn it in to park officials.

The cage at the top of the fire tower is locked, and the structure is unsafe in winds above 50 kph (31 mph).

Future Plans: A loop trail around Peskowesk Lake is being considered, but due to current budget constraints construction may not start soon.

Further Information: Both the Backcountry Guide and the Day Walking brochure outline this trail.

Gold Mines

Length: 3 km
 (2 mi) return
Time: 1 hr
Type: walking path,
 former road
Rating: 1

Uses: hiking
Facilities: outhouse,
 garbage can, picnic
 table, benches
Gov't Topo Map:
 Kejimkujik 21 A/6

Access: Follow the paved road from the park entrance to its end at the fish hatchery on Grafton Lake, approximately 11 km (7 mi). Follow the gravel road continuation another 3.5 km (2.25 mi). The parking area and trailhead are on your left and are well signed. The gate may be closed at Grafton Lake in winter, adding a total of 7 km (4.5 mi) of walking.

Introduction: In 1884, Jim McQuire, hiding in the woods to evade the law, discovered gold 9 km (5.5 mi) east of this spot. Soon gold fever spread, and mines were opened throughout south central Nova Scotia. A Caledonia businessman, Nelson Douglas, was the first to work this area, claiming the land from 1888 to 1890. However, he soon sold his interests to Charles Ford, a Maitland Bridge lumberman, whose family went on to work this claim for 30 years even though they found very little gold.

In 1922, John McClare, a former prospector who had worked for Nelson Douglas, found a 6 cm (2.5 in) vein of gold in the quartzite rock. Named "Blue Lead," this thin vein was not large enough to be profitable but too enticing to abandon. John McClare died in 1932, never having found the mother lode he expected, and until 1939 his son Horace continued to work the claim. But heavy rains that spring flooded the most promising sites, and the outbreak of World War II finally forced an end to the exploration. The claims lapsed, and the "big gold," if present, is still undiscovered.

Abandoned mine shafts, long narrow trenches from "snake diggin'," and remains of mining equipment can be found along the self-interpretive trail. This is a pleasant walk accessible to almost any fitness level. Recent work on the trail, new interpretive panels, railings, and benches make this an excellent choice for a short, interesting walk.

Kejimkujik

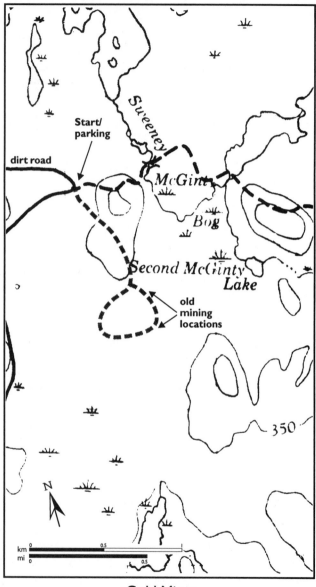

Start/
parking

dirt road

Sweeney

McGinty

Bog

Second McGinty
Lake

old
mining
locations

N

km
mi

350

Gold Mines

Those wanting a longer hike should add the McGinty Lake Trail to the Gold Mines route. Following an old road, McGinty Lake Trail crosses several brooks before ending at the park boundary. It crosses the site of an old farm on top of a drumlin, and the remains of an old mill can be found on the north shore of McGinty Lake. Combining the two hikes provides 8 km (5 mi) of walking and increases the difficulty level to 2. McGinty is a popular cross-country ski route, connecting to a series of wood roads outside park borders.

Trail Description: Two trails, McGinty Lake and Gold Mines, start from the parking lot. The former is an old road with a metal gate blocking vehicular traffic, while the latter is a narrow path entering the woods just to the right of the McGinty Lake route. A garbage can, picnic table, and outhouse are found by the parking area, but there is no water source anywhere on the trail.

The Gold Mines Trail is one of the nicest and best-maintained trails in the park. Although narrow and winding at first, the gravelled track provides excellent footing. An interpretive panel near the parking lot sets the scene for the story about gold mining in Kejimkujik. A second sign, 100 m/yd later, explains geographical features of the landscape. Climbing a small hill, notice the young pine flourishing beneath the protective shade of the hardwood forest. Eventually this hillside will become mature pine, replacing the birch, oak, and maple as they die out. Another panel, near the summit, explains the uses to which these various species of trees were put by the miners in their operations.

The path joins an old road emerging from the left, the direction of the McGinty Lake Trail. A rather large bench is positioned at this intersection. Turn right, and follow the gravel track as it leads gradually downhill to another sign. This panel also talks about geology; note that examples of the quartzite rock it mentions are piled at its base. At the top of a small rise 150 m/yd beyond, an arrow directs traffic left at a trail junction. You are now on a short loop that explores the actual mining site.

The trail becomes winding and narrow again, skirting water-filled holes that once were the mine entrances. In the next 500 m/yd, more interpretive panels outline the story of the men who searched for gold on this spot and the methods they used to achieve their dream. Moving from site to site, the trail circles through the debris of their digging, eventually returning to the old road that was their supply line. The last interpretive post, which I found particularly interesting, features old equipment: pump, ore bucket, shovel, and five stamp mill frame (whatever that is).

The loop ends a short distance past the old equipment, and walkers must retrace their path to return to the parking lot. Note that there is no arrow directing you left when the new path diverges from the former road, but if you follow the gravelled track, there should be no problem. If you do miss the turn, the old road soon intersects with the McGinty Lake Trail; turn left to reach the parking area.

Future Plans: The interpretive panels will soon be updated. They may be placed in new locations, and numbers may vary.

Further Information: Gold Mines is profiled on a separate park map showing all short hiking trails and day use facilities.

Hemlocks and Hardwoods

Length: 6 km
  (4 mi) return
Time: 2 hrs
Type: walking path
Rating: 2

Uses: hiking, cross-country
  skiing
Facilities: outhouses,
  garbage cans, campsites,
  firewood
Gov't Topo Map:
  Kejimkujik 21 A/6

Access: From the park entrance, drive along the pavement 5 km (3 mi) to the turnoff for Jeremys Bay Campground. Turn right and follow the road over the Mersey River. On the far side of the bridge the road divides, with a dirt road going right. Follow this 3 km (2 mi) to its end, a parking lot. The trail starts at the far end.

Introduction: Very little of the original forest in Kejimkujik survived the logging boom of the 1800s, but isolated groves of old-growth eastern hemlock can still be found, some of them as old as 300 years. A significant stand of these graceful softwoods is located along the northern edge of Big Dam Lake. A trail has been created to make these trees available to nature hikers, and it offers the most spectacular forest walk in the province. Relatively short, level, and well-maintained, this trail is excellent for families and people of most fitness levels.

Trail Description: This short loop begins at the Big Dam parking lot, which is also the trailhead for the Channel Lake Trail and the Loop Trail as well as a popular starting point for canoe trips. The initial kilometre features quite a few side-trails and path junctions. The first is a left turn just inside the woods that sends you toward Channel Lake. Moving past that, you quickly

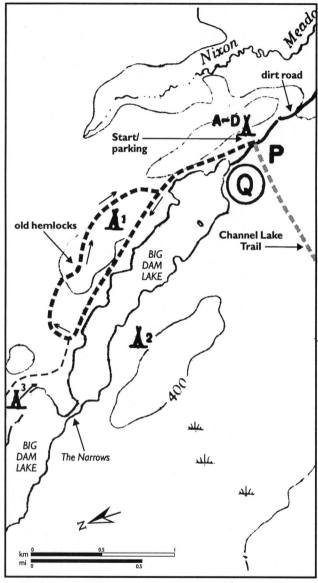

Hemlocks and Hardwoods

come to the intersection with the canoe portage trail. Keep to your right again, heading uphill. Following this, there are the connecting paths to campsites A-D, again all on your left.

The last junction in this series involves campsite #1, the inland path and the lakeshore route. I normally follow the lakeshore route—this path offers an easy stroll with the lake always in sight on your left—and save the hemlock stand for near the end. If you are in a hurry to see the big trees, you should turn right instead and follow the inland path.

The woods at first are the hardwoods of the trail's name. Large-toothed aspen, red maple, red oak, and white birch are common. After about 2 km (1.25 mi) the trees begin to change, with the hardwoods giving way to mixed spruce, hemlock, and pine. Within another kilometre, you will come to a well-signed junction. There should be no confusion: you want to turn right and head inland. Turning left sends you toward the backcountry, probably a longer trip than you intended.

The inland trail goes east for only a short distance before it turns another 90° and heads back in the direction you started from. The terrain ahead of you contrasts dramatically with the towering forest around it. A lengthy boardwalk crosses an open, swampy area of cinnamon ferns growing under black spruce. Suddenly you are transported into a completely different world. The low scrubs give way, and the leafy ceiling rises higher and higher. You are inside a massive arboreal cathedral, the huge trunks of the hemlocks the columns supporting the dome of the canopy far overhead.

Very little light penetrates here, giving an impression of perpetual twilight, and not much else can thrive in the thick carpet of decaying hemlock needles, so there are virtually no other plants on the forest floor. Only where one of the trees has been felled, admitting a shaft of

Kejimkujik

Campsite #38, near Poison Ivy Falls, Kejimkujik.
MICHAEL HAYNES

light, does new growth appear, either red spruce or hemlock saplings. Here are some of the painfully few remnants of the Acadian forest that many believe covered the New World of the first European explorers. I am always humbled in the presence of these magnificent giants.

If you have time, stop and spend a few quiet moments. Because of the popularity of this hike, such repose may not be possible during the busy summer season, but the spring and fall offer many low-use days. Few people are unaffected by these ancient guardians of the past.

Once past the hemlocks of Hardwoods and Hemlocks, you are just over half-way into hike, although to some the remainder may seem anticlimactic. In fact, you still pass through some attractive forest on your way back into the hardwoods you started with. At the next junction, turn left, and in less than a kilometre you are back to the Big Dam parking lot.

Cautionary Notes: There are many trail junctions in this area, and first-time visitors are often confused. Should you accidently take the Channel Lake Trail, you can tell that you are on the wrong path because you will not see any other junctions. If you walk for five minutes without seeing another side-trail or sign, turn back. Some people take the wrong turn at the junction at the far end of the Hemlocks and Hardwoods Trail. Campsite #3 is less than a kilometre along this path, on the lake shore. If you arrive here, turn around and retrace your steps immediately. Carefully check all trailhead signs.

This location is a Special Protected Area in the park. Be particularly careful not to cause damage.

Remember that this is tick country from April to July.

Further Information: An interpretive brochure called *The Forests,* particularly useful on this trail, is available at the information centre at the park entrance.

Liberty Lake: Big Dam — Campsite #43

Length: 18 km
  (11.25 mi) one way
Time: 6-7 hrs
Type: walking path,
  dirt road, former road
Rating: 4

Uses: hiking, cross-country
  skiing
Facilities: outhouses,
  campsites, firewood,
  garbage cans
Gov't Topo Map:
  Kejimkujik 21 A/6

Access: From the park entrance, drive 5 km (3 mi) to the turnoff for Jeremys Bay Campground. Turn right and follow the road over the Mersey River. On the far side the road divides, with a dirt road going right. Follow this

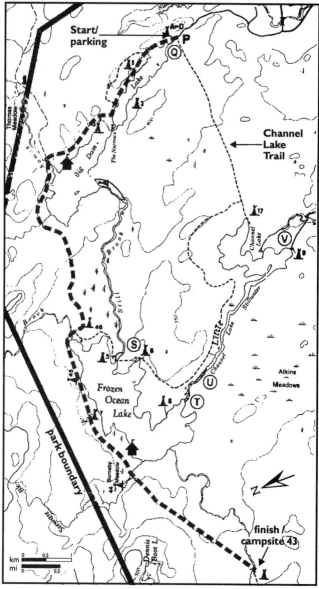

Liberty Lake: Big Dam — Campsite #43

5 km (3 mi) to its end, at Big Dam Lake. The trail starts on the far end of the parking lot.

Note that the Liberty Lake Trail is not a complete loop; Big Dam Lake is a considerable distance from the trail's end at Mersey River. The bridge over the Mersey is gated. From mid-June to Labour Day this gate is closed, and hikers must leave their cars in the lot at Mersey River. At other times of the year, however, the gate is open and cars can be driven as far as the Peskowesk lot, shortening the Liberty Lake hike by about 8.5 km (5.25 mi). You will have to use a two-car system, leaving one car at Big Dam and one at Mersey River, or be prepared to hitchhike back to your starting point.

Introduction: This trip can be undertaken either as the first part of the Liberty Lake Trail around the entire park, with several side-trip possibilities, or as an overnight campout. I have suggested camping at site #43, but sites #44 and #45 are common alternatives, especially if you plan to return along the same route the next day. The total loop trail is 59.5 km (37 mi).

Trail Description: At the beginning the trail offers several choices that you might find confusing. The first left, just inside the woods, is the path to Channel Lake; the second left takes you to the canoe launch. Then several paths connecting the main trail to campsites tempt the unwary, and about 500 m/yd into the walk is the junction to the Hemlocks and Hardwoods Trail. Read the trail markers carefully and follow the path beside Big Dam Lake.

After about a kilometre you can relax and begin to enjoy your surroundings. The trail is well maintained, comfortable to walk, and quite easy to follow. Big Dam Lake is on your left, usually visible through the mature hardwoods you start your walk in. Note that they are protecting their eventual successors, a thick undergrowth of white pine. Soon you move into spruce, pine, and hemlock stands, a hint of the magnificent old-growth hemlocks nearby. You are in one of the park's Special Preservation Areas, so declared because these trees are among the few remaining fragments of Nova Scotia's original forest, a tiny spot that was never logged.

Continue straight through the next junction; a right turn here takes you back to the parking lot, although if you can spare an hour, following this path for a short time also takes you into the middle of the area of 300-year-old hemlocks. Three kilometres (2 mi) from the start of the Liberty Lake Trail, you sight campsite #3 on your left. Like all the prepared sites, it has toilets.

Continue through these magnificent softwoods, but be prepared for the next junction, because it fools many. At 4.5 km (2.75 mi), the trail joins a dirt road. Left takes you to a warden's cabin and a dead end, so turn right. But watch carefully, because in a short distance a fairly small sign tells you to turn sharply left again. If you haven't found the bridge at Thomas Meadow Brook after 500 m/yd, you missed the turn.

You now have a former logging road for the next 5 km (3 mi), and it leads you toward Frozen Ocean Lake. A little rocky from time to time, and wet in one or two places, it is also wide enough for two to walk side by side. The road ends at another junction, your last today. Walk left for 50 m/yd and you will find campsite #46, and beyond that the Channel Lake Trail. Straight ahead is a clearing and a good view of the lake. Our route turns right, crosses over lively Torment Brook on a footbridge, and narrows into a path once again.

The trail follows the shoreline through beautiful hardwoods. Campsite #45, a popular bivouac for hikers and canoeists alike, marks the 11 km (6.75 mi) point of the day's walk. Beyond #45 the trail gets rockier and narrower, indication of the less frequent use of this path. It also strays more frequently from the water's edge. Past campsite #7, another lakeside site, the trail moves several hundred metres inland to avoid a huge swampy area. It also briefly follows an esker, a long narrow ridge of sand and boulders deposited by a glacier stream.

Campsite #44, at Stewart Brook, is well back from Frozen Ocean and just past the warden's cabin on the lake. From here, the trail moves inland onto higher, drier ground and into the park's Designated Wilderness Area. Comprising 41% of Kejimkujik, almost 163 km² (60 mi²), this area was deemed to need more federal regulatory protection of its natural environment. Only rudimentary facilities are provided within this zone, including foot trails and small dispersed campsites.

Although bracketed by stands of old growth hemlock at Dennis Boot Lake, and old growth red maple at the mouth of Inness Brook, the trail passes through fairly ordinary mixed woods for the remainder of the hike. Campsite #43, located just over the bridge at Inness Brook, appears suddenly. But it is in a beautiful location beside the brook, and after the day's hike it is certain to be a welcome sight.

Cautionary Notes: This trail will take you into the interior of Kejimkujik Park where there are few services and fewer people. Find out from park officials about animal sightings and ground conditions before you start.

An overnight stay in the woods requires different equipment from a day hike. Your load will be much heavier than usual, and you will tire more quickly. Schedule frequent short stops to permit recovery; I like a five to ten minute stop every hour.

Further Information: Anyone planning to hike the loop trail should purchase the *Backcountry Guide*. Not only

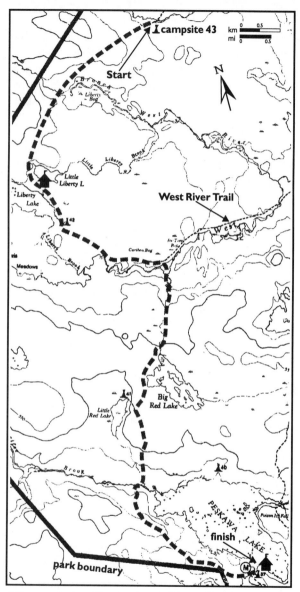

Liberty Lake: Campsite #43 — Campsite #37

is it a standard 1:50,000 topo map, but it shows the location of all trails, campsites, warden cabins, and other park services. Other park pamphlets, such as *You Are in Black Bear Country* and *Exploring the Backcountry*, will enhance your enjoyment of the whole Liberty Lake Trail.

Liberty Lake: Campsite #43 — Campsite #37

Length: 23 km
(14.5 mi) one way
Time: 9-10 hrs
Type: walking path,
former road, dirt road
Rating: 5

Uses: hiking, cross-country
skiing
Facilities: outhouses,
campsites, firewood,
garbage cans, water,
shelter with stove
Gov't Topo Map:
Kejimkujik 21 A/6

Access: To hike this trail you must have completed the Big Dam–Campsite #43 Trail first.

Introduction: This is the hike to do if you want solitude. Except for the busiest weekends in the summer, you can easily go the entire day without meeting another person. What this hike offers is an excellent example of inland Nova Scotia in an isolated wilderness setting but with all the comforts of a well-maintained national park. Who could ask for anything more?

Trail Description: Leaving westbound from Inness Brook, the path climbs for the next few kilometres. This will not create any undue hardship, however, even with nearly full packs. It takes nearly 3 km (2 mi) to climb about 35 m (15 ft). But do not expect any views. The entire loop system, except around the lakes, is under

Kejimkujik

thick foliage which severely limits the horizon. In most cases, a 200 m/yd skyline is the maximum. Make sure that you have prepared a safe supply of water for the day. There is no shortage of water, but you should not drink it untreated.

Moving up onto the higher, drier ground between the start and Northwest River also means moving into pine forest. These trees are not very old yet, because the park is still somewhat new and they have not been protected for long. As the years pass, they will have the opportunity to develop and may someday be like the trees the first loggers found: white pine 35 m (115 ft) high and .6 m (2 ft) in diameter. Come back again in 20 years; they will be more spectacular then.

The trail then descends toward the Northwest Branch West River. On the other side of the brook, you pass through more significant pine and spruce stands, but then you settle down into fairly ordinary mixed forest for the next several kilometres. The trail stays reasonably level through this section and gradually starts curving towards the south.

Your first clue that you are approaching Liberty Lake is a fairly messy boggy area. During the leafless seasons, you will detect Little Liberty Lake on your left; in the summer, you probably will not. After several hundred metres of wet feet, you'll see Liberty Lake on your right. The warden's cabin is easy to spot, and although it's locked it has a well and outhouses for general use. About a kilometre past that, at the south end of Liberty Lake, is campsite #42, approximately 7.5 km (4.5 mi) from your starting point.

Your next landmark is 4 km (2.5 mi) away, the trail junction with the West River Trail. The side trail along the West River is a trip you may wish to add to extend your stay in the park. Following it to campsite #22 and back will add 13 km (8 mi) and a full day to your itinerary. From the junction, the loop trail descends to cross the West River and follows Red Lake Brook. Fortunately there are sturdy bridges at every crossing; unfortunately, there is a large wet area before you cross the river that floods with every heavy rain. This must be the wettest spot in the park. I have never come out of there with dry feet.

The walk along Red Lake Brook is lovely. The brook has several cascades, and the trail climbs almost steeply up a rocky hillside toward Big Red Lake and a final crossing over the brook. The path becomes a former logging road, although not one in very good shape. Big Red Lake is visible on your left for most of the next kilometre, and about 500 m/yd beyond the lake you will find the junction to campsite #41 and Little Red Lake.

The next kilometre is fairly level walking, but the kilometre after that descends almost 50 m (165 ft) as you approach Peskawa Lake. If the weather is wet, expect this stretch to be a creek bed. A large bridge crosses Lucifee Brook, and about 200 m/yd beyond that the trail becomes a wide, dry dirt road used only by maintenance and emergency vehicles. Perhaps 5 km (3 mi) remain in your hike, but from now on it will be very easy walking. Once across Lucifee Brook you have also moved out of the Designated Wilderness Area of the park.

The trail actually comes within a few hundred metres of the Shelburne River. This is on your right side and outside the park, but it has been nominated a Canadian Heritage River and is definitely worth consideration if you enjoy canoeing.

Campsite #37, informally known as Mason's Cabin, will probably be a welcome sight. Located on Portage M between Peskawa and Pebbleloggitch lakes, it boasts a well, toilets, firewood, a new wood stove, indoor tables, and bunk frames. This is a popular camping area,

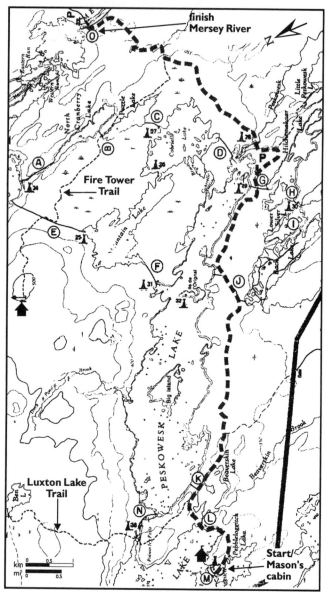

Liberty Lake: Campsite #37 — Mersey River

so make your reservations early in the year. It is the perfect spot to put up your feet, especially if the weather is at all cold or wet, and it concludes this day's excursion.

Cautionary Notes: On this section of trail, you are about as far away from everything as you can be in Nova Scotia. Do not be misled by the well-maintained trail and camping facilities into thinking that you can wander anywhere. Stay on the trail, both for safety and because of the sensitive environment.

This hike will require a full day to complete. I do not recommend it in late fall and early spring when fewer than 10 hours of daylight are available.

Note that this is tick country from April to July.

Liberty Lake: Campsite #37 — Mersey River

Length: 18.5 km
(11.5 mi) one way
Time: 6-7 hrs
Type: dirt road,
gravel road
Rating: 4

Uses: hiking, cross-country skiing
Facilities: outhouses, campsites, firewood, garbage cans, water, shelter with stove
Gov't Topo Map:
Kejimkujik 21 A/6

Access: To hike this trail you must first have completed both the other Liberty Lake Trail hikes, Big Dam–Campsite #43 and Campsite #43–Campsite #37.

Introduction: Canoeists love this area of the park. Both the Mersey and the Shelburne river networks converge here, and they are connected by a series of closely spaced lakes. Canoeing, far more than hiking, is the principal recreation activity in Kejimkujik National Park. In fact, more than half of the backcountry sites are accessible only by water (or bushwhacking), and eight of those are on islands.

The trail from campsite #37 (Mason's Cabin) to the Mersey River provides some of the easiest walking in the park and it is ideal for newer hikers. Alternative campsite are available, so shorter efforts can be planned. New campers may wish to try this walk in reverse, from the Mersey River to Mason's Cabin, for their first overnight experience. Numerous side-trips, such as the Fire Tower and Luxton Lake trails, provide opportunities to extend the expedition to several days while remaining in the same general area.

Trail Description: If you spent the night at Mason's Cabin, you may not be in a hurry to leave, especially if the weather is miserable. On a cool, late fall day, with the wood stove radiating comfort and the smells of breakfast filling the air, I have refused to venture out into the wind and drizzle without an argument.

If you have time before you start, venture down to Pebbleloggitch Lake and stick your arm in the water. It will seem to disappear into the murky liquid. Much of the water that flows into this lake passes through low-lying bogs, where it picks up dissolved organic substances including tannins. It is stained dark brown, almost the colour of tea. Many of the lakes and streams of the park are so affected, Pebbleloggitch most of all.

Fortunately, the trees on the way to Mersey River have grown up along the dirt road that is your route, and you will enjoy a leafy canopy overhead most of the time. At 1.5 km (1 mi) into the walk, Portage L, connecting Peskawa and Beaverskin lakes, crosses the trail. Beaverskin is a completely clear lake, being spring fed. The junction with the Luxton Lake Trail is 500 m/yd further, and a few hundred metres beyond that Portage K connects Beaverskin Lake with Peskowesk. The lakes are so numerous that you often can see them on both sides of the trail.

From the end of Beaverskin Lake to the gate at the Peskowesk parking lot, the trail is fairly unremarkable. It runs several hundred metres back from the lake and out of sight of the water. Portage J, connecting Peskowesk with Back Lake, provides a nice diversion, and after that the road moves closer to the lake edge. Portage G, which permits access to Hilchemakaar Lake, gives warning of the upcoming Peskowesk parking lot. I have to pass along a small anomaly: the *Backcountry Guide* published by Kejimkujik Park says the distance between campsite #37 and the Peskowesk parking lot is 8 km (5 mi). This is a printing error, and the actual distance is 11 km (7 mi).

Once past the gate, the road becomes gravel surfaced and remains so for the remainder of your walk. Within a kilometre you reach the junction of the Little Peskowesk Lake Trail. Those interested in a longish side-trip that goes outside the park can use this to connect to a road that will lead them eventually to Lake Rossignol, the largest body of fresh water in mainland Nova Scotia. Continuing on the road another kilometre, you reach Peskowesk Brook and campsite #28. The remainder of the hike is a pleasant walk through a mostly hardwood forest. With the exception of the junction with the Fire Tower Trail, 3.5 km (2.25 mi) from Peskowesk Brook, and the bridge at Square Camp Brook, there is little variation. But I have often seen hawks and owls patrolling this road, cruising beneath the trees in search of dinner. In its last kilometre, the trail climbs to the top of a drumlin-like ridge that parallels the Mersey River. When it starts to turn to the right and descend, you have only about 200 m/yd remaining.

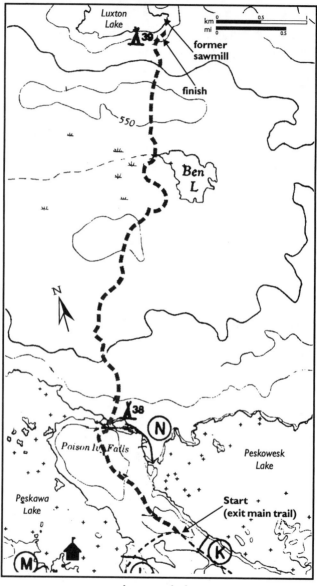

Luxton Lake

Cautionary Notes: You pass through several environmentally sensitive areas containing rare plants. Stay on the trail, and pick nothing. And do not forget that registration for all overnight trips is mandatory.

Note that Kejimkujik National Park is tick country from April to July.

Luxton Lake

Length: 14 km
  (8.75 mi) return
Time: 4-5 hrs
Type: former road,
  walking path
Rating: 3

Uses: hiking, cross-country
  skiing
Facilities: outhouse,
  campsite, firewood
Gov't Topo Map:
  Kejimkujik 21 A/6

Access: Luxton Lake is a side trip from the Liberty Lake Loop Trail. Otherwise, it can be reached from the Mersey River parking lot, adding 16.5 km (10.5 mi) each way (47 km [29.5 mi] total trip), or from the Peskowesk parking lot, adding 7.5 km (4.75 mi) each way (29 km [18 mi] total trip).

Introduction: When the Europeans first landed in Nova Scotia, it was to establish bases to dry the fish they caught off the coast. Later generations pursued beaver and other fur-bearing animals. Later still, settlers interested in agriculture cleared lands near the coast and in the fertile valleys. However, none of these had a larger influence on the face of the land than the loggers.

It is difficult to visualize what the woods of those days must have been like, because so few fragments remain. But we do know that for more than a hundred years the lumber of this region flowed to Europe in an unending stream, and that the interiors of all the Maritime provinces were gutted. Indeed, despite the population increase from the late 1800s, more than half the land in Nova Scotia that was clear then has grown back.

Queens County once supported nearly 60 sawmills, and evidence of their activity can be found in some of the place-names in Kejimkujik: Big Dam Lake and Mill Falls, for example. Luxton Lake features another artifact from that period, the remains of one of these sawmills. Actually, the mill still exists, having been moved when the park was established, and it operates on Mill Lake outside the park boundaries near the village of Northfield. The Luxton family still operates the sawmill, and locally Mill Lake is often referred to by their name: Luxton.

Trail Description: A sign indicates the turnoff onto the former logging road to Luxton Lake. This trail is in somewhat worse shape than the Peskowesk-Pebbleloggitch road, but it remains quite distinct. The first 2 km (1.25 mi) pass through some beautiful white birch, first climbing, then descending the hill that separates three lakes from each other. Arrive at campsite #38, located at Portage N connecting Peskowesk and Peskawa lakes near Poison Ivy Falls. The falls are so named with good reason, and this is one of the few areas in Kejimkujik where you are likely to find this justly feared plant. However, this is also one of the most attractive camping locations in the park and well worth a visit if you want to stay a night. A stream runs between tent-pads, and a sturdy, wide bridge connects its banks.

An interesting option is to follow Portage N downstream (to your right) on the north side of the small pond below #38. Midway, almost a kilometre along, near the canoe rest on the banks of Peskowesk Lake, lies a massive granite boulder left by glacier action. Ca-

Channel Lake Trail. MICHAEL HAYNES

noeists, on the other hand, may wish to stretch their legs with a jaunt from #38 to Luxton Lake. They may anticipate a 10-km (6.25-mi) four-hour round trip.

Across the brook, the Luxton Lake trail narrows once again, becoming almost a footpath. It also begins to climb: 50 m (165 ft) within the next kilometre. Every little rise seems to be capped with a jumble of boulders. Almost hidden by summer foliage, huge rocks loom on either side of the trail. You are now in the park's Designated Wilderness Area, 163 km² (60 mi²) of natural habitat within the most protected portion of the national park.

Nearly 3 km (2 mi) past campsite #38, the path descends toward tiny Ben Lake. The trail crosses the outflow, but there is a good plank bridge. Even so, expect boggy patches in this area. The path narrows further, and branches on both sides brush against you. The final 1.5 km (1 mi) only vaguely resembles a road,

Kejimkujik

although a well-defined path remains. This is also the nicest walking of the hike, through some of the prettiest woods. You face another brief climb immediately after the bridge, then the trail descends rapidly toward Luxton Lake.

Watch carefully for the turnoff to campsite #39. It is marked with flagging tape, but it is a new path built at right angles to the old road and is easy to miss. You probably will have already spotted the lake, however, so you know that the campsite must be nearby. This path ends on the shore of Luxton Lake in the middle of the tenting area.

Continuing past the entrance to #39 leads you to the ruins of the sawmill. Large piles of sawdust and the remains of a few structures cover a substantial area and create an artificial beach-like scene at the water's edge. Standing there looking at the tall pines bordering parts of the lake, it is easy to understand why the loggers were so active in this portion of the province. Unless you are camping overnight, it is time to retrace your steps back to the main loop trail.

Cautionary Notes: Watch out for old nails in the sawmill ruins. The wood of the structures is also quite rotten. Be cautious around it.

This trail is an "add-on" to the main loop system. Remember to reserve your campsite, or you may face a nasty surprise when it is time to stop for the night. Registration for all overnight trips is mandatory.

Future Plans: Park plans include a loop trail around Peskowesk Lake whenever budgets permit.

Peter Point

Length: 3 km
  (2 mi) return
Time: 1-1.5 hr
Type: former road
Rating: 1

Uses: hiking, cross-country
  skiing
Facilities: garbage cans,
  picnic table
Gov't Topo Map:
  Kejimkujik 21 A/6

Access: Follow the paved road from the park entrance to its end at Grafton Lake, approximately 11 km (7 mi). Follow the gravel road continuation for another 2 km (1.25 mi). The parking area and trailhead is on your right, well-signed. The gate may be closed at Grafton Lake in winter, adding 4 km (2.5 mi) to the return trip.

Introduction: Once the site of a cabin, Peter Point, a narrow peninsula 1.5 km (1 mi) long and barely 500 m/yd wide, juts out of the southern shore of Kejimkujik Lake. The trail is the remains of the road formerly connecting the camp with the outside world, and it provides easy walking for two side by side on comfortable, dry footing. Running up the middle of the point, the path offers access to the Snake Lake Trail, a gorgeous hemlock stand, and a wonderful panorama of Kejimkujik Lake. At the very tip, a small sandy beach invites sunbathing and swimming.

Rare coastal plain plants such as bartonia and panic grass may be found in an excellent habitat between the base of Peter Point and Snake Lake, and Peale Island, just off Peter Point, contains one of the park's few stands of climax sugar maple and white ash. The rare (but harmless) ribbon snake has also been spotted on Peale Island and at Snake Lake.

The walk to Peter Point is suitable for all age groups and all fitness levels. Campers at Jeremys Bay can easily

Kejimkujik

Peter Point

bicycle to the trailhead, and the gentle hills and wide trail make it suitable for novices. Adding the 3-km (2-mi) Snake Lake Trail permits more ambitious hikers to double the distance of their walk.

Trail Description: A single garbage can and picnic table stand on the fringes of the parking lot, and signs indicate hiking (but no bicycling) on the trail. A large rock is positioned to prevent vehicular travel down the former road. The trail starts rolling up and down a series of little hills through mixed woods, although there is quite a bit of young pine lining the path. Only a few hundred metres after the start, the Snake Lake Trail branches left. A sign indicates the direction for each route.

As you continue up a small rise, Kejimkujik Lake becomes visible on your left. In summer, low water exposes a stony beach, sometimes extending out 5 m/yd from the vegetation. But in spring the lake laps up almost against the trail, and there's a swamp on your right. For a small stretch, the dry ground extends only the width of the trail. Past the swamp, you enter an area of hemlocks. In summer, you'll find it much cooler under the hemlocks' twilight shelter than walking down the open trail.

The path descends gently to a narrow neck with the lake on both sides. Just past this point, the only modest climb of the hike begins, a 15-20-m/yd rise to the top of a drumlin. After 250 m/yd uphill, the path begins to descend again to the end of the hike. The trees on top of the hill are mostly old-growth hardwoods: sugar maple, yellow birch, and beech. Young hemlocks border the edges of the path on the downslope, growing where the sunlight comes in.

The headland is at the bottom of the hill and is a cleared space underneath mature hemlocks. Peale Island dominates the centre of your view, but you can

Kejimkujik

clearly see the public beach at Merrymakedge on your right and as far up as Bear Island and the mouth of the Mersey River. On your left the view includes Cape Split, Norway Island, and the Mersey River where it exits Kejimkujik Lake. In the summer this can be a delightful spot, although sometimes windy and cool. Canoeists are frequently visible on different parts of the lake. The shallow, warm water invites swimming (remember that there is no help nearby), and the tiny sand beach encourages dawdling. Sunsets here can be spectacular, and the broad path makes dusk walks safer than on many other trails. The return route is identical; retrace the path 1.5 km (1 mi) back to the parking lot.

Cautionary Notes: The area around Peter Point is a breeding ground for the rare Blanding's turtle as well as the painted and snapping turtles. In late June, females emerge from the water to lay their eggs in sand or gravel soil. Drive especially carefully from the vicinity of Grafton Lake. Should you see a turtle on land digging or laying her eggs, watch from a distance but please do not disturb her. Do not attempt to return her to water.

Note that this is tick country from April to July.

Further Information: One of the park's interpretive brochures, *The Turtles*, is particularly useful when walking on this trail.

Seaside Adjunct

Length: 12 km
  (7.5 mi) return
Time: 4 hrs
Type: former road, beach
Rating: 3

Uses: hiking
Facilities: garbage cans
Gov't Topo Map:
  Port Mouton 20 P/15

Access: From Liverpool, drive 25 km (15.5 mi) on Highway 103 toward Yarmouth. At Port Joli, turn left toward St. Catherines River, and drive 7 km (4.5 mi) on the dirt road to the parking area on your left. The trail starts at the far end of the lot.

Introduction: The Seaside Adjunct of Kejimkujik National Park, located about 100 km (62 mi) from the inland section, officially opened in 1988. The 22 km² (13.75 mi²) adjunct is an undeveloped headland separating Port Mouton Bay and Port Joli Bay. Along with Thomas Raddall Provincial Park, the Port Joli Migratory Bird Sanctuary, Summerville Beach, Port L'Hebert Pocket Wilderness, and the nearby Sable River and Liverpool rail trails, it belongs to a concentration of recreation and conservation properties rare in Nova Scotia.

Visitor services are few; there is no water, washroom or outhouse, no picnic tables or prepared picnic sites; and this location has not been extensively promoted both for this reason and to ensure its protection. However, there has been a steady increase in use since the adjunct's opening and awareness of its beauty has become fairly widespread among nature hikers.

Expect to see dozens of harbour seals lying on the rocks off St. Catherines River Beach, and be prepared to notice signs of deer, snowshoe hare, fox, raccoon, and even black bear. This is a tremendous location for

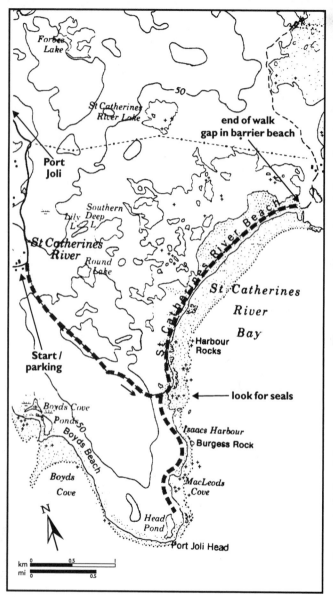

Seaside Adjunct

birdwatching, and as many as 10 pairs of the endangered piping plover nest on the sandy beaches here. Signs of former human habitation are also common: stone fences, rock foundations, old clearings, and cattle trails.

The best time to visit is September through November, although anyone who has never walked an ocean beach during a wild winter day is missing an exceptional, if somewhat untamed, experience.

Trail Description: From the parking area at St. Catherines River, the trail follows the old cart track that connected the former homesteads on Port Joli Head with the rest of the community. Starting out in a mixed forest heavy with oak and maple, the rough track soon passes into barrens dominated by spruce and balsam fir. Around frequent wet areas, dense stands of alder provide hiding places for inquisitive common yellowthroats and other warblers. Like much of the Atlantic coastal fringe, the adjunct is a granite finger, carved and shaped by glacier action, thrusting into the ocean and surrounded on three sides by the water. Although the view is superb, with white sand beaches, lagoons, and fierce waves breaking over exposed granite, the conditions at the point are far more rugged than they are just a few miles inland. Fog, high winds, and salt-laden spray kill all but a few hardy plants, so the terrain takes on a tundra-like aspect.

The trail continues down the middle of Port Joli Head, staying near the highest elevations. On clear days you can see across the bay to Sandy Bay, part of Thomas Raddall Provincial Park. Cranberry and bog rosemary become more common as you approach the ocean, and frequent bridges help you cross the wettest areas. After nearly 3 km (2 mi), the old track arrives in

Kejimkujik

tiny Isaacs Harbour, very close to the location of a former house-site and now home to dozens of harbour seals.

From here, two options are available. Turning right and following the coastline leads, after 2 km (1.25 miles), to Port Joli Head. On this route you'll find another abandoned field and house-site and a small brackish headpond at the very tip of the point. Turning left, following the more distinct path, leads along the rocky shore for about 1 km (.5 mi) to St. Catherines River Beach. Watch closely for "Area Closed" signs, and please respect them when present. Anywhere along here is perfect for a snack and rest, and even though the beach may look inviting, during plover nesting season it must be avoided.

Should you be able to continue along the beach, you will enjoy another 2 km (1.25 mi) of effortless walking until you reach the narrow, deep channel that separates the halves of the adjunct. There is no connecting bridge or path, so you must return to the parking lot along the same route. Given the beautiful setting, I doubt this will be any cause for complaint.

Cautionary Notes: St. Catherines River Beach is a nesting site for the endangered piping plover. Perhaps only 2300 pairs of the tiny shore birds still survive in North America, and only 50 pairs visit Nova Scotia. Laying their eggs on the flat beach just above the high water line, they are at risk from beachcombers and sunbathers. Between May and August, any disturbance threatens their breeding success. Should you see park signs warning of nests, do not cross the beach. Plovers are so well camouflaged that their nests can rarely be detected before they're destroyed. Never take a dog onto the beach during these months; dogs will destroy both eggs and young.

Future Plans: The present access to the Seaside Adjunct will be supplemented by access from the St. Catherines River side via Southwest Port Mouton. Plans to build a parking lot and improved trail there await further financing.

Camping has been prohibited for the foreseeable future.

View of Black Point from Meat Cove Campground.
MICHAEL HAYNES

AFTERWORD

Trails change over time. I have described the hikes as I found them in 1994 and early 1995, but even before I finished writing I heard of alterations, some substantial, to seven of the trails included in this book. Expect this to occur more frequently to old roads and hikes outside maintained parks. Do not be discouraged if you find things a little different than described. Exploration can be half the fun, as long as you know how to use your map and compass.

The spectacular natural beauty of Nova Scotia is a big attraction for urban visitors, and nature tourism is a growth industry. However, unless more hiking opportunities are created, the current network may prove insufficient to handle the demand. This has happened in other parts of Canada: the popular West Coast Trail on Vancouver Island is booked more than a year ahead. Kejimkujik already requires reservations early in the season to ensure a campsite on a holiday weekend, and one drizzly October day I encountered 49 people on a well-known route near Halifax.

I hope you enjoy the hikes found in these pages, and I hope that they encourage you to add more outdoor activities to your life. If you have a favourite path you think should be included in the 8th edition of *Hiking Trails of Nova Scotia*, or if you're curious about one of the trails I have described, contact me through the

Nova Scotia Trails Federation, PO Box 3010 South, 5516 Spring Garden Road (4th Floor), Halifax NS B3J 3G6.

Of course, we might meet out in the woods.

Michael Haynes

Baby moose crossing the road at Benjie's Lake, Cape Breton Highands National Park. MICHAEL HAYNES

USEFUL ADDRESSES

Annapolis County Recreation Department
PO Box 100, Annapolis Royal NS B0S 1A0   (902) 532-2331

Bowater Mersey Paper Co. Ltd.
PO Box 1150, Liverpool NS B0T 1K0   (902) 354-3411

Canadian Wildlife Service
PO Box 1590, Sackville NB E0A 3C0   (506) 364-5039

Cape Breton County Recreation Department
865 Grand Lake Road, Sydney NS B1P 6W2
(902) 563-2700

Cape Breton Highlands National Park
Ingonish Beach NS B0C 1L0
(902) 285-2691 (winter), (902) 285-2535 (summer)

Colchester YMCA, c/o Ken Cavanaugh
752 Prince Street, Truro NS B2N 1G9   (902) 895-2871

Extension Services, Department of Natural Resources
PO Box 698, Halifax NS B3J 2T9   (902) 424-4321

Friends of McNabs Island
21 Willowdale Drive, Dartmouth NS B2V 1B9
(902) 465-8708 (fax)

Hostelling International–Nova Scotia
PO Box 3010 South, Halifax NS B3J 3G6
(902) 425-5450 ext. 324

Inverness County Tourism Dept.
PO Box 179, Port Hood NS B0E 2W0   (902) 787-2274

Kejimkujik National Park
PO Box 236, Maitland Bridge NS B0T 1N0   (902) 682-2772

Les Amis du Plein Air
PO Box 472, Cheticamp NS B0E 1H0   (902) 224-2306

Musquodoboit Railway Museum
PO Box 303, Musquodoboit Harbour NS B0J 2L0
(902) 889-2689

Musquodoboit Valley Forest Nursery & Education Complex
PO Box 100, Middle Musquodoboit NS B0N 1X0
(902) 384-3420

Nature Conservancy of Canada
PO Box 8505, Halifax NS B3K 5M2   (902) 454-2049

Nordic Ski Nova Scotia
PO Box 3010 South, Halifax NS B3J 3G6
(902) 425-5450 ext. 316

Nova Scotia Government Bookstore
1700 Granville Street, PO Box 637, Halifax NS B3J 2T3
(902) 424-7580

Nova Scotia Museum of Natural History
1747 Summer Street, Halifax NS B3H 3A6
(902) 424-7353

Nova Scotia Trails Federation
PO Box 3010 South, Halifax NS B3J 3G6
(902) 425-5450 ext. 325

Parks and Recreation Division
Department of Natural Resources
R.R.#1, Belmont NS B0M 1C0   (902) 662-3030

Queens County Recreation Department
PO Box 1264, Liverpool NS B0T 1K0   (902) 354-5741

Richmond County Recreation Department
PO Box 120, Arichat NS B0E 1A0   (902) 226-2400

Route 223 Forest Management Co-op
R.R.#2, Box 17, Iona NS B0A 1L0   (902) 725-2061

Yarmouth Recreation Department
PO Box 152, Yarmouth NS B5A 4B2   (902) 742-8868

SELECTED BIBLIOGRAPHY

The popular field guides to birds, plants, animals, rocks and minerals, and geology of eastern North America will provide many people with sufficient knowledge about their surroundings. However, a growing body of excellent local publications covering all of these areas substantially enriches the outdoors experience for both the Sunday stroller and the more serious hiker.

The following list includes some of the texts I used as research for my hikes, but it omits all of the brochures, management plans, and other similar documents that were invaluable in my studies. In addition to the written materials, I enjoyed many conversations that proved as helpful as any book. I acknowledge my debt to them all.

Anon. *Canoe Routes of Nova Scotia*. Halifax: Canoe Nova Scotia and Camping Association of Nova Scotia, 1983.

Anon. *Fishing Guide to Nova Scotia*. Halifax: Nova Scotia Departments of Fisheries, Tourism, and Lands and Forests, 1987.

Anon. *Hiking Trails of Nova Scotia: 6th Edition*. Halifax: Hostelling International - Nova Scotia, 1984

Anon. *Notes on Nova Scotia Wildlife*. Truro: Nova Scotia Department of Lands and Forests, 1980.

Anon. *Nova Scotia Nordic Ski Trails*. Halifax: Nordic Ski Nova Scotia, 1993.

Anon. *Where to Find the Birds in Nova Scotia*. Halifax: Nova Scotia Bird Society, 1976.

Beardmore, R.M. *Atlantic Canada's Natural Heritage Areas*. Ottawa: Canadian Government Publishing Centre, 1985.

Davis, D.S. *Natural History Map of Nova Scotia*. Halifax: Nova Scotia Museum and Department of Education, 1987.

Donahoe, H.V. and Grantham, R.G. *Nova Scotia Geology Map*. Halifax: Land Registration and Information Service and Department of Supply and Services, 1994.

Erskine, J. *In Forest and Field*. Halifax: Nova Scotia Museum, 1971.

Gilhen, J. *Amphibians and Reptiles of Nova Scotia*. Halifax: Nova Scotia Museum, 1971.

Lawley, David. *A Nature and Hiking Guide to Cape Breton's Cabot Trail*. Halifax: Nimbus, 1994.

Nova Scotia Department of Natural Resources. *A Map of the Province of Nova Scotia, Canada*. Halifax: Formac, 1992.

O'Neil, Pat. *Explore Cape Breton: A Field Guide to Adventure*. Halifax: Nimbus, 1994.

Public Archives of Nova Scotia. *Place-Names and Places of Nova Scotia*. Belleville: Mika, 1974.

Roland, A.E. *Geological Background and Physiography of Nova Scotia*. Halifax: Nova Scotian Institute of Science, 1982.

Roland, A.E. and E.C. Smith. *Flora of Nova Scotia*. Halifax: Nova Scotia Museum, 1969.

Roland, A.E. and A.R. Olsen, *Spring Wildflowers*. Halifax: Nimbus and Nova Scotia Museum, 1993.

Saunders, G.L. *Trees of Nova Scotia*. Halifax: Nova Scotia Department of Lands and Forests, 1970.

Simmons, M., D. Davis, L. Griffiths and A. Muecke. *Natural History of Nova Scotia*. 2 vol. Halifax: Nova Scotia Department of Education and Nova Scotia Department of Lands and Forests, 1989.

Tufts, R. *Birds of Nova Scotia*. 3rd edition. Halifax: Nimbus and Nova Scotia Museum, 1986.

INDEX

A

Abrahams Lake   *128*, 129-131, 133
Advocate Bay   58
Advocate Harbour   57, 59
Amherst   31, 69
Amherst Point   31
Amherst Point Migratory Bird Sanctuary   *30*, 31-33, 35
Annapolis Royal   87, 119
Annapolis Valley   115
Anse aux Cannes   181
Antigonish   35
Aspotogan Peninsula   95
Aspy   *226, 227-229*, 231
Aspy Bay   253
Aspy River   228

B

Back Lake   301
Baddeck   205, 215
Baddeck River   215
Baddeck River, North Branch   216, 217
Baleine   179, 181
Baleine Harbour   180
Baleine Head   180
Bar Point   181
Barren Lake   166
Bateston   179
Bay St. Lawrence   201
Bayer Lake   149

Beachwalk Trail   170; *see also* Taylor Head Provincial Park
Bear Cove   190
Bear Hill   203
Bear Island   310
Bear Trap Trail   199; *see also* Mabou Highlands
Beaver Mountain Provincial Park   *34, 35-37*
Beaverskin Lake   300-301
Beinn Bhiorach Trail   198; *see also* Mabou Highlands
Belfry Gut   190
Ben Lake   305
Bennetts Pond   180
Beulach Ban Falls   227
Big Brook   198
Big Dam Lake   273, 275, 285, 291
Big Five Bridge Lake   154
Big Indian Lake   153
Big Red Lake   297
Black Brook   235, 236, 238
Black Brook Beach   236
Blackberry Lake   162
Blandford   95
Blomidon Provincial Park   *78, 79-82*

Bob Bluff Trail 171-172;
  see also Taylor Head Provin-
  cial Park
Bohaker Brook 90
Bohaker Falls 90
Bohaker Loop 89, 91; see
  also Delaps Cove
Borden Brook 80
Borden Brook Trail 79
Bottom's Up 194; see also
  Highland Hill
Bras d'Or Lake 219
Broad River 113
Browns Mountain 39
Bull Beach Trail 171-172;
  see also Taylor Head Provin-
  cial Park
Bull Hill 189

C
Cabot Trail 183, 201, 205,
  227, 231, 235, 238, 251, 257
Cains Mountain 194
Camerons Brook 36, 37
Canning 79
Canso 161, 195
Canso Barrens 161
Canso Causeway 209, 219
Cape Breton 178, 179-181,
  183
Cape Breton Highlands Na-
  tional Park 183, 223-268
Cape Canso 161
Cape Chignecto 61, 81
Cape Chignecto Provincial
  Park 61
Cape d'Or 59
Cape Gabarus 190
Cape North 201, 227,
  251, 254
Cape Smokey 183, 185,
  250, 258, 259

Cape Smokey Provincial
  Park 182, 183-186
Cape Split 81, 310
Cape St. Lawrence 202-
  203
Capstick 201
Caribou Island 55
Catalone 179
Chance's Pool 267
Channel Lake 273-274,
  291
Channel Lake Stillwater
  274
Channel Lake Trail 272,
  273-275, 277, 285, 292
Charlies Brook 91
Charlies Cove 90
Charlies Loop 90-91
Chebogue Meadows Inter-
  pretive Trail 83, 84,
  85-87
Chebogue River 83,
  85, 86
Chebucto Head 134
Chedabucto Bay 162
Chester 94, 95
Cheticamp 261
Cheticamp River 265-,
  268
Chignecto Bay 58
Clyburn Brook 231,
  233, 235, 249
Clyburn Valley 230,
  231-233, 235, 249
Coastal Trail 234, 235-
  238
Cobequid Mountains
  49, 65
Codline Cove 136
Cole Harbour 161
Convict Point 181
Coote Cove 157

Corberrie   83
Corney Brook   239, *240*, 241-242
Corney Brook, South Branch   241
Cover, The   33
Crowbar Lake   167
Crystal Crescent Beach   155
Cutie's Hollow   *38*, 39-41, 43

D
Daisleys Lake   254, 255
Dartmouth   115, 147, 165
Deep Cove   95, 158
Delaps Cove   87, *88*, 89-93
Dennis Boot Lake   293
Digby Gut   90
Diligent River   65
Diligent River, North Branch   65, 67
Dingwall   251
Douglas Brook   113
Duck Reef   135
Duncans Cove   132, 133-136
Duncans Reef   135

E
East Pennant   159
East River   44
Eastern Cove   135
Eastern Head   135
Eastern Passage   139
Economy Mountain   43, 46
Economy Mountain Trail   46; *see also* Five Islands Provincial Park
Effies Brook   254
Elmsdale   143
Estuary Trail   44, 47; *see also* Five Islands Provincial Park

F
Falls Brook   216, 217
Falls Trail   216; *see also* Usige Ban Falls
Faribault Creek   267
Fern and Moss Trail   145; *see also* Middle Musquodoboit
Finlay Point   197
Fire Tower   *276*, 277-280, 300, 301
First Cow Lake   162
Fishing Cove   243, *244*, 245-247, 263
Fishing Cove Creek   245
Five Bridge Runs   154
Five Islands   43
Five Islands Provincial Park   *42*, 43-47, 80
Five Mile Pond   154
Five Rivers   99
Forks Baddeck   213
Fort Ives   139
Fort McNab   140
Fortress Louisbourg   180
Franey Mountain   247, *248*, 249-251

G
Glasgow Lakes   251, *252*, 253-255
Gold Mines   280-281, *282*, 283-284
Graves Island Provincial Park   *92*, 93-97
Green Island   190
Gulf of St. Lawrence   261, 262
Gull Cove   187, *188*, 189-191
Gully Lake   47, *48*, 49-51

Gully Lake Brook   50
Guysborough   161

H

Hadleyville Shore   162
Halfway Brook   235, 238
Halifax   93, 115, 133, 137,
  151, 155
Halifax Harbour   136, 140,
  157, 159
Hangman's Beach   140
Hardwood Trail   145; see
  also Middle Musquodoboit
Hardwood Trail   122; see
  also Upper Clements Pro-
  vincial Wildlife Park
Hardys Point   189
Harris Beach   189
Harris Lake   189
Headland Trail   170; see
  also Taylor Head Provincial
  Park
Hemlocks and Hardwoods
  285, 286, 287-289, 291;
  see also Channel Lake Trail
Highland Hill   191, 192,
  193-195
Hilchemakaar Lake   301
Hummocky Point   180
Hunts Point   99, 113

I

Ile aux Cannes   181
Indian Springs Brook   80
Ingonish Bay   257
Ingonish Beach   183, 186,
  258
Ingonish Centre   247
Ingonish Island   259
Inness Brook   293, 295
Isle Haute   59, 81
Ives Cove   139

J

Jack Pine Trail   236,
  237, 238; see also
  Coastal Trail
James River   39
Jamesville West   191
Jamieson Brook   161
Jamieson Lake   162
Jeremys Bay   307
Jigging Cove   236, 237
Jigging Cove trails   237;
  see aslo Coastal Trail
John MacLeods Brook
  208
Joudrey Trail   80; see
  also Blomidon Provin-
  cial Park
Jumping Brook   262
Juniper Brook   49

K

Kejimkujik Lake   279,
  307, 310
Kejimkujik National Park
  269-315
Kejimkujik Seaside Ad-
  junct   111, 311, 312,
  313-315
Kelly Meadow   149
Kelpy Cove   181
Kemptown   47
Keppoch Mountain   35
Ketch Harbour   134, 136
Ketch Head   134
Klondike Mountain   233

L

La Prairie   267
Lac à Pic   103
Lake Martha (see
  Uniacke Lake)
Lake Rossignol   301

Larrys River   161
Laytons Lake   32
Lewis Lake   154
Liberty Lake   275, 296, 303
Liberty Lake: Big Dam —
   Campsite #43   289, 290,
   291-293, 295
Liberty Lake: Campsite
   #37— Mersey River   298,
   299-301, 303
Liberty Lake: Campsite #43
   — Campsite #37   294,
   295-297, 299
Liberty Lake Loop Trail
   278, 285, 303
Little Indian Lake   153
Little Liberty Lake   296
Little Narrows   191
Little Peskowesk Lake Trail
   301
Little Red Lake   297
Little Southwest Brook   228
Liverpool   97, 98, 99, 105,
   107, 109, 111, 311
Liverpool Rail Trail   96, 97-
   99, 101, 111, 311
Long Lake   254
Look-off Trail   81; see also
   Blomidon Provincial Park
Lorne   129
Louisbourg   179
Louisbourg National Historic
   Site   187
Lowell Point   189
Lower Economy   43
Lower Prospect   159
Lowland Brook   203
Lowland Cove   203, 204
Lowland Point   203
Lucifee Brook   297
Luxton Lake   300, 302, 303-
   306

M
Mabou   195
Mabou Harbour   195
Mabou Highlands   195,
   196, 197-199, 201
Mabou Mines   197
MacDonalds Glen   195,
   197
MacDougalls Lake   250
MacIntosh Lake   50
MacIsaacs Glen Brook
   199
Mackerel Cove   157
MacKinnons Brook   198
MacKinnons Little Brook
   194
Mad Rock   157
Magdalen Islands   263
Mahone Bay   95
Main-à-Dieu   179
Main-à-Dieu Passage   181
Marble Mountain   221
McAlpines Brook   99,
   101
McCurdy Trail   145; see
   also Middle Musquo-
   doboit
McDonald Lake   212
McGinty Lake Trail   283-
   284; see also Gold
   Mines
McKinnons Harbour   191
McNabs Island   137,
   138, 139-141,143
McNabs Lagoon   140
Meadow Brook   149
Meat Cove   200, 201-
   204
Merrymakedge   310
Mersey River   273, 277,
   278, 285, 291, 299,
   300, 301, 303, 310

Mica Hill 254
Middle Head 186, *256*, 257-259
Middle Musquodoboit *142*, 143-145, 147
Mill Brook 195
Minards Bay 279
Minas Basin 79, 80
Minas Channel 59
Mink Cove 258
Mitchell Creek 113
Money Point 253
Montaigne Noire 267
Moose Island 46, 47
Mount Trail 117; *see also* Uniacke Estate
Mount Uniacke 115, 117
Munroes Island Provincial Park 51, *52*, 53-55
Mushaboom Harbour 170, 172
Mushpauk Creek 103, 104
Mushpauk Lake *100*, 101-104
Musquodoboit Harbour 147
Musquodoboit Harbour Rail Trail *146*, 147-151
Musquodoboit River 148, 149

N
Nappan 31
Neils Harbour 235, 238, 251
Neils Harbour Pond 237
New Glasgow 35, 47, 129
New Harbour 161
New Waterford 184
New Yarmouth 58, 59, 61
Nine Mile River 153, 154
Norman Lake 116
North Bay Ingonish 259
North Cranberry Lake 279

North Mountain 227
North River 207-208
North River, East Branch 208
North River Bridge 205
North River Falls 215
North River Provincial Park 205, *206*, 207-209, 215
Northumberland Strait 62
Northwest River 296
Norway Island 310

O
Oak Ridge Trail 198; *see also* Mabou Highlands
Oban 209
Old St. Margarets Bay Coach Road 151, *152*, 153-155
Old Wife 46
Orangedale 221
Otter Lake 162, 166
Otter Run Lakes 162

P
Paquette Lake (*see* Paquets Lake)
Paquets Lake 251, 253
Parrsboro 43, 57, 65, 79, 80
Peadair Custie's Trail 193; *see also* Highland Hill
Peale Island 307
Pebbleloggitch Lake 297, 300
Pennant Barrens 134
Pennant Point 155, *156*, 157-159
Peskawa Lake 297, 300, 304

Peskowesk Brook   301
Peskowesk Lake   280, 301, 304
Peter Point   307, *308*, 309-310
Pleasant Valley   39
Point Aconi   184
Points West Bay, The   209, 213
Poison Ivy Falls   304
Porcupine Lake   167
Port Joli   113, 311
Port Joli Bay   311
Port Joli Head   313-314
Port Joli Migratory Bird Sanctuary   311
Port L'Hebert   108
Port L'Hebert Pocket Wilderness   105, *106*, 107-109, 311
Port Mouton   111, 113
Port Mouton Bay   311
Post Road Trail   117, 118; *see also* Uniacke Estate
Prescesky Trail   121, 122; *see also* Upper Clements Provincial Wildllife Park
Pringle Brook   209, 212
Pringle Lake   212
Pringle Mountain   209, *210*, 211-213
Prospect River   153
Psyche Cove   170
Pugwash   61
Puzzle Lake   279

Q
Quarter Moon Lake   32
Queensport   163
Queensport Road   *160*, 161-163
Quinan   101

R
Rabbit Run   195; *see also* Highland Hill
Red Head   46
Red Head Trail   46, 47; *see also* Five Islands Provincial Park
Red Lake Brook   297
Refugee Cove   *56*, 57-59, 61
Refugee Cove Brook   58, 59
River Trail   216, 217; *see also* Usige Ban Falls
Rocky Lake   162
Ross Brook   49
Rush Lake   189
Ryerson Meadow   121
Ryerson Trail   121, 122; *see also* Upper Clements Provincial Wildlife Park

S
Sable River   109, 111, 113
Sable River Rail Trail   98, 109, *110*, 111-113, 115, 311
Salmon River (Central - Eastern Shore)   *164*, 165-167
Salmon River (Cobequids - North Shore)   49-50
Salmon River Long Lake   167
Salt Mountain   219, 221
Sambro   133, 155
Sambro Harbour   157
Sambro Island   135, 157
Sandy Bay   313
Saunders Trail   145; *see also* Middle Musquodoboit
Scatarie Island   181

Scots Bay   80
Seaside Adjunct (see Kejimku-
    jik Seaside Adjunct)
Second Cow Lake   162
Seine Cove   258
Shag Rock   157
Shag Roost   263
Sheet Harbour   129, 169
Shelburne River   297, 299
Sight Point   198, 199
Sisters, The   157
Skir Dhu   184
Skye River Valley   219
Skyline   260, 261-263, 265
Sloans Brook   90
Snake Lake   307
Snake Lake Trail   307, 309
Sols Meadows   113
South Bay Ingonish   185, 250
South Highlands Trail   198-
    199; see also Mabou
    Highlands
South Meadow   149
South Mountain   227, 229
Southwest Pond Brook   163
Southwest Port Mouton   315
Sparrow Lake   149
Spicers Cove   61
Springhaven   101
Spry Bay   169
Spry Bay Trail   170; see
    also Taylor Head Provincial
    Park
Square Camp   301
Square Camp Brook   278
Squeaker Hole   237
St. Andrews Channel   191
St. Catherines River   311,
    313, 315
St. Catherines River Beach
    311, 314
St. Margarets Bay   151,
    153, 154

St. Patricks Channel
    191, 219
St. Paul Island   203
St. Peter's   209
Stanley Point   185
Stellarton   129
Stewart Brook   293
Still Brook   275, 277
Strawberry Battery   140
Summerville   99, 101
Summerville Beach   113,
    311
Summerville Beach Pro-
    vincial Park   99
Sydney   179, 187, 209,
    219
Sydney Mines   184

T
Tancook Island   95
Tatamagouche   61
Taylor Head   172
Taylor Head Bay   171
Taylor Head Provincial
    Park   168, 169-173
Terence Bay   159
Thomas Meadow Brook
    275, 292
Thomas Raddall Provincial
    Park   111, 311, 313
Tidney River   109, 111
Tittle Point   203
Titus Smith Trail   144;
    see also Middle
    Musquodoboit
Trafalgar   129
Tree Identification Trail
    145; see also Middle
    Musquodoboit
Trous de Saumon   264,
    265-268
Truro   43, 47, 69, 80
Turtle Lake   149

U

Uniacke Estate   *114*, 115-118

Uniacke Lake   116

Upper Clements Provincial Wildlife Park   119, *120*, 121-123

Usige Ban Falls   213, *214*, 215-217

V

Victoria Beach   237

W

Wallace Bay   61

Wallace Bay National Wildlife Area   *60*, 61-64

Wallace Harbour   62

Wallace River   61

Wards Falls   65, *66*, 67-69

Warner Brook   113

Wentworth   61

Wentworth Hostel Look-off   69, *70*, 71-73

Wentworth Valley   71

West Advocate   57, 61

West River, Northwest Branch   296

West River Trail   296

Wetlands Trail   117, 118; *see also* Uniacke Estate

Wharton   65

White Lake   150

White Point   99

Whycocomagh   191, 219, 221

Whycocomagh Bay   219

Whycocomagh Provincial Park   *218*, 219-221

Wildlife Trail   145; *see also* Middle Musquodoboit

Wilkins Lake   112, 113

Winging Point   190

Woodens River   151, 154

Woodland Trail   81; *see also* Blomidon Provincial Park

Woody Lake   167

Wreck Cove   140, 183

Y

Yarmouth   83, 97, 101, 102, 105, 107, 111, 119, 311

York Redoubt   140